Critical Media Literacy and Fake News in Post-Truth America

Critical Media Literacies Series

VOLUME 2

Series Editor

William M. Reynolds, *Georgia Southern University, USA*

Scope

The series critically investigates and informs the construction of youth identity and identity in general through the study of various forms of contemporary media. It will expand the notions of critical media literacy and its implications for multiple understandings of culture and youth. Since popular culture (including media texts) is one of the primary sites of education for all of us, it is crucial for those scholars involved in critical media studies to discuss these issues in book form. The scope of books in this series will include scholarly investigations into the connections among the symbolic order, various forms of cultural artifacts and multiple critical readings of these artifacts within the context of critical/transformational media literacy. How do multiple interpretations of popular culture within conceptualizations of media enhance our understandings of education and how can critical pedagogy, in the Freirean sense, be expanded to develop a student's critical consciousness of the texts (books, films, games, social media, etc.) that surround them in popular culture?

The titles published in this series are listed at *brill.com/cmls*

Critical Media Literacy and Fake News in Post-Truth America

Edited by

Christian Z. Goering and Paul L. Thomas

BRILL
SENSE
LEIDEN | BOSTON

All chapters in this book have undergone peer review.

Library of Congress Cataloging-in-Publication Data

Names: Goering, Christian Z. editor. | Thomas, P. L. (Paul Lee), 1961- editor.
Title: Critical media literacy and fake news in post-truth America / edited by C. Z. Goering and P. L. Thomas.
Description: Leiden; Boston: Brill Sense, 2018. | Series: Critical media literacies series; volume 2 | Includes bibliographical references.
Identifiers: LCCN 2017060422 (print) | LCCN 2018000749 (ebook) | ISBN 9789004365360 (E-book) | ISBN 9789004365353 (pbk. : alk. paper) | ISBN 9789004365377 (hardback : alk. paper)
Subjects: LCSH: Media literacy--United States. | Fake news--United States.
Classification: LCC P96.M42 (ebook) | LCC P96.M42 U583 2018 (print) | DDC 302.23--dc 3
LC record available at https://lccn.loc.gov/2017060422

ISBN: 978-90-04-36535-3 (paperback)
ISBN: 978-90-04-36537-7 (hardback)
ISBN: 978-90-04-36536-0 (e-book)

This book is printed on acid-free paper and produced in a sustainable manner.

CONTENTS

WILLIAM M. REYNOLDS

FOREWORD

Fantastic Statements, Ridiculous Tweets and the Necessity of Critical Media Literacy

> In an ever-changing, incomprehensible world the masses had reached the point where they would, at the same time, believe everything and nothing, think that everything was possible and that nothing was true. … Mass propaganda discovered that its audience was ready at all times to believe the worst, no matter how absurd, and did not particularly object to being deceived because it held every statement to be a lie anyhow. The totalitarian mass leaders based their propaganda on the correct psychological assumption that, under such conditions, one could make people believe the most fantastic statements one day, and trust that if the next day they were given irrefutable proof of their falsehood, they would take refuge in cynicism; instead of deserting the leaders who had lied to them, they would protest that they had known all along that the statement was a lie and would admire the leaders for their superior tactical cleverness. (Arendt, 1973, p. 382)

> The FAKE NEWS media (failing @nytimes, @NBCNews, @ABC, @CBS, @CNN) is not my enemy, it is the enemy of the American People! (@realDonaldTrump, February 17, 2017)

I am thrilled to have *Critical Media Literacy and Fake News in Post-Truth America* as the second book in the series, *Critical Media Literacies*. It is a stellar contribution. Critical media literacy is important to me because I grew up immersed in media. I would beg my father to stay up longer at night so I could watch more of the black and white images on the screen of our television. He would always let me because he know that I would promptly fall asleep. To this day, I fall asleep watching something on the screen whether it is a movie or television series streamed from Netflix or Amazon Prime. Not only was I tied to television but also movies and music. Media was always present. Although the technology has become more sophisticated and advanced, we all are immersed in media from our smartphones to our tablets. The longer I teach and write the more I realize the significance of media writ popular culture in maintaining the cultural hegemony Antonio Gramsci explained in *Selections from the Prison Notebooks* (1971). My students have informed me that there is little or no discussion of media culture in the public or private elementary or secondary classrooms or even undergraduate college classrooms. Paradoxically then, critical discussions of media are absent in schools despite media's overwhelming presence in everyday life. Media envelops everyone's everyday existence. Steinberg (2007) alludes to the phenomenon of media surrounding youth and all of us:

> Media have become the oxygen of our existence, that which once was seen as a medium for the educated, the privileged, the initiated, has become the essence upon which surrounds our daily existence…for good, for bad, or for the ugly, media affects us all. It becomes our responsibility, then, as educators to prepare our students/citizens, to learn how to use it, consume it, and to have personal power over it. (Steinberg, 2007, p. xiv)

As the editors and authors of this text indicate, it is difficult in the present historical moment to move beyond the election of November 2016, T-Day (see Taibbi, 2017). On November 9, 2016, we awakened to the nightmare that is now. Therefore, we can view, listen and watch the daily litany of horrible tweets and bombasts from the man who would call himself president. What will he do or say next? Life has become the new reality show with its preeminent game show, funny haired host. Media is saturated with this 24/7 reality-game show. In addition, while Trump wallows in the attention of the media, he is just clever enough to use that attention to denounce that very same media at every turn and in a fascistic manner attempt to personify the media as evil in an attempt to destroy the freedom of the press and free speech. The media is the enemy. Trump is effective in using Twitter and the 24/7 news media as distractions from the truth. Critical attention to the actual truth is mired in the Trumpocalyptic, phantasmagoric reality. It has become as the title of the book indicates a world of post-truth.

I believe this book on Critical media literacy moves beyond the slacktivism of simply posting anti-Trump notes on Facebook or in a text. As Taibbi indicates, "despising Trump and his followers is easy" (Taibbi, 2017, p. 3). *Critical Media Literacy and Fake News in Post-Truth America* on the other hand moves beyond that despising and develops notions of the importance of developing with students a critical media literacy. Chapters move through writing classrooms, narratives, real world arguments, and youth activism as well as others. Schooling must immerse itself in critical media literacy pedagogy and consequently move schooling toward becoming a critical education that encourages a critical citizenry:

> As the current pressures for standardization, privatization, and high-stakes testing are driving public education to focus more on global competition than on democratic ideals, critical media literacy pedagogy can help educators to strengthen civic engagement and reassert the promise of democracy with an informed and empowered citizenry. (Share, 2015, p. 4)

Not only a smart, critical consumption of media, but also a resistant type of production of critical media. In education, critical media literacy becomes increasingly significant in this era of fake news and post-truth. As Arendt elaborates about totalitarianism, we are living in a time in which people believe in everything and in nothing. If studying the media remains exclusively centered on how to use smart boards, powerpoints and various other technology/media in the classroom, then media literacy has no criticality. As the editors indicate in their introduction, critical media literacy is not necessarily a "lifesaving tool." It is, however, a way, a line of flight (Reynolds & Webber, 2016, p. 35) to move toward a critical education. The point is that critical media literacy is not even a vague notion in most schools. The absence of critical media literacy in educational institutions is not simply an innocent gap or lapse in the curriculum. This is one of the ways corporate, neoliberal agenda in education works to remove and destroy critical thought. As Share (2015) indicates as schooling (it is no longer education) increasingly moves toward the continual assessment agenda emphasizing accountability and the bottom-line, a type of fascism (Pinar, 2004) the spaces for critical thought are eliminated. It is part of the process to develop consumer citizens. In the case of media, people will wait in line to buy the latest smartphone or tablet and are happy that they were able to "get one." Any dialogue concerning a questioning of this immersion in consumer culture or the consumption of media is not covered in the schooling, testing, and accountability schema. Corporations such as Pearson rule the curriculum in schools and the universities and make this mindless schema possible. In education the type of teachers and students we produce are varieties of technocrats. Hedges (2016) indicates that these technocrats rule us and demonstrate the product of this type corporate education. He mentions elite schools; I believe the process he describes is in most schools/universities:

> Technocrats rule us. They are trained and indoctrinated in elite schools. They function as system managers. They only know how to serve the system. They cannot critique it or challenge it. They are devoid of creativity or the ability to think independently. They will maintain the system at all costs. They will plunder and squander resources to serve global capitalism, even as these resources are being destroyed or exhausted. (Hedges, 2016, p. 132)

That nightmare is our present lived moment and our current schooling. Again, schooling ignores what is the primary educational site for youth and all of us – media. Media not discussed in any critical way. Media is simply not discussed with the exception of how to consume it and use it. After students endure a meaningless curriculum of memorizing discrete bits of forgettable information (information is not knowledge), they are at the same time thrust into a media saturated society. They do not have critical dispositions to analyze what they are facing and no idea or reason(s) that there could be critical ways of analyzing what they are facing that move beyond mere acceptance and consumption.

Critical Media Literacy and Fake News in Post-Truth America addresses all of these issues in an in-depth manner. The book is a critique of the present moment and an invitation to confront and address the issue of critical media literacy.

REFERENCES

Arendt, H. (1973). *The origins of totalitarianism.* New York, NY: Harcourt, Brace, Jovanovich.

Gramsci, A. (1971). *Selections from the prison notebooks.* New York, NY: International Publishers Co.

Hedges, C. (2016). *Unspeakable: Chris Hedges talks with David Talbot about the most forbidden topics in America.* New York, NY: Skyhorse Publishing.

Pinar, W. F. (2004). *What is curriculum theory?* New York, NY: Routledge.

Reynolds, W. M., & Webber, J. A. (Eds.). (2016). *Expanding curriculum theory: Dis/positons and lines of flight* (2nd ed.). New York, NY: Routledge.

Share, J. (2015). *Media literacy is elementary: Teaching youth to critically read and create media* (2nd ed.). New York, NY: Peter Lang.

Steinberg, S. R. (2007). Reading media critically. In D. Macedo & S. R. Steinberg (Eds.), *Media literacy: A reader*. New York, NY: Peter Lang.

Taibbi, M. (2017, November 8). A year after Trump's election, nothing has changed. *The Rolling Stone*. Retrieved from http://www.rollingstone.com/politics/features/taibbi-a-year-after-trumpselection-nothing-has-changed-w511229

ACKNOWLEDGMENTS

Academic projects like books are rarely possible without a concerted group effort and this one is no exception. This being an edited collection, we first must thank the various contributors who have made this volume what it is. Bringing insights and expertise from their spheres, each helps to unpack the critical issues that rest at the heart of the book—what to do in a fake news and post-truth America. Both of our academic institutions—the University of Arkansas and Furman University respectively—provided support for this project in form of time and resources. Speaking of which, Seth French, a Distinguished Doctoral Student at the University of Arkansas, invaluably assisted this project in the form of layout and first round copyediting. Series editor, William Reynolds provided the eventual home for these ideas which, in turn, served as a source of inspiration. Finally, the team at Sense—now Brill—including Michel and Jolanda—were wonderful to work alongside throughout this process.

CHRISTIAN Z. GOERING AND P. L. THOMAS

1. AN INTRODUCTION

Can Critical Media Literacy Save Us?

INTRODUCTION

This edited collection is not a response to the 2016 United States Presidential Election so much as it is a response to the issues highlighted through that single event and since when incredibly smart, sophisticated, and intelligent members of our society were confused by misinformation campaigns. While media literacy and critical media literacy are ideas we've both interacted with leading up to this point, including using activities in teaching K-12 students and in methods of teaching courses we've taught at our respective universities, the need for increased attention to these issues has, we argue, never reached a flash point like the present.

Trying to write about these topics at this particular point in American history feels akin to trying to run out of a high rise hotel during an earthquake. Each step that lands finds the hallway floor in a bit of a different place than it was a split second earlier, bouncing us into the walls that may or may not be crumbling down around us. Other times it feels like the floor is altogether gone and we must suddenly leap to where a floor remains. What we meant when we said "fake news" in late 2016/early 2017 was clearly very different than what we mean now (November 2017) or what it may mean when this book is released. What we meant then was that fake news was the misinformation and literally untrue news stories that swirled in the political toilet that was the 2016 election cycle, stories with enough truth to be believable but that misrepresented—or completely falsified—the facts. A particularly famous case of this is referred to as "Pizzagate." *The New York Times* summarizes the event in the opening to an article:

> Edgar M. Welch, a 28-year-old father of two from Salisbury, N.C., recently read online that Comet Ping Pong, a pizza restaurant in northwest Washington, was harboring young children as sex slaves as part of a child-abuse ring led by Hillary Clinton.
>
> The articles making those allegations were widespread across the web, appearing on sites including Facebook and Twitter. Apparently concerned, Mr. Welch drove about six hours on Sunday from his home to Comet Ping Pong to see the situation for himself, according to court documents. Not long after arriving at the pizzeria, the police said, he fired from an assault-like AR-15 rifle. (Kang & Goldman, 2016, n.p.)

 | DOI 10.1163/9789004365360_001

Needless to say, Hillary Clinton and Comet King Pizza were not running a child-abuse ring but the story that prompted Mr. Welch to open fire—a story equal parts outrageous and inflammatory—did not need to rely on truth to have an impact, it just needed to be circulating in the world, to be shared and re-shared on social media platforms in order to mislead and incite a violent response. This was fake news that could have killed but the concept of fake news continues to evolve in front of our eyes. No questions asked, fake news, whichever version of it, is potentially deadly.

In July 2017 President Trump released a video showing him in a professional wrestling scenario taking down a person wearing a CNN icon over their face. For posterity's sake, let us say that again: the President of the United States of America shared a video that depicts him body slamming someone representing the media, one he frequently refers to as "fake news," and "fake news media." We often feel as though we can tune into a real life reality television show by simply turning on the daily news.

But let's take a serious historical look at this. Genocides have frequently relied on misinformation and complete control of the media to enact atrocities. The Cambodian Genocide began in earnest when the Khmer Rouge evacuated cities, announcing that the cities needed to be evacuated in advance of American bombings. Cambodians were marched outside of their cities literally to their deaths or to agrarian work camps (and then to their deaths) under the guise of a fake news story—that the Americans were coming to bomb their cities. Between 1.5 and 3 million people were killed.

Is critical media literacy a potentially lifesaving tool? We hope that sentiment is an overstatement but teaching the current school-aged generation to be more savvy consumers and creators of media should become an absolute priority of schooling in America. But, as Kellner and Share (2007) relate, "for most students in the United States, critical media literacy is not an option because it is not available; it is not even on the radar" (p. 59). What's become clearer in our efforts to edit this book and collect some outstanding thinking on these issues is that the concepts of fake news and existing in a post-truth society are constantly changing, sometimes daily. So whatever is said in the pages that follow and how we start looking at these issues throughout the education profession, we must be quick to first acknowledge that what we know today and what our students can do today may only help them for today; nefarious and/or profit-minded forces are inventing ways to our wallets, hearts, and minds as we meekly type this introduction.

As a high school teacher in the early 2000's, Chris used the backs of *Rolling Stone* magazines to introduce students to the concept of media literacy, prompting students to identify the messages portrayed by companies like Smirnoff Vodka and Camel Cigarettes. Students—through a process of understanding the semiotics of the magazine back covers—found it surprising that they almost all targeted adolescents, despite their products being illegal to that age group. Teaching media literacy skills then included having students identify messages in media, analyze those messages for underlying meanings, and eventually create media with embedded messaging. We should say that what Chris did in his classroom was not something overtly mentioned in the standards or expectations for a 9th or 11th grade English class but rather something he brought into school because he felt it was important.

In the fall of 2016, just after the U.S. elected Donald Trump president, a black female first-year student of Paul's submitted an essay on the prospects for Trump's presidency. The course is a first-year writing seminar focusing on James Baldwin in the context of Black Lives Matter; therefore, throughout the course, students have been asked to critically investigate race, racism, gender, sexism, and all types of bias related to the U.S.—through the writing of Baldwin, Ta-Nehisi Coates, Roxane Gay, Teju Cole, and Arundhati Roy, among others.

The student's discussion of Trump's policies, however, were hyperlinked to Trump's campaign website. Discussing the draft with the student revealed that the current post-truth America is a significant issue among youth who seem unable to distinguish between facts and so-called fake news. Here, Paul is attempting to employ critical media literacy but is met with resistance from his promising and thoughtful students.

A longtime advocate of media literacy, Renee Hobbs, summarizes the situation we presently face: "Not only are we seeing more emotionally manipulative online content, but it is also more challenging to find and validate the source of the information we consume" (2017, n.p.). She continues, "The quality of civic education and civic learning in public education must be continually responsive to the lived experience of the students we serve," and those experiences happen "in the face of increasing polarization" (n.p.).

Turning finally to Kellner and Share (2007), we define critical media literacy for the purposes of this volume as "an educational response that expands the notion of media literacy to include different forms of mass communication, popular culture, and new technologies" (p. 59) and "focuses on the ideology critique and analyzing the politics of representation of crucial dimensions of gender, race, class, and sexuality" (p. 60). It is the goal of this volume to build the aptitude and skill set of students and their teachers for critical media literacy in hopes for a better tomorrow.

CHAPTERS IN THIS VOLUME

Our contributors range from professors of English education, social studies education, communication, and English to practicing K-12 teachers, and we are certainly indebted to them for the quality of this edited collection. Similar to their unwillingness to be categorized in any sort of neat and orderly fashion, the chapters they contributed—while all relating directly to our goals of this book—take very different approaches to critical media literacy, fake news, and teaching in post-truth America. We've put the chapters in an order that felt natural to us and that grouped authors speaking to similar audiences. In Chapter Two, Co-Editor Paul Thomas foregrounds the rest of this book with a foundational offering that lays bare much of what has contributed to the current situation. In "An Educator's Primer: Fake news, Post-Truth, and a Critical Free Press," Thomas defines the terms and contexts for teaching critical media literacy, addresses the mainstream media and their responsibility in post truth disocurse, and offers an explanation of how we arrived at the present situation through a metaphor: crossing the Bigfoot line. He calls for a critical free press and for critical literacy education to address the issues afoot, ending with a dire warning: "We are a people without critical literacy and that may result in our being the pawns we deserve to be."

In Chapter Three, "Reconsidering Evidence in Real World Arguments," Troy Hicks and Kristen Hawley Turner harness argumentation to address the new reality of a post-truth world. In this extended consideration of what qualifies as evidence and how, Hicks and Turner offer practical advice for writing teachers seeking to address social media, ending with the acronym MINDFUL to help students consider and reconsider evidence. Next, "What is the Story? Reading the Web as Narrative" by Sharon Murchie and Janet Neyer offers an age old solution to a modern problem in encouraging teachers to have their students unpack the narrative in their lives, in this case, their digital lives. Their classroom practice and trials and errors with students in Michigan convey the struggle as well as several methods for finding the essence of these current stories.

"Fighting 'Fake News' in an Age of Digital Disorientation: Towards 'Real News,' Critical Media Literacy Education, and Independent Journalism for 21st Century Citizens," Chapter Five, by professor and practitioner of media Rob Williams, unpacks a culture of disinformation by defining "real news," outlining what all "fake news" exists, summoning Chomsky and Hermann's "propaganda model of news," and finally charting a course for "real news" to win the day. In Chapter Six, "Educating the Myth-Led: Critical Literacy Pedagogy in a Post-Truth World," Robert Williams and Daniel Woods, colleagues at Radford University, invoke and build on the work of Paulo Freire (and many others) to deal with the present intellectual and practical issues by calling for the use of multiple texts—including psychology and offerings from canonical literature—to analyze and crtique and act. Joanne Addison's "Teaching Critical Media Literacy as a Social Process in Writing Intensive Classrooms" (Chapter Seven), offers theoretical and practical advice for writing instructors to "empower students as agents in a participatory democracy."

Chapter Eight's team of authors—Jason Endacott, Matt Dingler, Seth French, and John Broome—takes on those people in our social networks guilty of sharing fake news and further propogating propaganda. "Before You Click 'Share': Mindful Media Literacy as a Positive Civic Act" advocates for processes and approaches to use with students that will enable them to engage in social spaces carefully and with eyes wide open to the nature of post-truth America. "Engaging the Storied Mind: Teaching Critical Media Literacy through Narrative" by Erin O'Neill Armendarez provides a complementary approach to addressing CML through narrative to the one offered by Murchie and Neyer in chapter three. By providing examples of stock stories as they exist throughout popular culture, especially how vastly different stories or approaches tell essentially identical stories, O'Neill Armendarez offers her students opportunities to identify when stories are used for nefarious purposes.

Mark Lewis' "Supporting Media-Savvy Youth-Activists: The Case of Marcus Yallow" invokes young adult literature to provide a counter-narrative to much of what was said following the election, something to the effect of blaming the youth or the schools for America's inbilitiy to distinguish between fact and fiction. Grounded in a youth lens (Petrone, Sarigianides, & Lewis, 2014) that counters the deficit model thinking about youth, Lewis traces Marcus Yallow through eerily similar circumstances in fiction to challenge and advance our view of youth. Chapter Eleven, "Creating Wobble in a World of Spin: Positioning Students to Challenge Media Poses," begins with the acknowledgement that the blurred lines of fact and fiction are a reality, one that we'll suggest won't change. Sarah Bonner, Robyn Seglem, and Antero Garcia build on the practical implementation (in Sarah's classroom) of Antero's 2015 book *Pose, Wobble, Flow: A Culturally Proactive Approach to Literacy Instruction*. Sarah's students work through the framework in regards to critical media literacy using the book *unSpun: Finding Facts in a World of Disinformation* to help them unlock meaning in language and identify how it can be used to distort the truth.

We encourage you to pick up this book as a whole and read it through to the end or find individual chapters that fit your interests and applications. While your classroom teaching situation may not look like each of those collected here, we find the lessons to be universal and, as we mentioned, never more important than right now. Can Critical Media Literacy save us, as the title to this introduction provokes? In short, we will only know if we try.

REFERENCES

Hobbs, R. (2017, November). Teaching and learning in a post-truth world. *Educational Leadership, 75*(3), 26–31. Retrieved from http://www.ascd.org/publications/educational_leadership/nov17/vol75/num03/Teaching_and_Learning_in_a_Post-Truth_World.aspx

Kang, C., & Goldman, A. (2016, December 5). In Washington pizzeria attack, fake news brought real guns. *New York Times.* Retrieved from https://www.nytimes.com/2016/12/05/business/media/comet-ping-pong-pizza-shooting-fake-news-consequences.html

Kellner, D., & Share, J. (2007). Critical media literacy is not an option. *Learning Inquiry, 1*(1), 59–69.

Petrone, R., Sarigianides, S. T., & Lewis, M. A. (2014). The youth lens: Analyzing adolescence/ts in literary texts. *Journal of Literacy Research, 46*(4), 506–533.

Christian Z. Goering
Department of Curriculum & Instruction
University of Arkansas
Fayetteville, Arkansas

P. L. Thomas
Department of Education
Furman University
Greenville, South Carolina

P. L. THOMAS

2. AN EDUCATOR'S PRIMER

Fake News, Post-Truth, and a Critical Free Press

INTRODUCTION

Being an educator at any level—K-12 through undergraduate and graduate education—has always been a challenge in the U.S. since formal education *in theory* is linked to preserving our democracy. Being a critical educator at any level in the U.S. has always been and remains nearly impossible because formal education *in practice* is more about enculturation and maintaining the status quo than seeking the social equity that remains elusive despite our claimed ideals as a people.

With the election of Donald Trump as president in 2016, the media punditry has become obsessed, as has Trump, with fake news and post-truth public discourse. In this volume committed to investigating and interrogating fake news and post-truth discourse in the context of curriculum and instruction grounded in critical media literacy goals, below we offer the foundational opportunity for educators to consider and reconsider the nature of truth/Truth, knowledge, and facts both in the teaching/learning dynamic and throughout mainstream media and all sorts of public discourse, notably by and about political discourse.

First, let's establish the terms and contexts essential to understanding and then teaching *critical media literacy*:

- "Fake news" is a technical term (although most public discourse fails to adhere to this technical distinction) that identifies mostly on-line information that is intentionally false and provocative, designed to be click-bait and drive internet traffic and thus revenue.
- "Satire" is purposefully distorted information that assumes readers/viewers recognize the information is not factual, but intended to make larger points. *The Onion*, Saturday Night Live's *Weekend Update*, *The Daily Show*, and John Oliver's *Last Week Tonight* are examples of satire packaged in seemingly credible formats, parodies of traditional news media.
- "Post-truth" is a relatively newer term for the popular and often right-wing embracing of (and misunderstanding) post-modernism's challenge to the objective nature of truth/Truth. Not to oversimplify, but post-modernism argues that truth/Truth is defined by whoever is in power (not an objective reality), while

 | DOI 10.1163/9789004365360_002

the contemporary popular and right-leaning political embracing of "post-truth" is more akin to "the truth is whatever I say it is regardless of any evidence or the credibility of evidence."

- Mainstream journalism functions under two important and corrupting norms: (1) journalists (just as educators are implored to be) maintain a stance of objectivity and neutrality, an apolitical pose, and thus (2) most mainstream examinations of topics, debates, and events are framed as "both sides" journalism, rendering all positions as equally credible and valid. For example, the mainstream media, as John Oliver has exposed, gives the general public the false notion that climate change has as many scientists for as against the "theory," a term read by the public as "hypothesis."

As noted parenthetically above, to embrace teaching critical media literacy (in conjunction with critical pedagogy and critical literacy) is disrupting the traditional norm that educators remain apolitical. This volume's authors recognize that educators face tremendous hurdles for teaching critical media literacy: eroding job security with the dismantling of unions (and absence historically of unions in many regions of the U.S.), increasing accountability for student test scores on exams that are reductive and demand of students far less in their literacy than critical media literacy (in other words, our efforts to teach critical media literacy can be disregarded with "that isn't on the test"), and deteriorating teaching and learning conditions such as overcrowded classrooms and more teachers inadequately prepared to teach (such as Teach For America candidates).

None the less, if we genuinely believe in universal public education as a key mechanism for democracy and individual liberty then we educators must be well versed in critical media literacy, and then we must make that central to our classrooms. Throughout this chapter, the intersections of media and education are examined in order to highlight the power and dangers inherent in fake news, post-truth discourse, and traditional calls for educators and journalists to be objective, apolitical.

MAINSTREAM MEDIA, NOT FAKE NEWS, SPAWNED POST-TRUTH DISCOURSE

Journalist Sarah Kendzior (2016) confronts the histrionics about fake news are distracting us from a very real and very ugly truth echoed by Hedges (2016): having crossed the Bigfoot line (see below), mainstream media, not fake news, spawned post-truth discourse. Let me illustrate.

Consider the lede from "Woman A Leading Authority On What Shouldn't Be In Poor People's Grocery Carts" (2014):

> With her remarkable ability to determine exactly how others should be allocating their limited resources for food, local woman Carol Gaither is considered to be one of the foremost authorities on what poor people should and should not have in their grocery carts, sources said Thursday.

From 2014, this is satire from *The Onion*, a publication often *confused* for fake news, although satire has not the malicious intent of the more recent purposefully placed fake news designed to be click-bait and make money (Shane, 2017).

What this satirizes, however, is incredibly important since it challenges the mostly misguided and nasty stereotypes (Gorski, 2013) that many if not most Americans *believe* about people who are poor: it is the fault of the poor, laziness, that they are impoverished, and thus, they do not deserve the same material pleasures hard working people do deserve (as in luxuries such as sweets). We might argue that no reasonable person would believe a story from *The Onion* to be true, but it happens (Mackey, 2015), and well before all the hand-wringing about fake news and presidential politics.

Yet, what is far more disturbing is that despite concurrent charges the sky is falling because the expert is dead, the U.S. still functions with an expert class of media, the primary cable news networks such as Fox and CNN as well as the last surviving newspapers, notably *The New York Times*. While many reject the "liberal media," most people remain solidly faithful that the NYT is reporting credibly. And here is the problem: the NYT and mainstream media are overwhelmingly meeting the standards of mainstream media, and those standards of "both sides" and objective journalism are far more harmful and dangerous than fake news.

For example, just one week before Trump's inauguration, the NYT published "In the Shopping Cart of a Food Stamp Household: Lots of Soda" (O'Connor, 2017), which in only a few days prompted this from state government:

> A lawmaker in Tennessee wants to ban people from using food stamps to buy items that have no nutritional value. The bill was proposed by Republican Rep. Sheila Butt.[1]...House Bill 43 would prohibit people from using food stamps to purchase items high in calories, sugar or fat, according to the Tennessean. That would include soda, ice cream, candy, cookies and cake. (Padilla, 2017)

However, there is more *indirect* truth in the satirical *The Onion* article than in the NYT article, as Joe Soss (2017) reports:

> In a New York Times story over the weekend, Anahad O'Connor massages and misreports a USDA study to reinforce some of the worst stereotypes about food stamps. For his trouble, the editors placed it on the front page. Readers of the newspaper of record learn that the end result of tax dollars spent on food assistance is a grocery cart full of soda. No exaggeration. The inside headline for the story is "What's in the Shopping Cart of a Food Stamp Household? Lots of Sugary Soda," and the front-page illustration shows a shopping cart containing almost nothing but two-liter pop bottles.

Yes, the key words above are "misreports" and "stereotypes." Soss explains:

> Let's be clear here: this is nonsense. It's a political hack job against a program that helps millions of Americans feed themselves, and we should all be

> outraged that the New York Times has disguised it as a piece of factual news reporting on its front page.

There are two major problems here. First, O'Connor misrepresents the findings of the USDA report. Second, O'Connor's article is a case study in the dark arts of making biased reporting appear even-handed. Let's start with the facts.

Not as sexy, and not what the general public believes, the USDA report actually has a much different message:

> A November 2016 study by the U.S. Department of Agriculture examined the food shopping patterns of American households who currently receive nutrition assistance through the Supplemental Nutrition Assistance Program (SNAP) compared with those not receiving aid. Its central finding? "There were no major differences in the expenditure patterns of SNAP and non-SNAP households, no matter how the data were categorized." (Vallas & Robbins, 2017)

Vallas and Robins note as well that the NYT/O'Connor misreporting is about more than feeding misguided stereotypes about people in poverty:

> Beyond the article's inaccuracies, there is a broader problem with this kind of reporting. It reinforces an "us versus them" narrative—as though "the poor" are a stagnant class of Americans permanently dependent on aid programs. The New York Times' own past reporting has shown that this simply isn't the case. Research by Mark Rank, which the paper featured in 2013, shows that four in five Americans will face at least a year of significant economic insecurity during their working years. And analysis by the White House Council on Economic Advisers finds that 70 percent of Americans will turn to a means-tested safety net program such as nutrition assistance at some point during their lives.

Now if we return to our concern about the rise of fake news and the death of the expert, we should be confronting a couple far more pressing facts ourselves as educators and then with our students:

- Mainstream media are mostly conducting press-release journalism, often bending to the market and not reaching for truth, justice, and the American way; and fail our democracy because of traditional norms of objectivity and "both sides" journalism.
- The public in the U.S. is not anti-expert, but seeking the *appearance* of expertise that confirms what they already believe[2]—even when what they believe lacks credibility, or worse (racism, sexism, homophobia, etc.).

Maybe we have a really ugly paradox here also: publications like *The Onion* and satirical programming such as work by John Oliver and Saturday Night Live are serving the American public and the ideal of democracy and freedom far better than even the so-called best mainstream media are doing. Satirists are not bound to simplistic conventions of objectivity (ironically, to be neutral is to endorse the status quo), and are critical instead. Journalists refuse to embrace the power of a critical free press (see below), and thus, are eager to blame fake news, to use it as a distraction.

Finally, then, we must wonder if O'Connor merely cribbed his NYT expose from *The Onion*, where three years ago they offered as satire:

> "All that junk she's buying is just loaded with sugar, too," said Gaither, identifying with uncanny speed another critical flaw in her fellow shopper's grocery selection. "No wonder her kids are acting out like that." … "The other day, I saw a woman who bought a box of name-brand Frosted Flakes because, apparently, the generic kind wasn't fancy enough for her," said Gaither, swiftly and decisively calculating that bagged cereal would have cost half as much. "And guess who's going to be paying the difference in the end?"

A speculation that does make sense because reading *The Onion* is far more entertaining and informative than plowing through a government report.

WHEN FAKE IS REAL AND REAL IS FAKE: ON CROSSING THE BIGFOOT LINE

Against the current focus on fake news and post-truth public discourse, and the renewed interest in postmodernism renamed "post-truth," human reality and facts are far more tenuous than we tend to admit in our day-to-day lives, and in our classrooms. 2 + 2 = 4 seems obvious and above any politics, but this formula is, in fact, relative to a base-10 math system, and that system has to be instilled and preserved by some power structure. Yet, as some of the garbled efforts to co-opt postmodernism has shown, while truth and facts are bound and controlled by power, while truth and facts are often contestable, we are certainly not served well as a people to make wild claims that no facts can ever exist (Holmes, 2016).

Here, let's consider these comments from journalists, one Tweet replying to me from Juana Summers (@jmsummers, 18 June 2014), then writing at NPR: "@plthomasEdD I'm not sure it's my place to say whether the study is credible, but we both note the significant criticism of the methods." And then one news article directly about Trump:

> Asked by host Chuck Todd whether he'd be willing to call out a falsehood as a "lie" like some other news outlets have done, [Wall Street Journal editor Gerard] Baker demurred, saying it was up to the newspaper to just present the set of facts and let the reader determine how to classify a statement.
>
> "I'd be careful about using the word, 'lie.' 'Lie' implies much more than just saying something that's false. It implies a deliberate intent to mislead," Baker said, noting that when Trump claimed "thousands" of Muslims were celebrating on rooftops in New Jersey on 9/11, the Journal investigated and reported that they found no evidence of a claim. (Gold, 2017)

Keeping traditional and current standards of mainstream journalism (poses of objectivity and neutrality) in mind, now consider how the mainstream media are addressing fake news directly:

> Established news organizations usually own their domains and they have a standard look that you are probably familiar with. Sites with such endings like .com.co should make you raise your eyebrows and tip you off that you need to dig around more to see if they can be trusted. This is true even when the site looks professional and has semi-recognizable logos. For example, abcnews.com is a legitimate news source, but abcnews.com.co is not, despite its similar appearance. (Davis, 2016)

To be blunt, helping *consumers of media* distinguish between the reality of fake news (abcnews.com.co) and "a legitimate news source" (abcnews.com) fails miserably because in essence these two present us with a very dangerous paradox: *fake news is real and real news is fake* (with the WSJ's odd twist on the false history of George Washington: "We cannot call a lie 'a lie!'"). Two ways this manifests itself are (1) mainstream media are rushing to cover fake news, but only to distinguish it from "legitimate" news, and (2) mainstream media refuse to take a stand on credible sources, warranted claims, and naming lies as "lies."

A popular media phenomenon exists that speaks to the essential problem with mainstream journalism:

> *Jumping the Shark* is the moment when an established long-running series changes in a significant manner in an attempt to stay fresh. Ironically, that moment makes the viewers realize that the show's finally run out of ideas. It's reached its peak, it'll never be the same again, and from now on it's all downhill. (Jumping the Shark, n.d.)

In mainstream journalism, I call our problem "crossing the Bigfoot line." In other words, and as I have been documenting for years in edujournalism, mainstream journalism has adopted and embraced a pose that allows them *to report on a real event without taking any stance on the finer elements of the event being reported.*

Just a few decades ago, tabloid journalism was distinct from mainstream journalism because tabloids used the "just reporting what we are being told" defense. If a person came to a tabloid with images or video and a wild story about Bigfoot ransacking their camp site, the tabloid eagerly and with outlandish headlines reported the *fact* that this person told them the story—while taking the pose I shared above: "I'm not sure it's my place to say whether the [story] is credible." There was a time when mainstream media balked at just reporting as fact that source A made claim X *if the journalists found claim X to be lacking in credibility*.

And while online click-bait has supplanted the outlandish grocery store tabloid in our increasingly virtual avenues for news and information, what is more troubling is that mainstream journalism has callously crossed that Bigfoot line, now brazenly using click-bait headline techniques (hard to distinguish from fake news) and remaining entrenched in their refusal to verify the claims of those about whom they are reporting.

Now there exists a great deal of fretting about the future of the free press under Trump; however, we have ample evidence that mainstream media and journalists had crossed the Bigfoot line long ago (Hedges, 2016), and not at the hands of rising fascism, but willingly as a natural development of capitalism and consumerism. The public in the U.S. and many voters hold provably false beliefs (Rampell, 2016) that guide how they live their lives and how they vote; this was pre-Trump, and this was in the context of how the media carelessly feed the masses.

Now that the Bigfoot line has been crossed by mainstream media, educators have a troubling challenge before us. Yes, the public and our students need much greater skills in critical media literacy, but those skills will mean little if we are left without a critical free press (see below) as an option. As it stands, on the other side of the Bigfoot line is the new mantra of mainstream journalism: "We are not fake news." This is a mighty low and ultimately irrelevant bar.

FAIR AND BALANCED EDUCATION AND JOURNALISM: ON THE DEATH OF DEMOCRACY

Through both my work as an educator (nearly two decades as a high school English teacher and another 15-plus years at the university level), I have rejected often calls for journalists and teachers to be objective, apolitical, focusing on Howard Zinn's brilliant metaphor of being unable to remain neutral on a moving train. Both calling for no politics in any context and taking a neutral stance are, in fact, political themselves—the former is a political strategy to deny some Others their politics while imposing your own and the latter is the politics of passively endorsing the status quo (in a society where racism and sexism, for example, continue to thrive, being neutral is an indirect endorsement of both).

Education and journalism—universal free public education and the free press—share many important and disturbing qualities: they are in theory essential to the creation and preservation of a free and equitable people, they remain mostly unachieved in the U.S. in practice because they are often the tools of powerful people and forces who distort their ideal contributions to democracy and equity, and at the heart of that failure (we have failed them; they have not failed us) is the shared traditional code of education/teachers and journalism/journalists assuming neutral poses, being forced into a state of objectively presenting both sides in a fair and balanced way.

Particularly in an era labeled "post-truth"—and I argue we are here *because* of our failures in education and journalism—demanding that educators and journalists remain neutral is not the right goal and not actually how either functions. In fact, education and journalism are always political, and in most contexts, educators and journalists routinely break the rule of neutrality—and thus, when anyone wags a finger and exclaims "We must be fair and balanced! Show both sides!" the truth is not that educators or journalists are being ideological or biased, but that someone in power feels that his/her politics is being challenged. Let me illustrate in both education and journalism, starting with the media.

When we compare the Ray Rice inspired public debate about domestic abuse to the Adrian Peterson motivated public debate about corporal punishment, the *neutral press myth* is completely unmasked because domestic abuse (men hitting and psychologically abusing women) was entirely examined throughout the media as wrong (no pro-abuse side aired) while that same media almost exclusively presented corporal punishment as a debate with a fair and balanced presentation of both sides to adults hitting children. What is clear here is incredibly disturbing: The media, in fact, make decisions about when to honor credible positions, when to reject or even *not cover* invalidated and unethical positions, and when to shrink back into the "both sides" cover.

While decades of research and the same ethical concerns about power and abuse related to rejecting domestic abuse *entirely refute* corporal punishment, the media routinely chooses to remain neutral on a moving train aimed at the health and well-being of powerless children. In other words, when media shirks its role in creating and maintaining a free and equitable people behind its tin shield of objectivity, this is a dishonest pose because the media routinely take sides.

Finally, I want to highlight that education represents this same dishonest dynamic—claiming to be apolitical, or aspiring to be apolitical, while often taking sides. Unless I am misreading the current mood of the country, the increased interest in *1984* and other works of literature similar to George Orwell's dystopian science fiction (such as the TV series adaptation of Margaret Atwood's *The Handmaid's Tale*) is along a spectrum of concern about fearing the rise of fascism and totalitarianism. Concurrently, with the public discussions about fake news and post-truth, we are experiencing a renaissance in examining how power and language are inseparable.

So what does it mean when teachers call for presenting both sides of this debate when we bring politically charged novels by Orwell or Atwood into high school and college classes? Before answering, let me offer a few examples from typical lessons found in high schools for virtually every student. Both the Holocaust and slavery in the U.S. are taught as foundational content in anyone's education; these are disturbing topics, and hard issues. When we teach the Holocaust, notably through *Night* by Elie Wiesel in an English course, do we rush to have students read Hitler's *Mein Kampf* to fairly represent both sides, treating each position as morally equivalent, allowing our students to choose whichever position she/he wishes? When we teach U.S. slavery, possibly having students read Frederick Douglass, do we also find eugenicists' and racists' declarations demonizing blacks to fairly represent both sides, treating each position as morally equivalent, allowing our students to choose whichever position she/he wishes?

As in the media, educators at all levels routinely take sides—the answer to the two questions above reveal. And thus, I am lost on how or why educators would find ways to present pro-fascist ideas to balance literature study about the threats of fascism and totalitarianism. Using Orwell and all sorts of powerful literature to help students on the cusp of or early in their roles as active participants in a democracy to better read the world through critical media literacy and better act on that world in informed and ethical ways is the very essence of politics, one not corrupted by simplistic partisan politics of endorsing Democrats or Republicans (which is worth resisting in education and journalism).

Currently, the U.S. and even the entire world are faced with whether or not we truly believe in freedom and equity, whether or not we are willing to invest in the institutions that can leverage both that freedom and equity—institutions such as formal education and the media. And we have been here before, in the same words and the same actions. If the answer is yes, then our resolve must be linked to demanding that our teachers and journalists are grounded in taking informed and ethical stands, not the dishonest and uncritical pose of objectivity. As I have shown above, neither is really being neutral now, but instead, pulling out the objective card only when it serves the interests of the status quo.

Critical educators and critical journalists must not serve the whims of power and money, and must be transparent in their pursuit of credible evidence and ethical behavior. To frame everything as a debate with equally credible antithetical sides is dishonest and insufficient for the promise of life, liberty, and the pursuit of happiness. Teachers and journalists are *always political agents*; both professions must choose in whose interest they are willing to work. The neutral pose by either is to take a seat on the train, to keep eyes down, and to allow the train to rumble along as if the tracks are not leading to a cliff. Pretending that cliff isn't now on our horizon will not stop the train from crashing on the rocks of the coming abyss.

ADICHIE'S "DANGER OF A SINGLE STORY" AND THE RISE OF POST-TRUTH TRUMPLANDIA

Focusing on fake news and post-truth discourse, then, often fails to confront that they are but extreme although logical extensions of a mainstream media and political elite existing almost entirely on false narratives—the denial of basic reality. The bootstrap and rising boat narratives, black-on-black crime, the pervasive threat of terrorism, the lazy poor, the welfare queen, and the relentless "kids today" mantra—these are all powerful as well as enduring claims but also provably false (Nightingale, 2016), if we practice critical media literacy.

As noted above, the media simply report that Source X makes Claim A—but never venture into the harder story that Source X is *making a false* Claim A—especially when false Claim A rings true within the Great American Myths (such as the stereotypes about people in poverty callously included in the soda story in the NYT) that Chimamanda Ngozi Adichie (2009) powerfully warns about:

> I'm a storyteller. And I would like to tell you a few personal stories about what I like to call "the danger of the single story." …

> I come from a conventional, middle-class Nigerian family. My father was a professor. My mother was an administrator. And so we had, as was the norm, live-in domestic help, who would often come from nearby rural villages. So, the year I turned eight, we got a new house boy. His name was Fide. The only thing my mother told us about him was that his family was very poor. My mother sent yams and rice, and our old clothes, to his family. And when I didn't finish my dinner, my mother would say, "Finish your food! Don't you know? People like Fide's family have nothing." So I felt enormous pity for Fide's family.
>
> Then one Saturday, we went to his village to visit, and his mother showed us a beautifully patterned basket made of dyed raffia that his brother had made. I was startled. It had not occurred to me that anybody in his family could actually make something. All I had heard about them was how poor they were, so that it had become impossible for me to see them as anything else but poor. Their poverty was my single story of them.

Adichie artfully shares more examples in her talk, but her message from 2009 rings much more horrifying today in the post-truth U.S., where the elected leader of the free world can say something one minute, deny it the next, and remain safely cloaked in the lies that endure as the "one story" many in the U.S. believe despite ample evidence to the contrary.

Part of teaching critical media literacy is to warn students about the failure of having only one story. The one story of black men as criminals that allows police to disproportionately execute those black men in the streets. The one story of the lazy poor that allows political leaders to avoid their moral obligations to provide social services, including health care even for children. The one story of objectified women that allows rape culture and the democratically elected leader of the free world to boast about his own cavalier behavior as a sexual predator.

And so: "Stories matter. Many stories matter," Adichie (2009) concludes: "Stories have been used to dispossess and to malign, but stories can also be used to empower and to humanize. Stories can break the dignity of a people, but stories can also repair that broken dignity." More recently for Adichie (2016), "now is the time" to confront post-truth discourse, and the media are on notice:

> Yet a day after the election, people spoke of the vitriol between Barack Obama and Donald Trump. No, the vitriol was Trump's. Now is the time to burn false equivalencies forever. Pretending that both sides of an issue are equal when they are not is not "balanced" journalism; it is a fairy tale—and, unlike most fairy tales, a disingenuous one.

A post-truth U.S. is creeping toward yet another of the very ugliest stories of a people claiming to embrace life and liberty but denying basic reality instead. The question before educators tasked with teaching critical media literacy is whether or not we have the capacity for changing that arc of history toward, as Adichie expresses, the possibility to "regain a kind of paradise."

U.S. AND EDUCATION REFORM NEED A CRITICAL FREE PRESS

As a powerful example of how fake news and post-truth discourse are less dangerous to our democracy than mainstream media is journalism's flawed coverage of education. Journalists, in their quest to maintain the traditional commitment to "fair and balanced" journalism, consistently *endorse* and perpetuate organizations without credibility and baseless claims (such as cries of "bad" teacher, "bad" teacher education, and "bad" unions).

With yet another report released by National Council on Teacher Quality (NCTQ), a right-leaning think tank, that failure of the mainstream media can be highlighted once again—specifically in coverage at *NPR* and *Education Week*, both of which are viewed as left-leaning mainstream media: "Study Delivers Failing Grades For Many Programs Training Teachers," Claudio Sanchez and Juana Summers (2014); "Alternative Certification Deemed Weak by NCTQ in New Teacher-Prep Report," Stephen Sawchuk (2014); "Most Teacher Preparation Falls Short on Strategies for ELLs, NCTQ Finds," Lesli A. Maxwell (2014).

First, the mainstream coverage of NCTQ's reports remains trapped inside *assumed crises* (the single-story mistake) that have no basis in fact; NCTQ's reports and then the media begin with the givens that education suffers under the burden of "bad" teachers, "bad" teacher certification, and "bad" unions. However, at the very least, these claims are disproportional, if not outright erroneous:

- If we maintain the current context that student achievement is accurately reflected in test scores (and it isn't), then we must acknowledge that teacher quality (10–15%) and school quality account for only about 20% of that measurement, but "60 percent of achievement outcomes is explained by student and family background characteristics (most are unobserved, but likely pertain to income/ poverty)," as Di Carlo (2010) details.
- If we accept that value-added methods (VAM) can accurately and consistently identify "good" and "bad" teachers (and the evidence is that it cannot [Amrein-Beardsley, 2017]) and if we accept the much repeated claim by Chetty et al. that teacher quality can add $50,000 to the lifetime earning potential of a student (and that also is a significantly contested claim [Thomas, 2014, June 16], as well as another example of advocacy and media hyperbole since that lifetime-earning figure equates to about 1.5–2 tanks of gas per month), the enormity of the claims about "bad" teachers and the urgency expressed about creating and implementing huge and expensive test-based systems to address teacher quality are at best *overstated*. No rational person would endorse the cost-benefit analysis of such schemes.
- Finally, claims that teachers unions are primary or significant *negative* influences on educational quality are powerfully refuted by the historical and current fact that the states in the U.S. with the lowest standardized test scores tend to be those that are right-to-work (non-union) states. Unionization correlates *positively* with measurable student achievement, in fact, while

poverty is the greatest correlation with low measurable student outcomes (for the record, union bashing is a straw man because U.S. public education has a poverty problem, not a union problem).

Next, NCTQ has established a sort of immediate *appearance* of credibility through three strategies: partnering itself with *U.S. News & World Report*, garnering significant and influential sources of funding, and bombarding the mainstream media with a series of reports without vetting those reports through blind peer review as is common in traditional scholarship, which slows down and greatly harnesses higher-quality research from reaching the public (Molnar, 2001; Yettick, 2009). And scholars don't issue press releases, and apparently, journalists respond primarily to press releases instead of conducting investigative journalism.

Further, once I engaged Sawchuck (*EdWeek*) and then Summers (NPR) on Twitter, several key aspects of this phenomenon were highlighted. Both journalists argued that their pieces on NCTQ were fair, and even critical—which I will examine below—but here I return to the comment quoted above by Summers on Twitter: "I'm not sure it's my place to say whether the study is credible, but we both note the significant criticism of the methods."

My two reactions to Summers deferring from examining the credibility of NCTQ are, first, to strongly disagree, and second, note that no journalists need to do any real investigative journalism to uncover that NCTQ has no credibility because all of that work has been done already by a number of scholars (see Thomas, 2014, June 17; Thomas & Goering, 2016). As disturbing, however, as that stance is, examining carefully the coverage of NCTQ reveals that the mainstream media do in fact *endorse* NCTQ implicitly (despite claims of impartiality) and also marginalizes the credible critiques of NCTQ.

All three articles (see above) have headlines that establish immediately for any reader that NCTQ's report is worthy of major media coverage. Next, all three articles have ledes that also present NCTQ positively:

> The nation's teacher-preparation programs have plenty of room for improvement, according to a new report. (Sanchez & Summers, 2014)
>
> Alternative-certification programs for preparing teachers suffer from many of the same problems that the National Council on Teacher Quality has identified in traditional, university-based programs, the Washington-based group concludes in a new pilot study. (Sawchuk, 2014)
>
> More than 75 percent of elementary teacher-preparation programs are failing when it comes to readying future teachers to work effectively with English-language learners, a new report from the National Council on Teacher Quality contends. (Maxwell, 2014)

Sanchez and Summers (again, recall that Summers argues it isn't her job to assign credibility to the study) certainly imply that the study is credible by using this language: "The study is a dismal read, given that the U.S. spends more than $6 billion each year to prepare teachers for the classroom."

The NCTQ study is only a "dismal read" if it is *accurate* (and it isn't). NCTQ has been carefully discredited in scholarship (for example, see Fuller, 2013) for serious conflicts of interest (Teach For America and KIPP leaders sit on the Advisory Board), for a flawed study design, and for shoddy methodology. So how are credible academic critiques of NCTQ characterized in the journalism that claims not to take evaluative positions?:

> When NCTQ released a version of this report last year, it was met with some skepticism among educators and those responsible for preparing teachers. Critics said the advocacy group should have visited individual teacher-prep programs and talked to graduates and students, rather than relying on syllabi. (Sanchez & Summers, 2014)

> Last year's inaugural teacher-prep review was immediately rejected by most teacher colleges and, especially, by their main membership body, the American Association of Colleges for Teacher Education.
>
> Criticism focused on the NCTQ's tack of reviewing syllabi and other course materials rather than visiting institutions; its use of open-records requests and current students to obtain documents; the complaint that its standards weren't agreed to by the profession; and the fact that its research products aren't peer reviewed. Additionally, critics have claimed that the project is ideologically driven, given NCTQ's role as incubator of an alternative-certification group, the American Board for Certification of Teacher Excellence (ABCTE), which received federal funding from the George W. Bush administration.
>
> The latter complaint seems less viable now that the NCTQ has turned its green eyeshade toward alternative-certification programs. (Sawchuk, 2014)

"Some skepticism" and "critics" clearly position credible scholarship negatively while maintaining the implied endorsement of NCTQ as an organization and NCTQ's reports. And while Sawchuk appears to address more directly NCTQ's lack of credibility, he still marginalizes scholars as "critics" and then in the last paragraph above, simply discounts the criticism.

Further in Sawchuk's (2014) piece, the contrast between lacking credibility (NCTQ) and credibility (scholarship discrediting NCTQ) is reduced to a simple misunderstanding and a matter of tone (not substance):

> Notably, the report's introduction this year contains a number of mea culpas regarding the bad blood between the NCTQ and teacher colleges. And Walsh agreed that her group bore some of the blame.
>
> "At times we were a bit arrogant about what it is we think teacher education should be doing," she said. "Even if we agree to disagree, we can be more respectful."

Again, this trivializes criticism of NCTQ and further equates NCTQ (an advocacy think tank) with scholarship—while also painting NCTQ as apologetic (despite the organization maintaining its *threat* of ranking programs whether they cooperate or not; a powerful tool afforded NCTQ because of its media partnership with *U.S. News & World Report*).

One of my strongest criticisms of teachers is that we far too often allow ourselves to be trapped within traditional calls that we take neutral stances; however, the U.S. needs *critical* teachers (political teachers) if our public schools are to be a foundation for our democracy. What I have detailed above is that journalists in the U.S. have bowed to the same call for neutrality, one that cannot be accomplished but can serve as a shield for maintaining the status quo. The U.S. needs *critical* journalists, ones who see their job as maintaining a commitment to seeking out and identifying the credibility of issues and events they report. Only those in power benefit when the free press is mostly free of taking to task those in power. Nowhere is that more apparent than in how the mainstream media fails the education reform debate.

WHY EDUCATION: CRITICAL LITERACY, FREEDOM, AND EQUITY

Along with the failures of mainstream journalism, the 2016 presidential election cycle provided another powerful and disturbing lesson in the U.S.: formal education has failed to accomplish the single most important aspect of why universal public education is essential for a free and just people, which includes grounding instruction in critical pedagogy, critical literacy, and critical media literacy. Often, we view formal education as a key to economic success, emphasizing the strong correlation between higher educational attainment and greater income. But we also remain committed to our mythologies and cultural narratives about education being the "great equalizer."

However, as this discussion will examine further, these beliefs are not supported by evidence. Yes, greater educational attainment correlates well with income, but schooling does not create equity (Thomas, 2014, December 4). While the relationship between formal education and any person's career and earning potential remains incredibly important in a capitalistic society, the *single most important aspect of why universal public education is essential for a free and just people* remains the relationship between formal education and freedom as well as social equity. Integral to the role of formal education as it contributes to individual freedom and societal equity is *critical literacy*: "challeng[ing] the status quo in an effort to discover alternative paths for self and social development" (Shor, 1999). For Paulo Freire (1993), a founding thinker in critical pedagogy, critical literacy is the ability to read and re-read the world along with the ability to write and re-write the world.

In more accessible language, critical literacy is the ability of any person to act on her/his world instead of being a slave to that world. Critical literacy is *living* instead of simply *surviving*. Here I want to offer one caveat: As I note often, formal schooling is not the only path to being educated. Many people (writers notably) have achieved a high level of awareness and education in spite of formal schooling. Yet, universal public education—as created by our very flawed founding fathers—was rightfully placed as essential if people were to achieve freedom and if a country were to ever become equitable (in our inception, we were far from that; today, equity remains a goal of the U.S., not something we have achieved).

But being well educated is not simply about the acquisition of knowledge (what Freire rejected as the "banking" concept of education). Being well educated is about being able to acquire knowledge in order to investigate and interrogate that knowledge: What is the source of that knowledge? Whose interest does that knowledge serve? Despite being economically and militarily powerful, the U.S. remains stagnated, when compared to other democracies, in a belief culture—stubbornly clinging to unwarranted beliefs despite an abundance of evidence easily accessible to anyone.

My public writing is dominated by interacting with well-educated people (often edujournalists) who are committed to provably false claims, and daily I interact with family, friends, and students who also cling to falsehoods and function while holding contradictory beliefs. These experiences are vivid to me because they reflect my own journey, having been raised in the South and indoctrinated with beliefs that I now reject strongly—racism, classism, sexism, homophobia. Much of my life over the past thirty years has been stepping back from beliefs that I discovered are false, flawed, unethical. That process is hurtful, disappointing, even embarrassing.

Even though I am approaching 60 and well educated, it still happens.

When teaching writing, I am so aware of the power of misconceptions and false beliefs, that I teach students to focus on misconceptions when doing public writing—a dependable pattern of "you likely think X is true, but consider this." And throughout all my teaching, grounded in critical pedagogy, I foster critical literacy and critical media literacy as a foundational commitment to individual freedom and equity.

Let me end with a couple examples.

Critical literacy is an awareness *and* investigation of codes. For example, why are blacks often called "thugs," but whites demonstrating similar behaviors are not? Because "thug" is a code for "nigger" that remains socially acceptable only because of a *lack of critical literacy*. And research shows that when whites are confronted with the fact of racism, they immediately emphasize their own hardships (Phillips, 2015). This also is a lack of critical literacy that allows an understanding of percentages: more whites are shot by police because whites outnumber blacks about 5 to 1, but blacks are more likely to be shot by police in terms of percentages—a fact of *racial inequity*.

Finally, as well, that whites suffer hardships isn't the issue—because whites do. Racism is about power, and the fact that white hardship is not because of being white while black hardship often is *because of being black*. Belief is dangerous because it oversimplifies the world to the point of being harmful. Critical literacy is about being able to step back from those simple beliefs in order to negotiate and even change the real and complex world.

This is the more important *why* of education, more important than what job or salary anyone will have or achieve. Education is about taking control of life so that it doesn't happen to you, so that it doesn't steamroll over you. Without critical literacy and increasingly critical media literacy, a people become pawns to demagogues and buffoons. We are a people without critical literacy and that may result in our being the pawns we deserve to be.

NOTES

1 I know this appears to read like a piece from *The Onion*, but Republican Rep. Butt is real; *The Onion* would have used Ophelia Butt.

2 Consider that the century-old debate between Creationism and evolution has morphed into the rise of Intelligent Design (replacing creationism) as pseudo-science to battle with traditional science, evolution.

REFERENCES

Adichie, C. N. (2009, October). The danger of a single story [subtitles and transcript]. *TED*. Retrieved from https://www.ted.com/talks/chimamanda_adichie_the_danger_of_a_single_story/transcript

Adichie, C. N. (2016, December 2). Now is the time to talk about what we are actually talking about. *The New Yorker*. Retrieved from http://www.newyorker.com/culture/cultural-comment/now-is-the-time-to-talk-about-what-we-are-actually-talking-about

Amrein-Beardsley, A. (2017, May 9). Also last thursday in Nevada: The "top ten" research-based reasons why large-scale, standardized tests should not be used to evaluate teachers [Web log]. *Vamboozled*. Retrieved from http://vamboozled.com/also-last-thursday-in-nevada-the-top-ten-research-based-reasons-why-large-scale-standardized-tests-should-not-be-used-to-evaluate-teachers/

Davis, W. (2016, December 5). Fake or real? How to self-check the news and get the facts. *NPR*. Retrieved from http://www.npr.org/sections/alltechconsidered/2016/12/05/503581220/fake-or-real-how-to-self-check-the-news-and-get-the-facts

Di Carlo, M. (2010, July 14). Teachers matter, but so do words [Web log]. *Albert Shanker Institute*. Retrieved from http://www.shankerinstitute.org/blog/teachers-matter-so-do-words

Freire, P. (1993). *Pedagogy of the oppressed* (M. B. Ramos, Trans.). New York, NY: Continuum.

Fuller, E. J. (2013, September 16). Shaky methods, shaky motives. *Journal of Teacher Education, 65*(1), 63–77.

Gold, H. (2017, January 1). New York Times, Wall Street Journal editors take on Trump and the media. *Politico*. Retrieved from http://www.politico.com/blogs/on-media/2017/01/embargo-new-york-times-wall-street-journal-editor-on-trump-and-the-media-233077

Gorski, P. C. (2013, October 28). Five stereotypes about poor families and education: The answer sheet [Web log]. *The Washington Post*. Retrieved from https://www.washingtonpost.com/news/answer-sheet/wp/2013/10/28/five-stereotypes-about-poor-families-and-education/

Hedges, C. (2016, December 18). "Fake news" in America: Homegrown, and far from new. *Truthdig*. Retrieved from http://www.truthdig.com/report/item/fake_news_homegrown_and_far_from_new_20161218

Holmes, J. (2016, December 1). A Trump surrogate drops the mic: "There's no such thing as facts." *Esquire*. Retrieved from http://www.esquire.com/news-politics/videos/a51152/trump-surrogate-no-such-thing-as-facts/

Jumping the Shark. (n.d.). *TV Tropes*. Retrieved from http://tvtropes.org/pmwiki/pmwiki.php/Main/JumpingTheShark

Kendzior, S. (2016, December 16). The fake war on fake news. *The Globe and Mail*. Retrieved from https://beta.theglobeandmail.com/opinion/the-fake-war-on-fake-news/article33347119/

Mackey, R. (2015, May 31). Ex-FIFA official cites satirical article from the onion in his self-defense. *The New York Times*. Retrieved from https://www.nytimes.com/2015/06/01/world/americas/ex-fifa-official-jack-warner-cites-onion-article-in-defense.html

Maxwell, L. A. (2014, June 17). Most teacher preparation falls short on strategies for ELLs, NCTQ finds: Learning the language [Web log]. *Education Week*. Retrieved from http://blogs.edweek.org/edweek/learning-the-language/2014/06/most_teacher_prep_falls_short_.html

Molnar, A. (2001, April 11). *The media and educational research: What we know vs what the public hears*. Milwaukee, WI: Center for Education Research, Analysis, and Innovation. Retrieved from http://epsl.asu.edu/epru/documents/cerai-01-14.html

Nightingale, J. (2016, November 27). Some garbage I used to believe about equality [Web log]. *The Co-Pour*. Retrieved from https://mfbt.ca/some-garbage-i-used-to-believe-about-equality-e7c771784f26

O'Connor, A. (2017, January 13). In the shopping cart of a food stamp household: Lots of soda. *The New York Times*. Retrieved from https://www.nytimes.com/2017/01/13/well/eat/food-stamp-snap-soda.html

Padilla, A. (2017, January 15). Tennessee could ban people from using food stamps to buy soda, ice cream, other junk food. *FOX 31*. Retrieved from http://kdvr.com/2017/01/15/tennessee-could-ban-people-from-using-food-stamps-to-buy-soda-ice-cream-other-junk-food/

Philips, L. T. (2015, November). The hard-knock life? Whites claim hardships in response to racial inequity. *Journal of Experimental Social Psychology, 61*, 12–18. doi:10.1016/j.jesp.2015.06.008

Rampell, C. (2016, December 28). Americans – especially but not exclusively Trump voters – believe crazy, wrong things. *The Washington Post*. Retrieved from https://www.washingtonpost.com/news/rampage/wp/2016/12/28/americans-especially-but-not-exclusively-trump-voters-believe-crazy-wrong-things/

Sanchez, C., & Summers, J. (2014, June 17). Study delivers failing grades for many programs training teachers. *NPR*. Retrieved from http://www.npr.org/sections/ed/2014/06/17/323032745/study-delivers-failing-grades-for-many-programs-training-teachers

Sawchuk, S. (2014, June 17). Alternative certification deemed weak by NCTQ in new teacher-prep report: Teacher beat [Web log]. *Education Week*. Retrieved from http://blogs.edweek.org/edweek/teacherbeat/2014/06/alternative-certification_deemed_weak.html

Shane, S. (2017, January 18). From headline to photograph, a fake news masterpiece. *The New York Times*. Retrieved from https://www.nytimes.com/2017/01/18/us/fake-news-hillary-clinton-cameron-harris.html

Shor, I. (1999, Fall). What is critical literacy? *Journal of Pedagogy, Pluralism and Practice, 1*(4), Article 2. Retrieved from http://www.lesley.edu/journal-pedagogy-pluralism-practice/ira-shor/critical-literacy/

Soss, J. (2017, January 16). Food stamp fables. *Jacobin*. Retrieved from https://www.jacobinmag.com/2017/01/food-stamps-snap-welfare-soda-new-york-times/

Thomas, P. L. (2014, June 16). The very disappointing teacher numbers from Chetty [Web log]. *Radical Eyes for Equity*. Retrieved from https://radicalscholarship.wordpress.com/2014/06/16/the-very-disappointing-teacher-impact-numbers-from-chetty/

Thomas, P. L. (2014, June 17). UPDATED: NCTQ: "Their remedies are part of the disease" [Web log]. *Radical Eyes for Equity*. Retrieved from https://radicalscholarship.wordpress.com/2014/06/17/nctq-their-remedies-are-part-of-the-disease/

Thomas, P. L. (2014, December 4). Grit, education narratives veneer for white, wealth privilege [Web log]. *Radical Eyes for Equity*. Retrieved from https://radicalscholarship.wordpress.com/2014/12/04/grit-education-narratives-veneer-for-white-wealth-privilege/

Thomas, P. L., & Goering, C. Z. (2016). *Review of "Learning about learning: What every new teacher needs to know."* Boulder, CO: National Education Policy Center. Retrieved from http://nepc.colorado.edu/thinktank/review-teacher-education

Vallas, R., & Robbins, K. G. (2017, January 16). In the shopping cart of a food stamp household: Not what the New York Times reported. *Talk Poverty*. Retrieved from https://talkpoverty.org/2017/01/16/shopping-cart-food-stamp-household-not-new-york-times-reported/

Woman a leading authority on what shouldn't be in poor people's grocery carts. (2014, May 1). *The Onion*. Retrieved from http://www.theonion.com/article/woman-a-leading-authority-on-what-shouldnt-be-in-p-35922

Yettick, H. (2009). *The research that reaches the public: Who produces the educational research mentioned in the news media?* Boulder, CO & Tempe, AZ: Education and the Public Interest Center & Education Policy Research Unit. Retrieved from http://epicpolicy.org/publication/research-that-reaches

P. L. Thomas
Department of Education
Furman University
Greenville, South Carolina

TROY HICKS AND KRISTEN HAWLEY TURNER

3. RECONSIDERING EVIDENCE IN REAL WORLD ARGUMENTS

Everyone is entitled to his own opinion but not to his own facts.

– Daniel Patrick Moynihan, 1927–2003
Senator, Ambassador, Presidential Advisor

INTRODUCTION

Decades ago, when we and our peers were still in our tweens and teens, on the journey through our K-12 schooling, we researched information in libraries. Carefully, we took our 3x5 notecards to the library; we found facts printed in books that had been, presumably, well-researched by authors, had been vetted by editors and publishers, and had finally found their ways onto the shelves. Lessons on the difference between fact and opinion were important, yes, especially when looking at the op-ed pages of the newspaper or tabloids at the supermarket checkout stand. However, any fringe ideas, lies, or hoaxes (while existent) were generally not found in school libraries, and we could rely on the premise that what we read was accurate. Reliable. True.

History was history.

Science was science.

Facts were, indeed, facts.

Fast forward to the 1990s, and the Internet opened new avenues for research. As the democratic ideals of the web gave way to the darker impulses of human nature, online spaces allowed anyone to publish anything, all without traditional vetting practices. In response, students learned to critically evaluate websites; checklists provided ways for them to consider the reliability of sources and potential bias of various domains by considering such criteria as the credentials of the author, the date of last update, and the domain's extension (Schrock, 2016). Questions about the quality of information on a website underscored this work, and comments like "don't trust a .com" or "*Wikipedia* is unreliable" entered classroom conversations. We established rules of thumb for how we could manage the web, sifting through the humorous deception of dihydrogen monoxide (Way, 2017) and pure fakery of northwest tree octopi (Zapato, 2017) to help students discern high quality information.

 DOI 10.1163/9789004365360_003

Except, we didn't do our job well. Or, at the very least, not well enough.

In the wake of the 2016 United States Presidential election, we now live in a "post-truth" world. Or, as host of *This American Life* Ira Glass lamented in the October 21, 2016 broadcast,

> The presentation of facts is seen as partisan opinion, and then every day a barrage of untruths are presented as truth, and we're just supposed to suck it up. That's the moment we live in. That's our country right now. And this is going to continue after this election, no matter who wins. Like, this is the rest of our lives, I think, this post-truth politics. With so many of us getting our news from social media and from sources that we agree with, it's easier than ever to check if a fact is true, and facts matter less than ever. (Glass, 2016)

These discussions about truth and reliability over the past few decades were, at the heart, centered on a question that has, in many ways, been with us since philosophers discussed it in an open air school of Athens: "What counts as evidence?" At a deeper level, these discussions make us wonder, "How is knowledge made?" And, to return to the task at hand, "How can writers use evidence in a manner that honors the context and purpose in which the evidence was gathered?"

Though questions about the nature of evidence have been around for centuries, in recent years the importance of evidence in students' compositions has taken center stage for a number of reasons. As social media encourages individuals to share unedited thoughts and popular media promulgates unsubstantiated claims, the need for evidence is becoming even more critical. Moreover, both the Common Core standards and the redesigned SAT have urged teachers to adopt evidence-based writing as a key component of instruction. While there are certainly many ways to critique both the CCSS and the SAT, the recent changes have invigorated a conversation about the importance of evidence in teaching writing (The College Board, n.d.).

Now, as always, evidence still matters. But what counts as evidence? For whom? And in what contexts? The nature of evidence—in light of ever-changing religious, political, scientific, and philosophical beliefs—is certainly up for debate, and it is too big a debate for us to tackle in this short chapter. However, the nature of evidence in light of traditional academic arguments, especially of the types of arguments written by students in school, is a topic worthy of time and attention. Creating five paragraph essays in which a predetermined thesis is supported with cherry-picked evidence is, if it ever really was, no longer enough for students to become critical, creative thinkers. Helping them understand the nature of evidence—and how certain kinds of evidence works rhetorically within a broader academic conversation—is necessary if we want students to become accomplished writers in a digital age.

THE NATURE OF EVIDENCE IN A DIALOGIC WORLD

Argument is about conversation, about engaging in a dialogue, not simply about having right and wrong positions. As Lakoff and Johnson (1980) pointed out in *Metaphors We Live By*, the "argument as war" frame sets up argument in an adversarial manner. However, from a different perspective, the act of argument is not about defending one's position, so much as it is about participating in an ongoing discussion.

Toulmin (1958) described a structure of argument that assumes individuals are engaged as conversational partners, and this framework is useful in analyzing how arguments are constructed in a digital age. Toulmin said that an argument begins with a claim, which presents an arguable position. This claim might be challenged by someone who asks, "What have you got to go on?" (Toulmin, 1958, p. 13). In essence, this challenge is asking for "data, facts, or other backing we consider to be relevant and sufficient to make good the initial claim" (p. 13). Claims cannot exist in a vacuum, and likewise, the evidence that supports the claim must be connected to the claim with an implicit or explicit warrant, or "the general principle that enables [a writer] to move from the reason to the specific claim" (Lunsford & Ruszkiewicz, 1999, p. 84).

Toulmin's model for argument describes thoughtful conversation, where challenges are rebutted using data, and claims are developed, explored, and revised through discussion. In a digital world, where these conversations happen through written form and multimedia, readers and writers are bound by a contract, or what Nystrand (1986) called a "reciprocity principle." Reciprocity assumes that readers and writers share norms of communication that embody shared meaning, purpose, and understanding. What happens, though, when the individuals in conversation do not operate with attention to reciprocity? What if they have disparate values that, seemingly, do not allow for thoughtful discussion?

Disparate values emerge for different reasons. Toulmin and his colleagues (Toulmin, Rieke, & Janik, 1984) acknowledged that arguments across fields vary in their *formality*, *precision*, *modes of resolution*, and *goals*. These differences sometimes make cross-disciplinary conversations challenging. For example, scientists construct arguments that are generally presented as claims that lead to a discernible fact. For example, the fact that the Earth rotates around the sun is one that has been proven through scientific inquiry and can be modeled mathematically (as well as through observation). For the arts or ethics, however, evidence and warrants are employed in different ways. In an ethical argument, there is a premise that one side could be "right" and another side could be "wrong." These types of arguments bring various legal, moral, and religious elements into them, and understanding the warrants becomes essential; warrants are the underlying assumptions that connect evidence to claims, ultimately making an argument valid.

These disciplinary differences are, however, not quite the same as what we are seeing in popular discourse today in a post-truth world where opinions are stated as fact, and facts themselves have come under fire. As many journalists and academics have lamented in the months since the 2016 election, there are still such things as "facts." See *The New York Times*' "The Truth Is Hard" (The New York Times, 2017) or National Public Radio's "Stand with the Facts" campaigns

(Cincinnati Public Radio, 2017) as two examples. For instance, in a move that risks breaking long-held norms of journalistic objectivity, the *New York Times* has even gone so far as to publish (and continually update) a page on their website devoted to documenting "nearly every outright lie" of President Donald Trump (Leonhardt & Thompson, 2017).

In all the descriptions of argument noted above, it is not the *evidence* itself that is in question. Recall Moynihan's quote at the opening of the chapter about the place of facts in argument. Though interpretations of the evidence may have differed, it was until very recently that scholars, journalists, politicians, and the general public would generally agree that evidence gathered in a rigorous and appropriate manner was, indeed, factual. Now, however, it seems impossible for us to agree on the facts, or the ways in which the facts are made, in everyday conversations.

In other words, we are now in a world where it is not only common to see evidence being fabricated, manipulated, or otherwise misused, but to see faulty evidence employed in a variety of arguments. In school, we would call this a violation of academic integrity. In the real world, where we live through internet searches, social media feeds, and popular media, we call this misuse of evidence something else: the new normal where, as Ira Glass put it, "facts matter less than ever." More than just teaching students to deconstruct an argument, it seems we now need for them to question the nature of evidence itself.

And, thus, we return to the core questions that can guide teachers and students:

What counts as evidence?

For whom?

In what context?

Exploring these questions of what counts as evidence is a critical piece of literacy instruction in a post-truth era. For many years we have relied on simplistic formulas or paradigms to describe the ways in which certain materials are good or bad, appropriate for referencing, or entirely unreliable. Trust a .org or .edu; never use *Wikipedia*. However, as recent discourse, fake news, and the over-reliance on unsubstantiated claims to make arguments, we must dig deeper into these questions about evidence. We must teach students how to analyze the evidence being used (or, perhaps, *not* being used) in the spaces they consume information and to consider how to present and warrant evidence in their own writing. In order to reach this goal and to help students become more critical and creative in the ways they think about the nature of evidence, we offer a framework for considering the use of evidence in various arguments.

TYPES OF EVIDENCE

First introduced to Kristen many years ago in a professional development workshop that focused on structured debates as a "hierarchy of evidence" (Turner, 2004, 2005), we have since acknowledged that "hierarchy" suggests a range in quality that may not hold true across disciplines. Therefore, we present "common types of evidence" (Turner & Hicks, 2016, p. 31) that can help students to consider how authors choose their evidence, as well as how they might present it in a digital text: scientific law, statistical data, expert opinion, opinion of noted individuals, and anecdotal evidence. For each type of evidence, we suggest that students consider the following questions:

- How is this kind of evidence generated?
- When is this kind of evidence used?
- What cautions should be taken when using/encountering this kind of evidence?

Scientific Law

Scientific law is established through a process of sustained, systematic inquiry. Scientists make hypotheses and design experiments to test them. Data is collected on an experimental condition, a natural observation, or some other situation in which change can be measured. Over time, conclusions about the data are drawn and scientists can create substantive claims about the ways in which a phenomenon occurs. Science is never fixed, but theories are constantly tested in order to uncover scientific "laws" that govern the physical properties of the universe and life itself.

When used as evidence. Using evidence accepted as scientific law can help a writer show gravitas. Though not all audiences will accept science at face value, for the most part, it is difficult to counter scientific law because of the rigorous testing and peer review that has contributed to its creation.

Critical questions and cautions. Bias or prejudice may influence a writer's selection of scientific laws or a reader's willingness to accept science as "truth." Science is often seen in conflict with issues of faith, and it is important to recognize the context in which an argument is made. Will the reader accept scientific law as evidence? In what contexts might this kind of evidence be less powerful? These questions are important to explore when taking scientific law into consideration as evidence to support a claim.

Statistical Data

Statistics are often the result of randomized controlled trials or surveys, and they are more powerful when they can be generalized to the population as a whole.

For statistics to be most effective as evidence, studies must include a large, randomly selected sample. Careful experiments will compare "experimental" and "control" groups. The experimental group will get the intervention—such as a drug, a training, or other opportunity/treatment—while the control group will not. In order to make statistically significant claims, effects of the intervention are measured and then compared with the control group. When testing a new medicine, for instance, Group A is given the drug, and Group B is given a fake (called a "placebo"). Then, the researchers measure changes in people's health to see if the new medicine caused a direct change. If there are changes, for good or bad, then it means that the drug, the variable in the experiment, had an effect.

A different kind of statistical data can be gathered in order to gain insights into people's thoughts, opinions, and behaviors. For this purpose, researchers will design and distribute surveys to a population. Surveyors will use a variety of scaled, multiple-choice, open-ended and other types of questions that have been designed to elicit responses from those taking the survey. We see them quite often in politics, and we are always presented with the "margin of error." Surveys do provide some insight on important issues, and can be tracked over time when offered to a randomized sample of the population.

When used as evidence. Using evidence from a randomized controlled trial can help a writer show that the scientific community, through ethical and appropriate research methods, have determined that changing a certain variable of a situation can lead to different results for a broad population. When the writer employs data from a randomized control trial, she shows the reader that she adheres to the principles of scientific inquiry and that the evidence has undergone sufficient testing to make it valid.

When the writer provides data from a survey, she shows the reader that the ideas, opinions, and concerns of a particular population are valuable in light of a given topic. The writer should make clear where, when, and how the survey data was collected, as different survey methods (face-to-face, by phone, online) offer different advantages and limitations.

Critical questions and cautions. Various studies could be designed without the appropriate controls, and the variable under examination may have exaggerated effects. Also, there are times when a certain company or organization funds research studies, and the results should be examined carefully to make sure that no bias affected the outcome. Reporting statistics without the context in which they were gathered may not reveal the entire story.

Surveys can be notoriously inaccurate, as many people reporting data in a survey—especially data on highly sensitive topics like race, class, and gender—are likely to misrepresent their true feelings in order to provide a socially-acceptable answer. Also, depending on when, where, and how the survey was delivered, the results may be representative of only a particular group of people, and the results may not be generalizable to a broader population.

Finally, statistics are often used to make a claim about a root *cause* of a given phenomenon. Though two things might be correlated (meaning they are linked in some way), correlation does not equal causality. See the site Spurious Correlations (Vigen, n.d.), for instance, to see how per capita cheese consumption correlates with the number of people who died by becoming tangled in their bedsheets!

Expert Opinion

Experts have some kind of advanced knowledge of a field, typically marked by graduate education or real-life experience. These individuals contribute to a growing body of knowledge through publishing. They are often asked to speak at conferences or events, and they are often quoted in media reports.

When used as evidence. Writers who are not experts in a field rely on the words or opinions of experts to support their claims. By deferring to someone who has studied the topic, a writer can support her argument with authority. Experts are often directly quoted, though paraphrases of their words can also be used with appropriate citations or references. Making the case for the expertise of the individual cited is, of course, an important part of using an expert's opinion.

Critical questions and cautions. Of course, citing an expert opinion is one of the surest ways in which a writer can build his/her own ethos, as we have done ourselves in this chapter. Figuring out exactly when to use an expert—and, perhaps more importantly, which expert to use—is particularly important. Some experts work for think tanks or other organizations that may have a stake in a societal issue or that may be biased in some other way. It is important for a reader to dig deeply into the background of the expert whose opinion is being used as evidence, just as it is important for a writer to make that expertise clear.

Credible news media often try to present experts with differing views in order to promote discussion of an issue. The credibility of all experts should always be presented and/or investigated in order to judge the quality of the evidence. In a digital world, the nature of expertise is changing. Whereas teachers used to question the value of *Wikipedia* as an expert source, now *Wikipedia* is viewed as a collaboration of experts who vet the knowledge that is contributed. Recognizing that expertise may lie not in one individual, but rather in a collective, is an important part of evaluating evidence in a post-truth era.

Opinion of Noted Individuals

Noted individuals, just like the rest of us, have their own biases and perspectives. They may come to their understanding of the subject in a variety of different ways including personal experience, substantive inquiry, or being informed by the opinions of others. Often, celebrities and professional athletes, who may not have particular expertise in a subject may be cited as notable individuals with strong opinions on a topic.

When used as evidence. When the writer employs data from a noted individual, she shows the reader that this person's ideas and opinions should be taken into consideration because of their social clout. Often this kind of evidence is used with an audience who will identify with or look up to the noted individual. The writer should ensure that the word of individuals—or people speaking on behalf of other individuals or groups—should be quoted accurately, and in context (from an interview, in an article, via social media, or from other sources).

Critical questions and cautions. Throughout history, and especially in the modern era where celebrity and social media have heightened the amplitude of individual voices, the opinions of noted individuals, like all kinds of evidence, should be explored on a case-by-case basis. Additionally, specific attention should be given to whether the person being quoted is noting an opinion or is attempting to articulate or interpret facts about a given situation.

Often celebrities, though entitled to their opinion, are driven by causes or endorsement deals, and these biases must be recognized when their opinions are employed as evidence. Bandwagon appeals may be persuasive, but in many contexts, when evaluated closely, they would not carry much weight.

Anecdotal Evidence

Personal experience can be a significant factor in coming to an opinion about an issue. Anecdotes are individual stories that are used to support a claim. And, while the gist of the story is based in a person's lived experience, we know that human memory is faulty, and that stories have ways of morphing and changing over time.

When used as evidence. Writers often use anecdotes to elaborate an example or to make an emotional appeal to the audience. When doing so, a writer should provide adequate context for the anecdote ("I recall a time when I was seven…") as well as appropriate caveats ("My mom was there, too, and remembers me saying…").

Critical questions and cautions. Returning to our note earlier in the chapter that the Common Core and SAT are now pushing writers to build arguments based on evidence, we believe that the role of personal experience in argument writing is still important. Still, the extent to which an author solely relies on personal anecdote to make an argument should be minimal.

THE NATURE OF EVIDENCE IN A DIGITAL WORLD: FROM EVIDENCE TO CONTEXT

Though the weight of each of these kinds of evidence varies by discipline, these categories can be valuable in discussing how evidence can be used, and how that evidence contributes to the overall quality of the argument being presented. But what happens when students begin to examine evidence in the texts they encounter daily—texts that are hyperlinked, multimodal, and digital?

Digital texts offer opportunities for direct conversation between writers and their readers. When making claims, then, remember that writers must expect that their readers will ask, "What have you got to go on?" (Toulmin, 1958, p. 13). The evidence presented in a digital text may come in many forms. A hyperlink may lead to a web page that shares an expert opinion; an infographic embedded in the text may present statistics; a video may relate a first-person anecdote. Each of these media can be used to marshal evidence, and it is incumbent upon a reader to question not only the quality of the evidence but why these particular forms of media were selected to present it. In this sense, thinking about the various options for hyperlinks as well as embedded images and media, digital arguments become nuanced and complex.

This layer of analysis requires that readers and writers consider the context in which the argument is being made. Figure 1 (available for you to download and modify as a .docx file through link: https://goo.gl/aoNzMx) offers a graphic organizer that can help students to expand their analysis from evidence to context. By asking questions about the conversation that may unfold between a writer and readers, students can begin to identify warrants that may (or may not) link the evidence to claims. This process helps them to judge the quality of the argument.

How Does the Evidence Contribute to the Conversation?

A Critical Thinking Guide for Considering Evidence in Argument Writing

As you read and interact with "A Month Without Sugar," describe how the writer has used various kinds of evidence from the common types of evidence to build his argument. Also, consider the form of the evidence. Record your ideas in the "Examining the Evidence" section.

Then, make a judgment: Do you share a contract of reciprocity with this writer? Do you share the same norms and expectations? If so, why? If not, why not? Record your reactions to that kind of evidence in the "Contributing to the Conversation" section.

Examining the Evidence			Contributing to the Conversation
Evidence (copy/paste a quote or screenshot here if appropriate)	**Type** Scientific Law Statistical Data Expert Opinion Opinion of Noted Individual Anecdote	**Form** Quote? Link? Image? Video? Other?	*What counts as evidence?* Why is the writer using this type of evidence in this manner? *For whom?* By using this evidence, what is the assumption that the writer makes about her/his readers? *In what context?* How might a reader disagree with or challenge the way the writer has used this evidence?

Figure 1. Contributing to the conversation: a critical thinking guide for considering evidence in argument writing

To illustrate how a student can use this guide to consider the context in which an argument is being made, we analyzed an op-ed from the *New York Times*, published just before the new year, David Leonhardt's "A Month Without Sugar" (Leonhardt, 2016). Figure 2 (available for you to download as a PDF file through this link: https://goo.gl/hbQQYi) shows a completed version of the thinking guide that can be used as a model for students as they identify other evidence from the piece.

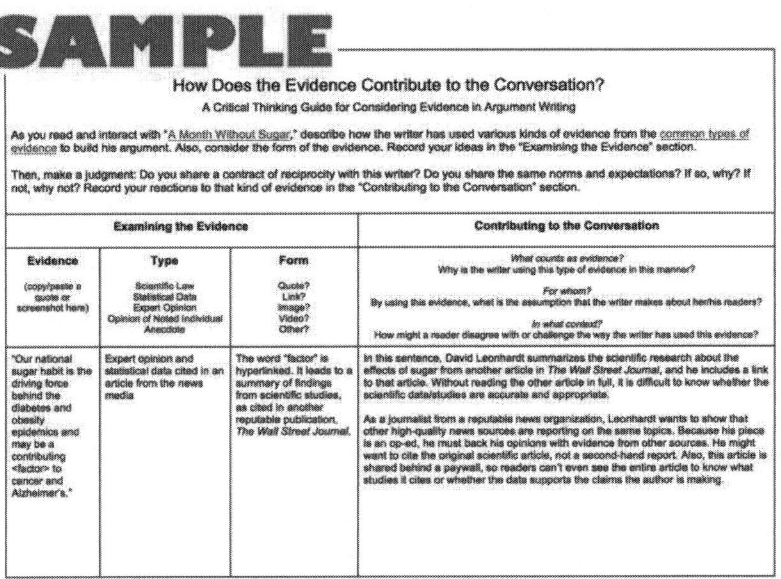

SAMPLE

How Does the Evidence Contribute to the Conversation?

A Critical Thinking Guide for Considering Evidence in Argument Writing

As you read and interact with "A Month Without Sugar," describe how the writer has used various kinds of evidence from the common types of evidence to build his argument. Also, consider the form of the evidence. Record your ideas in the "Examining the Evidence" section.

Then, make a judgment: Do you share a contract of reciprocity with this writer? Do you share the same norms and expectations? If so, why? If not, why not? Record your reactions to that kind of evidence in the "Contributing to the Conversation" section.

Examining the Evidence			**Contributing to the Conversation**
Evidence (copy/paste a quote or screenshot here)	**Type** Scientific Law Statistical Data Expert Opinion Opinion of Noted Individual Anecdote	**Form** Quote? Link? Image? Video? Other?	*What counts as evidence?* Why is the writer using this type of evidence in this manner? *For whom?* By using this evidence, what is the assumption that the writer makes about her/his readers? *In what context?* How might a reader disagree with or challenge the way the writer has used this evidence?
"Our national sugar habit is the driving force behind the diabetes and obesity epidemics and may be a contributing <factor> to cancer and Alzheimer's."	Expert opinion and statistical data cited in an article from the news media	The word "factor" is hyperlinked. It leads to a summary of findings from scientific studies, as cited in another reputable publication, *The Wall Street Journal*.	In this sentence, David Leonhardt summarizes the scientific research about the effects of sugar from another article in *The Wall Street Journal*, and he includes a link to that article. Without reading the other article in full, it is difficult to know whether the scientific data/studies are accurate and appropriate. As a journalist from a reputable news organization, Leonhardt wants to show that other high-quality news sources are reporting on the same topics. Because his piece is an op-ed, he must back his opinions with evidence from other sources. He might want to cite the original scientific article, not a second-hand report. Also, this article is shared behind a paywall, so readers can't even see the entire article to know what studies it cites or whether the data supports the claims the author is making.

Developed by Troy Hicks (@hickstro) and Kristen Hawley Turner (@teachkht). Permission granted for classroom use. More resources available at Argument in the Real World.

Figure 2. Sample thinking guide

(RE)CONSIDERING EVIDENCE: BEING *MINDFUL*

As we consider the ways in which we teach our students to be successful writers, especially those who can craft a variety of types of arguments in multimedia, we feel that it is important to include conversations about the evidence that our students might employ. It is no longer sufficient for them to grab a quotation or statistic to use in a formulaic, five paragraph essay; having just this one separate piece of evidence accumulate with other single pieces of evidence to prove the point that they have already set out in their thesis is not going to help them think critically or creatively. Instead, we must help them think about how different types of evidence can be employed across contexts, and how evidence gathered strategically from multiple sources can lead to a logical claim.

As we close this discussion about evidence and reiterate the main questions—What counts as evidence? For whom? In what contexts?—and we think about the ways in which digital arguments bring nuance and complexity to these questions, we know that sometimes arguments are not created through fully formed blog posts, academic essays, infographics, videos, or other forms of digital writing. Sometimes they are as quick and (not-so) simple as a post on social media. In using social media, writers can compose a brief message or simply share/retweet/reblog an item that someone else has created. Because students are both creating their own and (despite the claim that they may not be endorsements) authorizing the items they share, we again think about the nature of evidence and the principles of reciprocity evident in that action.

Here, we point to a thinking tool, a heuristic that we have developed for teachers and students to consider as they explore their own uses of argument in social media. Our MINDFUL acronym in Figure 3 offers writers and readers ways to analyze claims (available on the original Medium blog post with this link: https://goo.gl/JdnU8c).

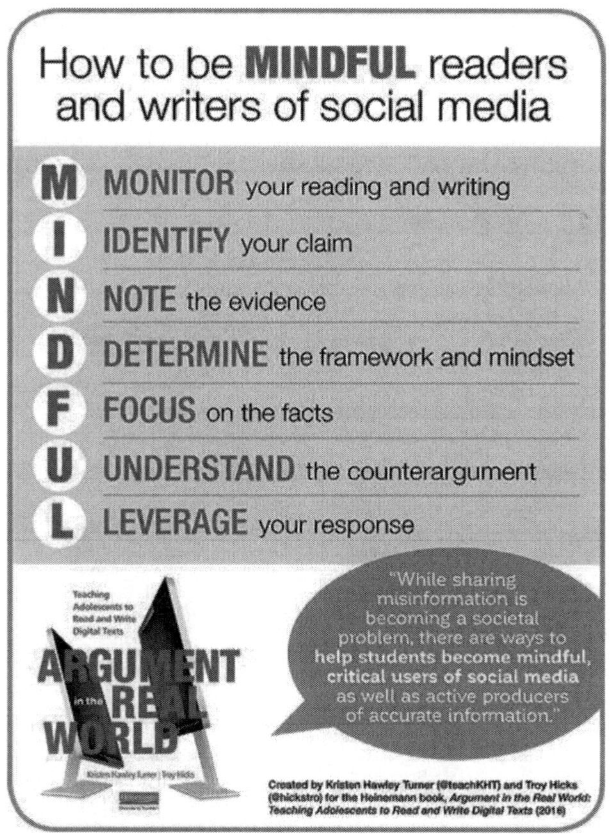

Figure 3. How to be MINDFUL readers and writers of social media[1]

While we encourage teachers to explore the entire heuristic with their students, specific sections of the acronym focus on issues of evidence. "N," noting evidence, "D," determining the framework and mindset (or context), and "F," focusing on the facts, are all key steps in carefully considering evidence. Whether a student is creating her own argument or evaluating the arguments of others, these practices will support mindful engagement in everyday life.

In short, evidence matters.

And, perhaps, being MINDFUL will encourage critical consumption and creation. Supporting students' critical literacy development may be the key to shifting public discourse away from the tendency to see argument as "winning" and instead promote productive conversations. By asking key questions we can encourage our students to think about the nature of evidence and how it matters when used in civic discourse and academic argument.

NOTE

[1] Adapted from *Argument in the Real World* by Kristen Hawley Turner and Troy Hicks for the Heinemann Blog – Medium – on January 11, 2017. Copyright © 2016 by Kristen Hawley Turner and Troy Hicks. Published by Heinemann, Portsmouth, NH. Reprinted with permission.

REFERENCES

Cincinnati Public Radio. (2017). *Stand with the facts*. Retrieved September 12, 2017, from https://www.cinradio.org/standwiththefacts/

College Board. (n.d.). *Chapter 6: Command of evidence*. New York, NY: The College Board.

Diaz, A.-C. (2017, February 23). The truth is hard. *New York Times*. Retrieved from https://www.youtube.com/watch?v=gY0Fdz350GE

Glass, I. (2016, October 21). *This American life episode 599: Seriously?* Retrieved September 12, 2017, from https://www.thisamericanlife.org/radio-archives/episode/599/seriously

Lakoff, G., & Johnson, M. (2003). *Metaphors we live by* (1st ed.). Chicago, IL: University of Chicago Press.

Leonhardt, D. (2016, December 30). Opinion: A month without sugar. *The New York Times*. Retrieved from https://www.nytimes.com/2016/12/30/opinion/a-month-without-sugar.html

Leonhardt, D., & Thompson, S. A. (2017, July 21). President Trump's lies, the definitive list. *The New York Times*. Retrieved from https://www.nytimes.com/interactive/2017/06/23/opinion/trumps-lies.html

Lunsford, A. A., & Ruszkiewicz, J. J. (1999). *Everything's an argument*. Boston, MA: Bedford/St. Martin's.

Moynihan, D. P. (2010). Daniel Patrick Moynihan: A portrait in letters of an American visionary (S. R. Weisman, Ed., 1st ed.). New York, NY: PublicAffairs.

Nystrand, M., Himley, M., & Doyle, A. (1986). *The structure of written communication: Studies in reciprocity between writers and readers*. Orlando, FL: Academic Press.

Toulmin, S. E. (2003). *The uses of argument* (2nd ed.). Cambridge: Cambridge University Press.

Toulmin, S., Rieke, R. D., & Janik, A. (1984). *An introduction to reasoning* (2nd ed.). New York, NY: Macmillan.

Turner, K. (2005). The one-stop shop: Addressing all five strands of language arts literacy with the practice of debate. *New Jersey English Journal*, 35–45.

Turner, K. H. (2005). *Toulmin and transfer: The impact of instruction in argument on students' writing across disciplines* (PhD Dissertation). Rutgers, The State University of New Jersey, New Brunswick,

NJ. Retrieved from http://search.proquest.com/docview/305429989/1402803DD8F6ED5256E/3?accountid=10181

Turner, K. H., & Hicks, T. (2016). *Argument in the real world: Teaching adolescents to read and write digital texts*. Portsmouth, NH: Heinemann.

Schrock, K. (2016). *The 5 W's of web site evaluation*. Retrieved September 12, 2017, from http://www.schrockguide.net/uploads/3/9/2/2/392267/5ws.pdf

Vigen, T. (n.d.). *Spurious correlations*. Retrieved September 12, 2017, from http://tylervigen.com/spurious-correlations

Way, T. (2017, September 12). *DMHO.org: Dihydrogen monoxide research division*. Retrieved September 12, 2017, from http://www.dhmo.org/

Zapato, L. (2015, May 17). *Save the Pacific Northwest tree octopus*. Retrieved September 12, 2017, from http://zapatopi.net/treeoctopus/

Troy Hicks
Central Michigan University
Mount Pleasant, Michigan

Kristen Hawley Turner
Drew University
Madison, New Jersey

SHARON A. MURCHIE AND JANET A. NEYER

4. WHAT IS THE STORY?

Reading the Web as Narrative

INTRODUCTION

Jayson was fired up. It was October, a few weeks before the presidential election, and he was much more interested in stirring up conflict than he was in writing about it.

"She defended a child rapist! And then she laughed about it!" he claimed.

"No, that is not even a thing!" Alisha jumped in. "She was a public defender! She HAD to defend him. That was her job! That's called defending the public! You don't get to just choose the good people to defend!"

"She laughed that he got off," Jayson insisted, "and then she laughed that he passed a lie detector test!"

"No, that is not even how that went down!" Alisha was hot, now. "You are so ignorant!" This was my[1] teacher cue to jump in, reminding them that the writing prompt on the board was about conflict they experienced in their lives, and this would be a good time to write about it. They clearly had a moment they could describe. And also, I had to add, we could argue ideas in the classroom, but not insult each other.

"Fine," Alisha snapped. "Your facts are so ignorant!"

WHAT IS THE STORY? SEARCHING FOR TRUTH

Heated discussions about "facts" like this one are becoming all too prevalent in our classrooms and in our lives. In a 2016 study by Stanford's History Education Group, researchers collected 8,000 responses from middle school, high school, and college students, asking them to evaluate online information presented in various platforms. The results were stunning: "Overall, young people's ability to reason about the information on the Internet can be summed up in one word: bleak" (p. 4). Students who have the world at their fingertips seemingly don't have the skills to decode that world and determine "facts" from "ignorant facts."

As noted in the introduction to this book, we currently live in a post-truth, fake news world. Our students are steeped in "truthiness" and "alternative facts." Satirist Stephen Colbert coined the word "truthiness" in 2005 on *The Colbert Report* and it later became one of Merriam-Webster's Words of the Year in 2006. Defined as "truth coming from the gut, not books; preferring to believe what you wish to believe, rather than what is known to be true" (Wikipedia Contributors, 2017), truthiness

 | DOI 10.1163/9789004365360_004

is grounded in feelings, not evidence. Kellyanne Conway, during a 2017 *Meet the Press* interview defending the White House's dubious claims of inauguration crowd size, coined the term "alternative facts" to explain the discrepancy between the White House's claims and the actual aerial footage and rapid transit ridership data from the event. Our students desperately need to develop the critical thinking skills to discern not only evidence-based facts from wishful thinking and feelings-based fiction, but also the many shades of grey that exist in between. Comprehensive media literacy instruction, that which includes "helping students learn to pick and evaluate the best resources for their personal learning networks from print, subscriptions, and free sources" (Hamilton, 2009, p. 5), has to be integrated into regular classroom instruction. Unfortunately, the common approach is often one that sets our students up against the scary enemy that is the media, especially the media online. The Internet is a "vast ocean," according to the European Association for Viewers Interests (2013), and we need a "golden lasso" in our superhero toolkit (Quijada, 2013) to "distinguish fact from fiction, argument from documentation, real from fake, and marketing from enlightenment" (Jenkins, 2006, p. 98). This "us versus the Internet" approach puts us as educators, and our students as consumers, on defense from day one. And a defensive mindset is never a foundation for critical thinking.

Hyperbolic metaphors aside, "discerning the validity of data or information can become very complicated when sources go to great lengths to prove that their take on an issue is the best, the most valid or corners the market on truth" (Laue, 2015, p. 1). The transition from print news to web-based news has created a media petri dish. As stories ricochet, they propagate; as they propagate, they mutate. As they mutate, we get Pizzagate.

The Center for Media Literacy explains, the "Internet [is] an international platform through which groups and organizations—even individuals—have ready access to powerful tools that can persuade others to a particular point of view, whether positive or negative" (Share, Jolls, & Thoman, 2007, p. 68). Because anyone with basic keyboarding skills can publish online, as illustrated by our recent explosion of fake news stories originating from Macedonia (Subramanian, 2017), evaluating the veracity of the news is paramount. Teaching students how to read the media and how to determine if their sources are quality is complicated, nuanced, and dynamic; students need to develop a skillset of discourse analysis that helps them discern not only the messages present in the written words but also the connotations and implications present in the iconography on the page.

In her 2014 book *It's complicated: the social lives of networked teens*, danah boyd states:

> Given the lack of formal gatekeepers and the diversity of content and authors, it's often hard to determine credibility online. Because youth do not learn to critically assess the quality of information they access, they simply look for new intermediaries who can help them determine what's valuable. For better

> or worse, they take Google's results for granted while also dismissing high-quality content from other sites that they have been taught to distrust. (p. 186)

Further, boyd stresses that "educators have an important role to play in helping youth navigate networked publics and the information-rich environments that the internet supports" (p. 180). Students "must become media literate," she states. "When they engage with media…they need to have the skills to ask questions about the construction and dissemination" of the information they are presented (p. 181). They must be able to "recognize propaganda, interpret rhetorical devices, verify sources and distinguish legitimate websites from bogus, hate or hoax websites" (Share et al., 2007, p. 68).

Many students do not have the media literacy skills needed to "identify the most credible information" (Purcell et al., 2012, p. 3). Responding to a National Writing Project survey, "A major challenge teachers cited in teaching effective research skills is getting their students to look beyond the first link in the search result list and to 'dig' for high-quality, reliable, and accurate resources" (Purcell et al., 2012, p. 3). Part of the issue at hand is that students treat the sources listed by Google as answers to their query; they don't have a clear understanding of what Google is and how it works. As boyd explains, the same lack of clarity of understanding can be applied to Wikipedia (2014, p. 186), or to any other online source of information. "Instead of looking at information and data as components of knowledge, and then understanding, [students] instead treat information in more binary terms: black or white, right or wrong, credible or not credible, good or bad" (Heick, 2014, para. 15). To make matters more complicated, our natural instinct is to treat the Internet like a "deliverer of answers"; we do a quick Google search to quickly answer the questions we have without considering the validity of the sources we consult or our own filter bubbles in accepting the answers we want to hear. Likewise, students don't apply the close reading and analytical skills they have learned in the classroom to their online reading. Students race through the pages, clicking without fully reading; they don't truly "see" what the images and iconography are presenting; they skim for answers and then quickly move on to the next hyperlink.

In order for students to be savvy consumers of online content, they need to slow down. They need to develop "the skills to question and rationally identify both overt and latent values"; only then will they be "more astute in…decision-making to accept or reject the overall message" (Share et al., 2007, p. 56). Part of the set of analytical skills that students must develop is that of multimodal critical discourse analysis; that is, looking closely at how "images, photographs, diagrams and graphics also work to create meaning" and understanding that "texts will use linguistics and visual strategies that appear normal or neutral on the surface, but which may in fact be ideological and seek to shape the representation of events and persons for particular ends" (Machin & Mayr, 2012, p. 9). Salisbury et al. (2012) argue that these skills "associated with research that lead to information seeking behaviour characterised by a high degree of discernment and scholarship…can be transferred beyond university to professional life and lifeline learning" (p. 4). The Center for Media Literacy claims that these skills are "vital for effective citizenship in a democratic society…as we negotiate our way each day of our lives through an increasingly multicultural world" (Share et al., 2007, p. 56).

This need for "effective citizenship in a democratic society" was glaringly obvious in the 2016 Presidential election cycle. The fact-checking couldn't keep up with the fact-inventing; meanwhile, memes and soundbites were posted and reposted, and the average citizen was surrounded by a filter bubble so secure that no contradictory evidence could get through. Jayson's "ignorant facts" in the classroom argument about Hillary Clinton's work as a public defender were, in fact, facts. They were out of context, and the premise of the argument was way off base. But there was truth there: Hillary Clinton did defend an accused child rapist when she was working as a public defender, the accused did accept a plea bargain, and later, Clinton did laugh in an interview when discussing the story. But clearly, the story he was quoting was framed for a specific audience with specific intent. It was playing right into his already established beliefs: that Clinton was a criminal. Jayson had already made up his mind about Clinton, and everything in his social media feed confirmed what he already knew. Like most adults, he didn't fact-check everything he read, because he believed that the media outlets publishing the stories had already done that. He wasn't thinking critically about what he was reading, or about why it was being published. He wasn't analyzing the discourse or questioning the narrative.

Traditionally, we have taught students to memorize rules and use checklists when reading the media. We used to ask students to determine the 5W's of websites in order to evaluate their sources, using checklists like the ones put out by Kathy Schrock at schrockguide.net. This used to be enough: if students could determine WHO the author was and if they were an expert; if students could determine WHAT the purpose of the website was; if students could verify WHEN the website was created; WHERE it was posted and hosted, and WHY the information was useful, then they could deem that website "verified" and use that information with confidence.

But, we quickly learned that methods like these turned the students into private investigators rather than critical thinkers and the internet into a scavenger hunt for "truth." Students would focus on URLs and copyright dates instead of the actual information on the page. Every year, students tell me the rules: "never use a .com; always use a .org." They truly believe that a .org is reliable and a .com is not. "A .com is trying to sell you something; a .org is an organization," they tell me. And when I point out that the NRA is a .org, and that the infamous martinlutherking.org website (hosted by Stormfront) is a .org, they are understandably confused. We have to stop making up rules about URLs and instead shift the focus to content. Had Jayson applied the 5W's checklist to his Clinton story, the website and the story would have passed as "verified." He could have easily determined the answers to each of the 5W questions and concluded that his source and the story were true.

More nuanced evaluation frameworks like the CRAAP test and RADCAB came into our classrooms with more thoughtful questioning of sources. The CRAAP test, designed by Meriam Library at California State University, Chico, asks students to question their sources' currency, relevance, authority, accuracy, and purpose. RADCAB, designed in 2002 by Karen Christensson, an elementary school library media specialist, asks students to question their sources' relevancy, appropriateness, detail, currency, authority, and bias. And, had Jayson applied the CRAAP test or RADCAB to his article on Hillary Clinton, perhaps he would have seen near the end of the question sets that the information and the article itself that he was quoting had an agenda. But, even if we expect him to ask 26 questions of every source, like with the CRAAP test, his article and source would have passed 23 of the 26 questions, surely a high enough pass rate to be deemed as credible. As Mike Caulfield (2016), director of blended and networked learning at Washington State University Vancouver and director of the Digital Polarization Initiative points out on his blog, *Hapgood*, The Pacific Northwest Tree Octopus hoax website passes the CRAAP test with flying colors.

KQED recently published an article with lesson plans on its website, under the headline, "The Honest Truth about Fake News…and How Not to Fall for It." Its "Breaking News Consumer's Handbook—Fake News Edition" has an 11-step process by which to fact-check and gut-check the news we see (Green, 2017). This is a more reasonable method to teach to our students. The News Literacy Project created its Checkology virtual classroom, "a place where students discover how to navigate today's challenging information landscape by using the core skills and concepts of news literacy" (Green, 2017, para. 2). The Daily Dot published a comprehensive list of fact-checking websites and groups, and their partisan alignments (Khalid, 2017). Teaching students to run what they read through a "fact-checker" step, like Snopes, is a simple way to determine if a news article is based in fact. And graphic organizers, like the one created by Vanessa Otero that went viral in 2016, have been widely shared that attempt to visually illustrate the spectrum of news organizations, their political leanings, and their reliability.

But all of these resources, although huge steps in the right direction, fail to successfully address the "ignorant facts" that Jayson had believed. In our attempts to help students discern between fact and fiction, we have inadvertently perpetuated the myth that news is either real or fake. We continually stress that news must be unbiased, that bias in reporting is wrong, and that only without bias can we uncover the truth. We acknowledge and repeat labels like the "liberal media" or the "conservative think tank" or the "corporate machine" but paradoxically demand that there must be some truly unbiased side to the story and that a "truth" remains, somewhere in the middle of all of the ideology. We insist that "objectivity" is possible. This tendency, unfortunately, can lead us to equate bias with "fake news."

Our demand for objectivity is hindering our abilities to teach our students to discern bias and ideology in the informational texts they read, whether it is the news or a textbook. And if our primary focus is that students determine if what they read is fact or fake, we limit their abilities to unpack and understand what is actually being said, and to learn to discern the bias and ideology in the message.

Instead of teaching our students to search for "unbiased information," we need to teach them to unpack the biases of everything they see, measure that information against their understanding of the world, and use that information to broaden their horizons.

2016 Kentucky Teacher of the Year and the founder and CEO of Curio Learning Ashley Lamb-Sinclair addresses this idea when she writes, "Now is the time for teachers to teach students not only to be critical thinkers who question the validity of facts, but also to analyze narratives" (2017, para. 12). In her piece published for *The Atlantic*, she eloquently explains that facts mean very little to people who are caught up in the storylines; that truth is actually subjective; and that teaching students to understand the narrative is the key to their abilities to unpack false narratives and confirmation bias.

WHAT IS THE STORY? ANALYZING THE NARRATIVE

Classroom English language arts teachers have always taught students to analyze the narrative, to find the essence of the story, regardless of what teaching methodology has been in vogue. Whether the strategies have focused on reader response or on close reading, figuring out what the storyteller is saying has always been a part of the pedagogy. In fact, we want students today to engage in discourse with the storyteller. We use strategies like Talk to the Text (from the Reading Apprenticeship Program) to encourage our students to talk back, question, and explore the story. We want students to enter into the conversation as Kenneth Burke first described it about literature and literary form:

> Imagine that you enter a parlor. You come late. When you arrive, others have long preceded you, and they are engaged in a heated discussion, a discussion too heated for them to pause and tell you exactly what it is about. In fact, the discussion had already begun long before any of them got there, so that no one present is qualified to retrace for you all the steps that had gone before. You listen for a while, until you decide that you have caught the tenor of the argument; then you put in your oar. Someone answers; you answer him; another comes to your defense; another aligns himself against you, to either the embarrassment or gratification of your opponent, depending upon the quality of your ally's assistance. However, the discussion is interminable. The hour grows late, you must depart. And you do depart, with the discussion still vigorously in progress. (1941, p. 110)

When we study literature, we want students to determine what the authors have to say about the world, and we want to encourage them to explore what they, as readers, have to say about the world in return.

If we want students to learn to read the world critically then learning to read literature critically is a solid starting point. Cognitive Psychologist Daniel Levitin says, "We are a storytelling species, and a social species, easily swayed by the opinions of others" (2016, p. 123). If we accept this, then it makes sense that we teach students—both explicitly and implicitly—to read the world as story.

Reading literature in the classroom presents a significant challenge for students. It requires not only time and effort but a shift in the essential way our brains work. Our students—and frankly, most adults—would much rather take everything at face value. Our Facebook feeds prove this as every single day the adults in our circles repost stories that are clearly false. Levitin says, "A big part of the problem here is that the human brain often makes up its mind based on emotional considerations and then seeks to justify them. And the brain is a very powerful self-justifying machine" (2016, p. 124). In our approach to reading literature in the classroom as well as our approach to teaching students to read the web, we are asking them to rewire their brains to take on an entirely new mindset: a different way to view the world. Teaching students explicit information to help them be better consumers and creators of media literacy helps them reframe their understanding of the world. Checklist approaches that offer heuristics are helpful in offering explicit instruction to students about what to look for; unfortunately, though, they fall short of the kind of shift in thinking that we ask of students.

Imagine if our discussions of literature stopped at the 5 Ws. Webb and Bloom would say we were at the most basic levels of their taxonomies—remembering, recalling, recognizing, maybe understanding rudimentary levels of the story but certainly not understanding with complexity and depth. Instead, when we discuss literature, we challenge students to think deeply, to synthesize what they know about the world with what they are reading, to extend their thinking beyond the surface features of the text, to recognize the subtleties of word choice and tone. This is the same level of thinking that we need to encourage students to use in reading online sources. This sort of mindset goes beyond the idea that "students should be taught to constantly question the validity of what they are reading, the strength of the source, the purpose of the author, and the overall authenticity of the information" (Bender & Waller, 2011, p. 66). In addition, students must talk to online text in all of its complexity. What do the images suggest? What is the author's claim and how do you know? Who is the audience and what emotional devices is the author using to reach them? They must enter into the conversation that the text offers much in the way they would do so in discussing a story.

As part of a final unit in my ninth grade English classes, students are given an assignment to explore the conversation around a self-selected topic. Previously, our units depended on teacher-selected text sets, but this time, students are on their own. The goal is not to form an opinion and cherry-pick information to support an opinion—an assignment that these students are used to from previous research experiences. Instead, they select a topic and then search out what experts have to say on the topic. This proves challenging. Even though they have been instructed to search for both sides of the conversation, students fall into only collecting articles that support their initial opinion, even when those articles are questionable. Mary, for example, decided to research whether students sit too much in school and what health effects that might have. As one of her two articles, Mary identified a blog on a website and came to ask about it. The title—"New Arrivals from the Collection"—was a clear hint at the story behind the blog post. This was a website that sold ergonomic furniture and footwear. When I pointed out that she should pay close attention to the title, she replied, "but the blog post is from a doctor." I asked her to dig into the site a bit more. Why would a doctor write blog posts for this site? What do you think his purpose is on this site? Does this affect the manner in which the data are used? What I am really asking her is, "What's the story here?"

WHAT IS THE STORY? ANALYZING THE IMAGES

A critical part of understanding the story being told is understanding what is portrayed by the images that accompany the stories. In their daily lives, our students are inundated with visual images, and this constant barrage often makes them unaware of the explicit message conveyed, although they are not immune to the influence of the implicit ideology of the images. Visual images both denote, showing "*particular* events, *particular* people, places, and things" and connote, portraying abstract ideas and ideals (Machin & Mayr, 2012, p. 49). Teaching students basic multimodal critical discourse analysis, as discussed in the beginning of this chapter, is an important skill, looking closely at how "images, photographs, diagrams and graphics also work to create meaning" and understanding that "texts will use linguistics and visual strategies that appear normal or neutral on the surface, but which may in fact be ideological and seek to shape the representation of events and persons for particular ends" (Machin & Mayr, 2012, p. 9). Attaching images to messages is part of the authorship of the piece, and part of the narrative that cannot be ignored.

When students in my class read *The Grapes of Wrath*, we look at and discuss Dorothea Lange's iconic 1936 photograph, "Migrant Mother," and discuss the story that is told through that photograph. What is the story in the woman's eyes? What is conveyed through her hands? What does the photographer want us to notice about the children? What does the photographer want us to *do*? This discussion of the storytelling of a photograph is the internal discussion that we need to have when we see media imagery.

In a unit that I built specifically to help students become more aware of the choices that authors make online (sourceanalysis.weebly.com), I have students discuss the story being told on three different websites on vaccinations. In one activity, I pull up the vaccination pages from the American Academy of Pediatrics' website healthychildren.org, the Centers for Disease Control and Prevention's website cdc.gov, and Dr. Joseph Mercola's website mercola.com. At first glance, students do not actually notice the visuals and the connotations and implications of the visuals of the three websites. Although most students notice that one of the three websites has a picture of a child getting vaccinated, and two do not, students do not immediately get the message. However, with discussion, students recognize that the Mercola website's primary image is a young child with red-rimmed eyes, a needle piercing his arm and a facemask over the doctor's face; whereas the AAP website's primary image is a cute child standing in a power pose. The immunization page of the AAP website shows a smiling child looking at the needle. The CDC's webpage on vaccinations shows smiling faces of all ages and races, no needles to be found. Before this activity, students were missing the story being told by the imagery; they did not realize the influence of the visuals on the message the websites were promoting. They didn't pick up on the multimodal message that the iconography was sending (Machin & Mayr, 2012) and, therefore, missed the obvious anti- and pro-vaccination ideologies of these respective websites. By looking at these images alone, void of any text, students were able to unpack the stance of the different organizations.

This type of thoughtful image analysis can and should be applied to every piece of "news" that we see. Whether it's a political story or a meme, thinking for a moment about the story being told through the image is just as critical as reading the text on the page. Does the politician look insane? Angry? Gloating? Dangerous? Like a caricature? And, does that image support our own established beliefs on that person?

My guess is that Jayson, when reading up on "criminal Hillary," also saw at least one version of the meme that was circulating on the story. One version of the meme had an image of Clinton with an expression that could be described as gloating. Another version of the meme had an image of a stunningly beautiful female adolescent, crying. What is the story being told by these two photographs? How does the creator of these memes want the audience to react? My goal is that Jayson will, by the end of the year, spend a moment looking at the imagery on memes and in the news and be aware of the emotional manipulation of these images. By becoming a discerning analyzer of images, he can begin to avoid playing into the hands of the ideology the authors are selling.

WHAT IS THE STORY? ANALYZING EMOTIONAL LANGUAGE

Reading images helps students to understand the emotional context of an author's message, just as reading the language for pathos helps them to deepen their understanding of the message itself. Pathos, one of the Aristotelian appeals, refers to the language that writers use to evoke an emotional response from readers. In studying narrative, we teach students to recognize authorial choices such as diction, figurative language, and detail as a means of understanding the content at a deeper level.

Take, for example, Harper Lee's *To Kill a Mockingbird*, and more specifically, Atticus's closing argument in the Tom Robinson case. In analyzing this speech for pathos, students begin to recognize the devices that Lee uses to hook the audience's emotions. Lee packs Atticus's closing with language that appeals to the jury's pity for both the victim and the accused, saying "I have nothing but pity in my heart for the chief witness for the state, but my pity does not extend so far as to her putting a man's life at stake" (p. 203) Atticus appeals to their sense of interconnectedness in saying, "There is not a person in this courtroom who has never told a lie, who has never done an immoral thing, and there is no man living who has never looked upon a woman without desire" (p. 204) And in his final words, Atticus appeals to the jury's human decency and even spirituality, calling for them to "In the name of God, do your duty…In the name of God, believe him" (pp. 205–206). Atticus uses pathos to appeal to his audience—the jury—but Lee, as author, is appealing to the readers. In both the novel and the movie versions, this scene has a powerful effect on students. They are emotionally moved by Atticus's words and that, coupled with their understanding of the logic in his defense of Tom Robinson, results in a collective gasp when the jury still finds Tom Robinson guilty. Over the years, countless students have responded with anger and frustration at the jury's failure to be swayed by the emotional power of Atticus's words. Helping them to understand the emotional effect as a result of the choices the author has made deepens their understanding of the message and of the power inherent in those authorial choices.

These rhetorical choices impact every aspect of our daily lives, from the wars that our country fights to the taxes we pay and the politicians we elect. Teaching students to recognize these attempts at emotional appeal is critical. For example, when discussing standardized testing with students, I always bring up the language of the policies that put all of this testing into place: No Child Left Behind and the Every Student Succeeds Act. What are the goals of these policies? To whom are these policies crafted to appeal? How do students push back against standardized gateway testing if the very policies that put it into place are phrased in ways that cannot be pushed back against? An eye-opening activity for students is to ask them to rename these policies in ways that convey their own beliefs about standardized testing. Asking students to consider these rhetorical moves and craft their own appeal to pathos helps them understand the moves that authors (and politicians and their speech writers) make.

George Orwell, in his essay, "Politics and the English Language," rails against the use of dying metaphors, operators or verbal false limbs, pretentious diction, and meaningless words. He then states, "A scrupulous writer, in every sentence that he writes, will ask himself at least four questions, thus: What am I trying to say? What words will express it? What image or idiom will make it clearer? Is this image fresh enough to have an effect?" (1946, p. 6). If Orwell were alive today, he would have much to say about the state of our current journalistic practices, with click-bait headlines and inflammatory language. He concluded his 1946 essay by pointing out, "Political language—and with variations this is true of all political parties, from Conservatives to Anarchists—is designed to make lies sound truthful and murder respectable, and to give an appearance of solidity to pure wind" (p. 10). Teaching our students to craft their own writing by making rhetorical choices to appeal to pathos will help them recognize when those in the news and those reporting on the news are making lies sound truthful and giving an appearance of solidity to pure wind.

WHAT IS THE STORY? A CONVERSATION

Teaching students to be discerning consumers of the news media involves conveying a mindset: not one of defense, but one of understanding. Reading the narrative is so much more involved than simply applying a heuristic; it means attempting to understand not only the story the author is telling, through their language and images, but also what the author wants us to do with that information. Reading the narrative forces us to consider our own relationship with the text, and have a conversation with it. Instead of searching for unbiased facts, like some sort of news "Where's Waldo," we should instead search for an understanding both of what is being conveyed and of our own positioning. Only then will we be able to step outside of our own filter bubbles and be discerning, thoughtful citizens, participating not in mud-slinging and the regurgitation of ignorant facts, but rather in engaged and respectful discourse.

WHAT IS THE STORY? GETTING STARTED IN THE CLASSROOM

Moving students into a thoughtful and discerning mindset requires deliberate identification and practice in the classroom. Below is one lesson to get students started on transferring what they know about reading stories in the classroom to the reading of stories on the web.

Objective

Students will recognize the word choices in literature that an author makes to put forward a theme or claim and will be able to transfer their understanding of authorial word choice to their reading of the web.

Materials

- a recently studied short work of literature
- butcher paper or whiteboard space for building an anchor chart
- computer access for students
- http://sourceanalysis.weebly.com/what-is-the-message.html

Context

Today students will re-examine a short work or works they have previously studied in class to determine how authorial world choice impacts the messaging in the work.

Lesson

Create an anchor chart with the title, "Authors use words with emotional connotations to tell a story."

Ask students to consider this and to dig back into the texts at their disposal to create a list of words with emotional connotations (or "juicy words," for younger students). Students may begin with a turn-and-talk before the teacher compiles the responses of the whole class on the anchor chart.

As students transition to computers, display the anchor chart prominently and remind students that the goal will now be to transfer what they know about author's techniques for messaging in literature to author's techniques in messaging on the web.

Direct students to http://sourceanalysis.weebly.com/what-is-the-message.html and have them open the three websites:

- Dr. Mercola: http://vaccines.mercola.com/
- CDC: https://www.cdc.gov/vaccines/index.html
- healthychildren.org (AAP): https://www.healthychildren.org/English/safety-prevention/immunizations/Pages/Vaccine-Safety-The-Facts.aspx

Ask students to work in pairs to identify words that carry emotional connotations.

Performance Task

What emotion-laden words do the authors of these three websites use in their beginning paragraphs? Choose 4 or 5 words with emotional connotations from each website. Define the words. Based on these specific words, what story is each author telling about vaccination?

NOTE

[1] Although we work 133 miles apart, throughout this chapter, we have chosen to write with the singular pronoun both for ease of narrative and also to reflect our collective experience.

REFERENCES

Bender, W. N., & Waller, L. (2011). *The teaching revolution: RTI, technology, & differentiation transform teaching for the 21st century*. Thousand Oaks, CA: Corwin.

boyd, d. (2014). *It's complicated: The social lives of networked teens*. New Haven, CT: Yale University Press.

Burke, K. (1941). *The philosophy of literary form*. Berkeley, CA: University of California Press.

Caulfield, M. (2016). Yes, digital literacy. But which one? [Blog Post]. Retrieved from https://hapgood.us/2016/12/19/yes-digital-literacy-but-which-one/

Christensson, K. (2017). RADCAB: Steps for online information evaluation. *RADCAB: Your Vehicle for Information Evaluation*. Retrieved from http://www.radcab.com/

European Association for Viewers Interests. (2013). *Media literacy concepts and metaphors: Critical thinking*. Retrieved April 19, 2015, from https://www.youtube.com/watch?v=BYKnfuFZ1pA&feature=youtube_gdata_player

Green, M. (2017). The honest truth about fake news … and how not to fall for it (with lesson plan). *KQED News: The Lowdown*. Retrieved from https://ww2.kqed.org/lowdown/2017/05/03/the-honest-truth-about-fake-news-with-lesson-plan/

Hamilton, B. J. (2009). Transforming information literacy for nowgen students. *Knowledge Quest, 37*(5), 48–53.

Heick, T. (2014). *How google impacts the way students think.* Retrieved May 27, 2017, from http://www.teachthought.com/critical-thinking/how-google-impacts-the-way-students-think/

Jenkins, H. (2006). White paper: Confronting the challenges of participatory culture: Media education for the 21st century by Henry Jenkins. *MacArthur Foundation.* Retrieved from https://www.macfound.org/press/publications/white-paper-confronting-the-challenges-of-participatory-culture-media-education-for-the-21st-century-by-henry-jenkins/

Khalid, A. (2016). *The best political fact-checking sites on the internet.* Retrieved May 27, 2017, from https://www.dailydot.com/layer8/best-fact-checking-websites/

Lamb-Sinclair, A. (2017). When narrative matters more than fact. *The Atlantic.* Retrieved May 27, 2017, from https://www.theatlantic.com/education/archive/2017/01/when-narrative-matters-more-than-fact/512273/?utm_source=eb

Laue, S. (2013). *"He said, she said" – Reliable sources.* Retrieved May 27, 2017, from http://www.schooljournalism.org/wp-content/uploads/2013/09/Reliable-Sources-by-Sue-Laue.pdf

Lee, H. (1960). *To kill a mockingbird.* New York, NY: Time Warner Company.

Levitin, D. J. (2016). *A field guide to lies: Critical thinking in the information age.* New York, NY: Dutton.

Machin, D., & Mayr, A. (2015). *How to do critical discourse analysis: A multimodal introduction.* Los Angeles, CA: Sage.

Meriam Library Staff. Tutorial for Info Power – CRAAP Test. (2010). Retrieved May 27, 2017, from https://www.csuchico.edu/lins/tip/evaluating/evaluating6.html

Murchie, S. (2016). *Source analysis.* Retrieved May 31, 2017, from http://sourceanalysis.weebly.com/

Orwell, G. (1946). Politics and the English language. *Horizon, 13*(76), 252–265. Retrieved from http://www.npr.org/blogs/ombudsman/Politics_and_the_English_Language-1.pdf

Otero, V. (2017). News quality. *All Generalizations are False.* Retrieved May 27, 2017, from http://www.allgeneralizationsarefalse.com

Purcell, K., Rainie, L., Heaps, A., Buchanan, J., Friedrich, L., Jacklin, A., Chen, C., & Zickuhr, K. (2012). How teens do research in the digital world. *Pew Research Center: Internet, Science & Tech.* Retrieved from http://www.pewinternet.org/2012/11/01/how-teens-do-research-in-the-digital-world/

Quijada, A. (2013). *Creating critical thinkers through media literacy: Andrea Quijada at TEDxABQED.* Retrieved May 27, 2017, from https://www.youtube.com/watch?v=aHAApvHZ6XE

Salisbury, F., Karasmanis, S., Robertson, T., Corbin, J., Hulett, H., & Peseta, T. (2012). Transforming information literacy conversations to enhance student learning: New curriculum dialogues. *Journal of University Teaching & Learning Practice, 9*(3), 1–14. Retrieved from http://ro.uow.edu.au/jutlp/vol9/iss3/4

Schrock, K. (2001). *5 Ws: Kathy Schrock's guide to everything.* Retrieved from http://www.schrockguide.net/

Share, J., Jolls, T., & Thoman, E. (2007). *5 key questions that can change the world: Lesson plans for media literacy.* Malibu, CA: Center for Media Literacy.

Stanford History Education Group. (2016). *Evaluating information: The cornerstone of civic online reasoning: Executive summary.* Retrieved May 27, 2017, from https://sheg.stanford.edu/upload/V3LessonPlans/Executive%20Summary%2011.21.16.pdf

Subramanian, S. (2017, February 15). Inside the Macedonian fake-news complex. *WIRED Magazine.* Retrieved from https://www.wired.com/2017/02/veles-macedonia-fake-news/

The News Literacy Project. (2017). *Checkology® virtual classroom.* Retrieved May 27, 2017, from http://www.thenewsliteracyproject.org/learn-channel/checkology%C2%AE-virtual-classroom

Wikipedia Contributors. (2017, July 1). *Lists of Merriam-Webster's words of the year.* Retrieved September 2, 2017, from https://en.wikipedia.org/w/index.php?title=Lists_of_Merriam-Webster%27s_Words_of_the_Year&oldid=788456915

Sharon A. Murchie
Bath High School
Lima, Ohio

Janet A. Neyer
Cadillac High School
Cadillac, Michigan

ROB WILLIAMS

5. FIGHTING "FAKE NEWS" IN AN AGE OF DIGITAL DISORIENTATION

Towards "Real News," Critical Media Literacy Education, and Independent Journalism for 21st Century Citizens

Journalism's job is not impartial 'balanced' reporting.
Journalism's job is to tell the people what is really going on.

– George Seldes

INTRODUCTION

"This is what makes covering Donald Trump so difficult," explained baffled CNN reporter John Corker to a national viewing audience in February 2017, shortly after Inauguration Day. "What does he mean when he says words?" (Badash, 2017). This bewildering statement reflects our increasingly disorienting digital landscape of 21st century U.S. news and information, in which the meanings of words, images and news stories seem to have become completely unmoored from reality. Trump is just the tip of the iceberg. Decades ago, journalist and *1984* author George Orwell famously warned readers to be wary of "doublethink" and "Newspeak" (from which we derive the modern term "doublespeak"), in which governments deploy phrases designed to disguise, distort or even reverse reality—think "war is peace," or "ignorance is strength." Post-2016 election, the term "fake news" is the latest phrase to capture what is an age-old phenomenon—namely, how powerful state and corporate actors work together to deploy news and information designed to distract and disorient the rest of us. It is no exaggeration to say that we now live in what I call an "age of digital disorientation," in which the very meaning of "reality" itself seems up for grabs in a "post-truth" digital media culture controlled by powerful corporate and state actors, and defined by speed, immediacy, and information oversaturation. Never before has independent critical media literacy education and the championing of independent journalism and "real news" been so vital.

In this chapter, I will unpack our 21st century news and (dis)information culture by (1) defining "real news," (2) classifying many varieties of 21st century "fake news," (3) updating Chomsky and Hermann's "propaganda model of news" for our 21st century digital age, and finally, (4) suggesting solutions for reviving "real news" in an "Age of Digital Disorientation." My hope is that this analysis will be

 | DOI 10.1163/9789004365360_005

of use to two global communities: (1) teachers and students interested in practicing "critical media literacy education," (CMLE); and (2) members of the world's journalism community seeking practical understandings and hands-on approaches to our contemporary culture of news and (dis)information. I also hope to challenge some long-held assumptions about the role of critical media literacy education and independent journalism within our educational and public spaces, offering a radical starting place for critiquing our US culture of contemporary news and (dis)information.

First, a quick summary of my professional background and political leanings, as these are germane to shaping my thinking about this chapter's themes. I write as both a long-time champion of CMLE (I co-founded ACME—the Action Coalition for Media Education—in 2002) and a working journalist here in Vermont since 2005, when we founded *Vermont Commons: Voices of Independence*, the state's first and only statewide radical news journal (now online as *The Vermont Independent*). For 15 years, I have approached our culture of news and information through both lenses, and I believe that critical media literacy education and independent journalism complement and strengthen one another in numerous ways. "Teachers and journalists are always political agents; both professions must choose in whose interest they are willing to work," explains P.L. Thomas at our book's beginning, referencing historian Howard Zinn's famous challenge to those who would embrace so-called Objectivity—one "can't be neutral on a moving train." "The neutral pose by either is to take a seat on the train, to keep eyes down, and to allow the train to rumble along as if the tracks are not leading to a cliff," he concludes (see Chapter Two).

As a U.S. media historian, furthermore, I understand that the framers of the U.S. republic (Thomas Jefferson chief among them) believed that the only way the United States might survive as a democracy was if "virtuous" (meaning public spirited and civic minded) citizens developed capacities to critically read, write, and think for themselves and in civic communities. As Italian semiotician Umberto Eco explained, channeling Jefferson on the eve of the digital age, "a democratic civilization will save itself only if it makes the language of the image into a stimulus for critical reflection—not an invitation for hypnosis" (Alvarado, 1993). Eco penned these words right at the moment in which images supplanted words as civilization's primary form of communication, and a rapidly expanding world wide web saw we media consumers ushering ubiquitous digital screens and corporately-coded social media platforms into the most intimate nooks and crannies of our daily lives. Has this new digital information age enhanced our capacity as "virtuous citizens"? This is a question open for vigorous debate, and central to the discussion is the role of news and (dis)information in both our public and private spaces. I imagine that Jefferson himself, were he alive today, would support this volume's focus on "critical media literacy," defined in these pages as "an educational response that expands the notion of media literacy to include different forms of mass communication, popular culture, and new technologies," focusing on "the ideology critique and analyzing the politics of representation of crucial dimensions of gender, race, class, and sexuality.” (see Chapter One).

Let me be clear here about my own politics. As a teacher and journalist both, I approach critical media literacy education and journalism, subjectively speaking, as a decentralist and a communitarian. When left-leaning liberals like members of the (post) #OccupyWallStreet movement complain about the influence of Big Business, and right-leaning conservatives like the (still stirring) TEA Party movement grouse about Big Government, they are both half right. The problem, as I see it, is BIGness, and the unholy alliance between powerful trans-national corporations (TNCs—including US-based news and digital media conglomerates) and U.S. government officials from both sides of the aisle (Democrats AND Republicans) who do TNCs' bidding, often with strategic nudges from what has come to be called the “Deep State” (more about this shortly). The United States is no longer a functioning republic but a dysfunctional Empire, and the chief role of our so-called US based “news and information” sources is to champion the continued expansion of said Empire, whether it is through news and (dis)information distributed from so-called “liberal” left-wing news sources like CNN or the *New York Times*, or news and (dis)information deployed from so-called “conservative” right wing news sources like FOX or *The Washington Post*. In my twenty years of CMLE experience, most media literacy educators tend to be well-meaning liberals and progressives who bring their own often-unexamined assumptions and biases to the table. As a decentralist communitarian, I challenge us to look past media manufactured binary frames—progressive/liberal versus conservative, Red versus Blue, Democrat versus Republican—and consider alternative and potentially more useful frames as we explore the relationship among our political views, our practice of CMLE, our culture of news and (dis)information, and our promotion of “real news”—“news we can use”—in our age of digital disorientation.

DEFINING “REAL NEWS”

Before we explore so-called “fake news” and from whence it comes, let's begin with a definition of “real news.” Anyone who has explored the concept of “news” knows that the term has a rich and storied definitional history. Here is a useful starting place, Tony Harcup and Deidre O'Neill's March 2016 article “What Is News? News Values Revisited (Again),” in which they conclude that “although there are exceptions to every rule, we have found that news stories must generally satisfy one or more of the following requirements” if they are to be selected as “news”:

1. *The power elite*: Stories concerning powerful individuals, organisations or institutions.
2. *Celebrity*: Stories concerning people who are already famous.
3. *Entertainment*: Stories concerning sex, show business, human interest, animals, an unfolding drama, or offering opportunities for humorous treatment, entertaining photographs or witty headlines.

4. *Surprise*: Stories that have an element of surprise and/or contrast.
5. *Bad news*: Stories with particularly negative overtones, such as conflict or tragedy.
6. *Good news*: Stories with particularly positive overtones, such as rescues and cures.
7. *Magnitude*: Stories that are perceived as sufficiently significant either in the numbers of people involved or in potential impact.
8. *Relevance*: Stories about issues, groups and nations perceived to be relevant to the audience.
9. *Follow-up*: Stories about subjects already in the news.
10. *Newspaper agenda*: Stories that set or fit the news organisation's own agenda.

This Top 10 list is useful, but I want to sharpen our definition of "news we can use" to consider our role as citizens charged with navigating our "age of digital disorientation" here in the US—the richest and most powerful Empire the world has ever seen. With this goal in mind, I suggest that "real news" stories are best defined by considering six ingredients.

First, a complete definition of "real news."

"Real news" stories are defined by "information that is recent, relevant, reliable, historically framed, hegemonically hip, and multi-perspectival."

Let's consider each element in turn. "Recent and relevant" simply mean that the news story in question has been recently introduced into the cultural conversation and is "in play" across multiple platforms and in various arenas. "Reliable," the third ingredient, refers to clearly verifiable and explicitly named "go to" sources (as opposed to vague, unclear, or unnamed "government officials" or "sources claimed" language.) Fourth, "historical framing" means that the news story is contextualized in some meaningful fashion, grounded in past precedents and events—it does not simply occupy what novelist Wallace Stegner called "the amputated present" (Stegner, 2017). By #5, "hegemonically hip," I mean that the news story makes transparent the power relations inherent in any discussion surrounding political events, including the biases and subjectivities of the news source reporting the story—foregrounding the political economy of news on a story by story basis is a vital intellectual task. "Multi-perspectival," finally, refers to the importance of news stories embedding multiple points of view within their narrative, not simply a binary "he said/she said" sort of framing typically found in much of what passes for "news" today.

Using this short list of six ingredients to define and then analyze "real news" stories makes possible a pedagogically rich conversation around the nature of real versus fake news, as well as setting high standards for independent "real news" story production. While these ingredients can be considered as a guide for defining "real news," and not an absolute, when applying these six ingredients as a simple analytical framework for analyzing stories produced and distributed within our 21st century digital news culture, it quickly becomes apparent how few "real news" stories are produced by our mainstream news outlets across print, television and the web. Despite the seemingly endless variety of news and information available to us, few so-called "news" stories meet all six of these criteria. This leads to our next question—why is "real news" so hard to find?

CLASSIFYING "FAKE NEWS"—A SIMPLE TAXONOMY

Before we answer this question, let's explore the many varieties of "fake news"—"false or counterfeit information published by news organizations," according to Merriam Webster—found in our 21st century news and (dis)information culture. This volume defines "fake news" as "purposefully false and provocative" "misinformation and literally untrue news stories," (see Chapter Two) even as scholars recognize the ever-evolving politicized nature of the term "fake news" in an era when powerful corporate, media and state players push terms (like this one!) for their own propagandistic purposes." I want to begin with a bold, even audacious, claim: the biggest purveyor of "fake news" is the U.S. "Deep State," the subterranean network of U.S. government officials, intelligence agencies, and corporate commercial "news" outlets who often collaborate to "manufacture consent" (as Edward Hermann and Noam Chomsky argue in their book of the same title) for U.S. imperial policies.[1] If we define "real news" as "information that is recent, relevant, reliable, historically framed, hegemonically hip, and multi-perspectival," than most of what is defined as "news" in the United States' imperial news'scape is better classified in one of the following categories—a taxonomy, of sorts.

1. "Infotainment"—Any "one off" "news" story that promotes fluffy "kitty in the tree" narratives falls into this category. Momentary glimpses of celebrities, sports figures, entertainers, as well as "feel good" stories (often referred to as "human interest" stories) or freakish "dog hit thrice by lightning" tales can all be classified as "infotainment." These stories keep audiences watching, cultivate a "buyers mood," and promote aspirational lifestyles and a culture of consumerism central to the ideological underpinnings of our U.S. news and (dis)information culture.
2. "Junk Food News"—"Infotainment" on serialized steroids, "junk food news" refers to ongoing "news" stories driven by "sensationalized, personalized, and homogenized inconsequential trivia," often filling space that otherwise could be occupied by "real news." Project Censored founder Carl Jensen coined the term in a 1983 edition of *Penthouse* magazine, and Project Censored has since devoted a chapter of their annual *Censored* book of top 25 censored news stories to an exploration of the top 10 junk food news stories from the previous year (Phillips, 2001). Jensen developed a humorous taxonomy for different kinds of "junk food news" that included (1) brand name/celebrity gossip, (2) sexposes, (3) show biz stories, (4) "yo yo" news (daily ever-changing statistics like stock market numbers); (5) fads and fashion; (6) anniversaries; (7) sports and celebrity athletes;

and (8) political campaign horse race "news"—which politician has raised the least or most money or is running ahead or behind in which state at any given moment.

3. "News Abuse"—Another term coined by Project Censored, "news abuse" refers to news stories that potentially have merit, but are presented by US corporate "news" outlets in a slanted or non-newsworthy manner. A classic example is the sensationalized and fabricated "Private Jessica Lynch" story as a stand in for more critical coverage of the U.S. invasion and occupation of Iraq. I could fill this chapter with dozens of other "news abuse" moments—see any annual *Censored* book for a laundry list of examples.
4. "Deep State Disinformation"—Refers to secretive "news" campaigns waged by the Deep State to "seed" U.S. corporate print, radio and television news outlets with public relations propaganda to manufacture consent for particular policy outcomes. U.S. wars of aggression are perhaps the most prominent examples of Deep State disinformation campaigns. U.S. public relations firms like Hill and Knowlton provided "news" content to justify the 2003 U.S. invasion of Iraq, and prominent national journalists like *New York Times*' Judith Miller provided front page (dis)information reporting on Iraq president Saddam Hussein's alleged weapons of mass destruction (WMD) programs, stories that turned out to be false, but in the moment helped provided the rationale for aggressive U.S. warmaking in the Middle East. Deep State U.S. intelligence services like the Central Intelligence Agency (CIA) have cultivated cozy relationships with a multitude of prominent U.S. journalists and publishers since the beginning of the Cold War, and now, even prominent Democratic Party operatives maintain intimate ties with U.S. journalists, publishers, and news outlets, as revealed by 2016 documents published by Wikileaks. The CIA's start up funding of Google, Amazon founder Jeff Bezos' recent purchase of *The Washington Post*, and Amazon's brokering of a $600 million web servicing contract with the CIA, are but three specific examples that provide further evidence of the intimate ties between new digital media companies, U.S. journalism outlets, and the Deep State (Ahmed, 2015).
5. "Click Bait"—broadly, this term refers to any web content that prioritizes the generating of click-through online advertising revenue over any attempt to provide accurate, detailed, nuanced, or complex news content, usually through the deployment of eye-catching graphics or titillating headlines. Some of the U.S.' information culture's most popular online "news" sites—*Huffington Post*, *Upworthy*, *Buzzfeed*, *Salon*, *Townhall*, and *Breitbart*—are driven by an obsession with providing "clickbait" content.

Tally up the collective impact of this taxonomy of "fake news," and U.S. citizens are facing an unprecedented situation my colleagues at Project Censored refer to as a "Truth Emergency." Writes Project Censored's Peter Phillips:

> There is a literal truth emergency in the United States, not only regarding distant wars, torture camps, and doctored intelligence, but also around issues that most intimately impact our lives at home. For example, few Americans know that there has been a thirty-five year decline in real wages for most workers in the country, while the top 10% now enjoy unparalleled wealth with strikingly low tax burdens. (Phillips & Kubiak, 2003)

At our independent news journal *the Vermont Independent*, we have offered a comprehensive top 10 list of underreported news stories that are vital to informing citizens of the US of Empire "what is really going on," in the words of journalist George Seldes. In the spirit of "clickbait," here is our brief "Top 10" "news we can use" list, drawn from our *Plan 'V'—Designing a 2nd Vermont Republic* pamphlet:

1. The U.S. financial sector's debt-driven predatory capitalism, featuring a global economy driven by Wall Street, unaccountable monied institutions like the IMF, the World Bank, and the WTO, and the Deep State.
2. The Pentagon's pursuit of a policy of "full spectrum dominance," global arms sales, drone warfare, and sequential energy wars and aggressive creation of "failed states" in the greater Middle East.
3. The gutting of the U.S. Constitution and the Bill of Rights in the name of "Homeland Security."
4. Electoral Dysfunction—our votes as U.S. citizens are no longer accurately counted.
5. A massive Orwellian surveillance apparatus—think Facebook meets Google meets the NSA—which spies on us all.
6. A bankrupt and oligopolistic two party Democratic/Republican political system that serves only the rich and powerful.
7. A mass media network controlled by for-profit multinational corporations that distracts and divides us.
8. A U.S. neo-colonial "empire of bases" (as many as 1,000) that seeks to control over the entire Planet and outer space, a space-age exercise in "imperial overreach."
9. A collective inability to face the civilizational challenges that confront U.S.—climate change, peak oil, and the threat of nuclear Armageddon.
10. Catabolic collapse—the Mother of all Dilemmas—systemic breakdown of a complex civilization that has overextended itself, a problem that has ultimately possessed and consumed every Empire over the past 10,000 years of world history.

All of these stories are dramatically underreported within U.S. mainstream news and (dis)information channels and outlets—to our collective detriment and ignorance. Without a basic factual "news"-driven understanding and an informational grounding in U.S. imperial policies, we as U.S. citizens cannot even begin to discuss and debate the vital issues of our time.

TOWARDS A "PROPAGANDA MODEL OF NEWS" FOR THE DIGITAL AGE

So why are we unable to access, produce and deploy more "real news"? To answer this question, let's build on Edward Hermann and Noam Chomsky's conceptual theory known as the "propaganda model of news," in which they provided extensive analysis of *The New York Times*' domestic and international news coverage and explained their findings in their landmark 1988 book *Manufacturing Consent: The Political Economy of The Mass Media.* Hermann and Chomsky proposed a list of five "filters" through which all news and information had to pass before being published by "respected" U.S. mainstream news outlets. I will briefly review them here, and then propose five additional filters for our digital age that enhance our conceptual thinking about our 21st century culture of news and (dis)information.

- Filter #1) Advertising: The lifeblood of our corporate commercial media culture, advertising—the ceaseless "to be you gotta buy" consumer-happy promotion of goods and services—provides the majority of funding for U.S. print, radio, television and web news media. Advertisers have tremendous power to shape stories that provide U.S. our news and (dis)information content. "He who pays the piper calls the tune," as the old nursery rhyme goes.
- Filter #2) Ownership: Many corporate commercial U.S. news and (dis)information outlets are in turn owned by much larger corporate entities that have a vested interest in maintaining the U.S. imperial status quo. As Ben Bagdikian's *Media Monopoly* research has chronicled, 90% of our media content—radio, movie, TV, web, magazine and newspaper outlets—are now ultimately owned by 6 transnational corporations with "little to tell but everything to sell," in the words of George Gerbner.
- Filter #3) News Makers: So much of our daily news content is shaped by the most visible persons and organizations deemed "newsworthy"—the POTUS, the FLOTUS, and the SCOTUS, to name but three examples from U.S. news and (dis)information culture. Even a seemingly mundane "news" story—"President Obama rearranges his sock drawer with the family dog!"—often trumps more vital stories that go underreported.
- Filter #4) News Shapers: Prestigious U.S. think tanks, foundations, and public relations firms are in the business of producing "research" designed to generate news and (dis)information for the voracious 24/7 news cycle. News organizations often find it easier and less provocative to simply source their information from these "news shaper" rather than conduct their own independent investigative research.
- Filter #5) "Flak": also called "negative criticism," this fifth filter refers to attacks on individual journalists or news organizations who stray beyond the boundaries of the accepted news and (dis)information *status quo*. The past few decades are littered with the careers (and occasional corpses) of U.S. journalists who got too

close to power in their dogged pursuit of a story they deemed the public had a right to know but offended the wealthy and powerful.

These five filters together comprised Hermann and Chomsky's "propaganda model of news," and their compelling conceptual use of these five interrelated "filters" is my starting place for expanding their model for the digital age. Here are five additional filters, based on what we know about how news and (dis) information is produced, deployed and "shared" through 21st century digital networks.

- Filter #6) Deep State Disinformation: As discussed earlier, the Deep State has for decades secretly partnered with both news organizations and think tanks to "seed" stories into mainstream news and (dis)information channels designed to promote US imperial agendas, protect corporate interests, and advance the goals of what retired U.S. general and departing Republican president Dwight D. Eisenhower famously called the "military industrial complex" in his 1961 farewell address. In the Age of the Internet, the concept of the "Deep State" is now cracking into mainstream cultural conversations in ways never seen before, and this phenomenon bodes well, perhaps, for independent news analysis and information access. An entire book could be written on the Deep State's relationship with the U.S. news media—I have mentioned several sources and examples here, and reference others in my footnotes. Certainly, the Deep State "filter" is difficult to spot, as it demands a deep and abiding knowledge of U.S. history and politics, and the ability to see beyond media-manufactured false binaries—Red versus Blue, Democratic versus Republican, "liberal" versus "conservative, "for us or against us."
- Filter #7) Algorithms: Contributing to our "Age of Digital Disorientation" is the widespread use of proprietary corporately-controlled news and (dis)information platforms built on sophisticated ever-evolving computer code programs known as algorithms. Google, Facebook, Twitter, Amazon and other powerful global digital media corporations are constantly exploring new and novel ways to harvest consumer data and capture networked content for their true customers—advertisers and the third party data harvesting companies who collect and share consumer information, often in secret. News and (dis)information provides vital content within the algorithmic mix, revealing intimate details about users' personal data and their connections with others. Becoming more aware of the Algorithm filter's power is a vital element of 21st century critical media literacy education, and CMLE educators are developing new curricula and approaches to teach this concept with students.
- Filter #8) Filter Bubbles: Best considered in conjunction with the algorithm, the "filter bubble," a term coined by MoveOn and Upworthy co-founder Eli Pariser, is another important digital news and (dis)information filter that impacts all of us as news consumers. Each of us develops a "filter bubble" through repeated news and information searches online, as a combination of platform-specific algorithms and our own personal search choices construct a particular digital

"reality" for each of us over time. Understanding the presence of our own "filter bubble" and taking active steps to push our search for news and information beyond the routine, habitual, or even comfortable is a vital element of critical 21st century media literacy education and thoughtful news consumption. Otherwise, we end up wrapping ourselves up in our own "news reality" that merely reflects our own agreed-upon tastes, choices, and consumption habits. By extension, our "trusted friends" (a popular phrase in the world of digital media marketing) simply become foils for networking back to us what we already think we know. Spotting the "filter bubble," like developing an awareness of algorithms, is vital for 21st century CMLE and independent news consumption and production.

- Filter #9) "Behavioral Microtargeting": What if private corporations could partner with political campaign strategists to reach into the web and use social media platforms to "massage" a citizenry's thinking, influence voter choices on particular issues, or encourage voters to support a particular candidate? Cambridge Analytica, a U.K.-based consulting company, claims they can engage in this sort of "behavioral microtargeting," using an astonishing 5,000 pieces of individual data on each of 220 million American voters. We can't know for sure, since their data is proprietary, but the use of "psychographic" data is sure to gain notoriety in the years ahead, and must be considered as a primary filter in shaping thinking and behavior regarding our news and (dis)information habits, particularly as our civic spaces become ever more intertwined with our digital spaces.
- Filter #10) Sock Puppets: Finally, imagine if corporations or governments could create thousands of fake social media accounts to create, share, promote or attack a particular candidate, campaign or ideological position? Already happening. "Sock puppets" is the term given to these fake and often anonymous social media accounts, which can be unleashed into digital and social media spaces via the power of the algorithm and then used to spread messages, stories, and real or imagined claims (including so-called "fake news" stories) virally through various networks. Surely, being aware of the presence and use of sophisticated "sock puppets," a powerful new digital filter in our brave new digital world of news and (dis)information in the 21st century, is of vital interest for all CMLE practitioners and independent journalists.

To conclude, Deep State disinformation, algorithms, filter bubbles, behavioral microtargeting, and the use of sock puppets constitute five new and powerful emerging digital filters that shape news and (dis)information in our 21st century digital age. When combined with the five analog filters posited by Hermann and Chomsky in their "propaganda model of news," we gain a deeper and more complex understanding of how news and (dis)information can be used to "manufacture consent" in our digital age, rather than promote dialogue, discussion, debate and information sharing about vital topics of interest, with Seldes' goal of telling the people "what is really going on."

CHAMPIONING "REAL NEWS" IN THE DIGITAL AGE

Fighting so many varieties of "fake news" with "real news"—"information that is recent, relevant, reliable, historically framed, hegemonically hip, and multi-perspectival"—is both our 21st challenge and opportunity as critical media literacy educators and independent journalists. The world is already awash in what I would consider NON solutions, alleged antidotes to the "fake news" phenomenon, a term that seemingly has now been weaponized and directed at any "news" outlet by any figure who feels attacked or threatened by a critical or alternative interpretation of events. Among a variety of "non solutions" for combatting "fake news" advanced over the past year? (1) The creation of online lists by organizations such as "PropOrNot," which aggregates "suspect" U.S. news sites that allegedly channel pro-Russian propaganda; (2) The algorithmic "policing" and censoring of suspected "fake news" accounts and stories by digital corporations such as Google and Facebook; (3) Calls for government regulation of "fake news"; (4) State legislation proposing fines and penalties for the purveying of "fake news" as well as top down legislated and mandated media literacy programs; and (5) third party providers contracting with existing news sites to label and marginalize so-called "fake news" sites. All of these proposed "solutions" rely on outsourcing critical thinking to some other agency, organization or party, rather than promoting the more challenging but ultimately more rewarding solution—teaching critical thinking skills to all students and citizens by fostering active and ongoing communities of inquiry.

Let me repeat—our best solution to fighting "fake news" and fomenting "real news" is an interdisciplinary one, with the teaching of critical thinking, history, writing and multimedia production at its core. Twenty-first century citizens must be both judicious news media consumers and skilled news media producers, and this pedagogical practice ought to be taught from cradle to grave. The good news? This kind of work is happening every day in thousands of classrooms and communities across the country and around the world. Speaking from my own experience, here are just three of my current favorite examples of CMLE and independent journalism in action.

1. The Jimmy Dore Show—Jimmy Dore is an LA-based nightclub comedian who espouses progressive values, but also asks critical questions of everything and everyone in ways that are at once thoughtful and irreverent. A member of the "Young Turks," Dore has built a sizeable YouTube following around his weekly "in studio" videos featuring fellow comedians and independent journalists doing on-the-ground investigative reporting. One of his favorite techniques is to deconstruct (analyze) a mainstream "news" story, either on television or in print, asking funny yet critical questions in conversation with his guests. Dore has a point of view, but he also promotes the free and open exchange of ideas, as well as tackling the Deep State, US imperialism, war, class warfare, and national politics in a way that is refreshing and stimulating. His honest comedic reporting has led to Google/YouTube "demonetizing" many of his videos focusing on U.S.

warmaking and other controversial topics, raising important questions about news, information and Internet censorship by Google/YouTube and other Lords of the Cloud.

2. "#BlackLivesMatter—Flag of Revolution"—Here at the University of Vermont (UVM) where I teach courses on CMLE, media, communications, and politics, I ask students to work in pairs to identify a national movement of any political stripe and explore how said movement is playing out here on our college campus. In my University of Vermont digital civic journalism course, for example, two of my students spotlighted our UVM #BlackLivesMatter movement chapter, focusing their 20 minute video news story around the theft of a BLM flag from a campus flag pole and the resulting impact on the campus community. Their final 20-minute news documentary featured the voices of more than two dozen community members—students and adults—with different perspectives on the flag stealing, and told a compelling story of how a single event rippled out through our campus community with unforeseen consequences. The student producers then decided to develop a curriculum for the film, and are planning to host a series of college community "critical conversations" around their news story when they return for the fall semester. This is CMLE and independent journalism in action.
3. The Global Critical Media Literacy Project (GCMLP)—A collaborative project of the Action Coalition for Media Education (ACME), Project Censored, and Sacred Heart University's Critical Media Literacy Education graduate program, the GCMLP provides a digital publishing platform for student-produced social and digital media news stories of interest. The project is still in pilot form, but early results have been encouraging, with students from a growing number of colleges and universities researching and publishing stories on a wide variety of global news topics of import, ranging from the #ArabSpring, to the promise and peril of self-driving cars, to the cultural impact of social media platforms on everything from individual self-esteem to national politics.

In summary, the best way to fight "fake news" in an Age of Digital Disorientation is to fuse critical media literacy education (CMLE) with the production of independent investigative news and information grounded in real issues unfolding in real places. This is our greatest challenge and opportunity. Our time is now. "Journalism's job is to tell the people what is really going on," explains George Seldes. Let us rise to the occasion, championing critical media literacy as a "potentially lifesaving tool" to navigate our 21st century age of digital disorientation (see Chapter One).

NOTE

[1] The literature on the "Deep State" is growing—the most accessible book-length introduction is Lofgren (2016).

REFERENCES

Ahmed, N. (2015, January 22). *How the CIA made google from insurge intelligence*. Retrieved from https://medium.com/insurge-intelligence/how-the-cia-made-google-e836451a959e

Alvarado, M. (1993). *The screen education reader: Cinema, television, culture*. New York, NY: Columbia University Press.

Badash, D. (2017, February 13). *'What does he mean when he says words?' John Oliver takes on Donald Trump and his lies: And does America a huge favor*. Retrieved from http://www.thenewcivilrightsmovement.com/davidbadash/_what_does_he_mean_when_he_says_words_john_oliver_takes_down_donald_trump_and_his_lies

Global Critical Media Literacy Project (GCMLP). Retrieved from www.gcml.org

Harcup, T., & O'Neill, D. (2001). What is news? Galtung and ruge revisited. *Journalism Studies, 2*(2), 261–280. Retrieved from http://www.tandfonline.com/doi/full/10.1080/1461670X.2016.1150193

Hermann, E., & Chomsky, N. (1988). *Manufacturing consent: The political economy of mass media.* New York, NY: Pantheon Books.

Jensen, C. (2001). Junk food news 1877–2000. In P. Phillips (Ed.), *Censored 2001* (pp. 251–264). New York, NY: Seven Stories Press.

Jimmy Dore Show. Retrieved from https://www.youtube.com/user/TYTComedy

Konkel, F. (2014, July 17). The details about the CIA's deal with amazon. *The Atlantic.* Retrieved from https://www.theatlantic.com/technology/archive/2014/07/the-details-about-the-cias-deal-with-amazon/374632/

Lofgren, M. (2016). *The Deep State: The fall of the constitution and the rise of the Shadow Government.* New York, NY: Penguin.

Merriam-Webster. (2017). *The real story of fake news*. Retrieved from https://www.merriam-webster.com/words-at-play/the-real-story-of-fake-news

Phillips, P., & Kubiak, D. (2010, May 2). *Truth emergency US*. Retrieved from http://projectcensored.org/truth-emergency-us/

Stegner, W. (2017). *The sound of mountain water: The changing American West*. New York, NY: Knopf Doubleday Publishing Group.

Williams, R. (2017, September). Plan "V": Designing a 2nd Vermont Republic. *Vermont Independence Press.* Retrieved from www.vermontindependent.org

Rob Williams
Community Development and Applied Economics (CDAE) Program
The University of Vermont
Burlington, Vermont

ROBERT WILLIAMS AND DANIEL WOODS

6. EDUCATING THE MYTH-LED

Critical Literacy Pedagogy in a Post-Truth World

> *We can take the role of agents, makers and remakers of our world in a permanent critical approach to reality in order to discover the myths that deceive us and help us maintain the oppressing, dehumanising structures.*
>
> – Paulo Freire

INTRODUCTION

In human societies trust and distrust are inescapably available as mechanisms or agents for manipulation of the social order (Valsiner, n.d.). From the mysterious goddess figurines of the earliest stone age civilizations to contemporary religious beliefs, leaders and social organizations have exploited the individual human drive to trust others like oneself, and to distrust others unlike oneself for as long as there have been human groups. Especially important to that impulse is a certain typical fear or ignorance of the unknown, and fear or ignorance of the unknown embodied in the concept of otherness. Certainly, fear and ignorance of unknown others is genetically set in humans as social creatures trusting of others like themselves, distrusting of others perceived as unlike themselves. Most importantly for teachers must be the recognition that schools always offer the capacity to serve those same forces of trust or distrust, or both, simultaneously. Organized, formal schools have always served as sites for enactment of the forces that simultaneously exhort students to learn new truths, to embrace intellectual otherness, while reinforcing the existing social order based in distrust of otherness in the social realm. Indeed, schools universally participate (often unwittingly) as reproductive agents in perpetuation of many of the myths that permeate the society in which the school exists. As members of society, the social order calls upon everyone to trust in the institutions, trust in the self-appointed guardians of those institutions, and to trust that society's leaders make decisions focused on the common good (Valsiner, n.d.).

In the same vein, most of the myths a society lives by are absolutely not malicious, or propagated for personal gain or other agendas (Lévi-Strauss, 1963). In fact, many of the myths handed down through generations are actually intended to be curative, or protective. From admonishments about adequate clothing, avoiding chills and dampness, or covering one's head, to directives for handling and cooking

 | DOI 10.1163/9789004365360_006

food, many of the prescriptions debunked by modern science originally served a beneficial purpose. And many such directives survive the most rigorous attempts at debunking. Pop culture continues to be rife with references to the mythical, but seemingly sensible. The myth of the sugar high (Hoover & Milich, 1994) continues to permeate pop culture and literature. Recent work in science education further documents the persistence of so-called neuromyths among educators, myths ranging from those that appeal to our intuition—learning styles—to myths that are grounded in solid neuroscience but that are inappropriately extrapolated or overgeneralized in the popular culture—being right- or left-brained (Macdonald et al., 2017). Most parents still caution their children against getting wet when the weather is cool. "Bless you" continues to follow sneezes everywhere one turns, and whether one believes that the blessing is prophylactic against the plague, or the separation of one's soul from one's earthly body, the tradition continues.

Additionally, misinformation about calamity, catastrophe, and personal failure circulate widely, whether over backyard fences, in the common fifties stereotype, or over backyard Facebook, Instagram, Twitter, or Whisper, or Yik-Yak. Large percentages of the population revel in gossip (Foster, 2004), although not necessarily in a dysfunctional way (Baumeister, Zhang, & Vohs, 2004). Conspiracy theories are no different in that the whole nature of conspiracy invokes some element of moral or ethical failing, including greed, or a desire to advance an interest through unethical means. From the theory that some in 18th century Britain sought to weaken the British military by sending troops to America in order to open the door for a French invasion (Bell, 2006), to the infamous 200-mpg-carburetors of the seventies, eighties, and nineties (Snopes, n.d.), to contemporary Birther conspiracies, deviousness and nefariously ill-gotten gains drive the people involved, and thus show the moral and ethical failings of those same people. And willing believers believe every word, or perhaps every other word, knowing that some aspects of the tale seem too salacious to be true.

On another level entirely, however, are the myths and misinformation propagated for the benefit of those in power. A short tour of history offers plenty of examples, from the most cliché—biblical proscriptions grounded in the threat of eternal damnation, or monsters who eat little children in the night—to the most subtle—can we really trust anyone who reads all those books, those elites? More specifically, Kovacs (2008) points to the burgeoning class of neo-intellectuals who attempt to use pseudoscience and fear to further their own (often corporate) agendas. Fast forward to 2017, and Kovacs analysis seems most prescient in light of everything from calls for more border security, calls based in inflated or misleading reports of criminal elements in immigrant populations (Pérez-Peña, 2017) to May, 2017's Presidential Executive Order on the Establishment of Presidential Advisory Commission on Election Integrity, an order that has been characterized as an outright attempt to justify voter suppression on a grand scale (Wines, 2017). This is not to propose the need for the populous to resort to tinfoil hats to curtail a New World Order, but is instead an exhortation that we must explore the power of myths and legends and misinformation and pseudoscience when they are used to create or maintain power structures.

Emphatically, we are proposing a critical literacy approach to addressing these issues. Behrman (2006) notes that "critical literacy can foster social justice by allowing students to recognize who language is affected by and affects social relations" (p. 409). He also asserts that the "aims of critical literacy are to have students examine the power relationships inherent in language use, recognize that language is not neutral, and confront their own values in the production and reception of language" (p. 409).

WHY CRITICAL LITERACY, WHY NOW?

The written word and the power it is ascribed have a long history of acting as a tool for division and injustice, for denying some groups of people while validating others, whether because of gender, age, race, religion, sexual orientation, or political affiliations (Apple, 1995, 2003; Foucault, 1980; Ladson-Billings, 2003; Morrison, 1993; Shor, 1992). This is not meant to suggest or advocate an ideology that writing is bad or that the practice of writing as a whole is in anyway unjust. It is an effort to express the reality that unless all people come to *the word* (written or spoken) with an equal opportunity, injustices can and do occur. Kutz and Roskelly (1991) insist, "No one's language is neutral. The forms chosen, at any instance, place them in relation to others and assert their meanings and intentions" (p. 148). As such, considering the *intent* of the word is as important as the consideration of the word in the first place. It is desirable (to those interested in social justice) that those ruled by the word come to understand the word and the multitudes it can contain (Freire, 1998). In short, if the word is to be an authentic element of a democracy, that same word must be available to all.

So, too, while *the word* in the form of myths and legends clearly creates a repository of cultural mores (Lévi-Strauss, 1963), there are many myths in the guise of fairytales that have led to the perpetuation of false or unrealistic expectations being placed on those outside of the dominant class. Additionally, because the dissemination of knowledge is often guided by, if not completely controlled, through the dominant social class of a society (Apple, 1995; Freire & Macedo, 1987; Giroux, 1992; hooks, 1994), it is a matter of consequence that it is the world of the dominant social classes that is reflected most deeply in the majority of our public schools (Giroux, 1983; hooks, 1994).

As recently as 2016 a social studies textbook for fourth graders in Connecticut was whitewashing the horrors of slavery by claiming that when "compared to other colonies, Connecticut did not have many slaves" and that slave owners "cared for and protected them like family; [sic] even educated some of them" (Grochowski, n.p.). In 2015 a world geography textbook in a 9th grade class in Texas came under fire as the authors denoted the immigration of slaves throughout the southern US as a migration pattern of workers (Wang). Workers. WORKERS! And while it is often difficult, if not impossible to ascertain an author's intent, it is easy to delineate an author's effect and the concept of renaming slaves, people who had been sold into bondage and treated as livestock, as *workers*. Manifestly, the term "workers," no matter how bad the conditions, could not capture the horrendous institution of slavery. But of course, who else to rename slaves as migrant workers than the textbook publishers who must cater to the textbook buyers Texas and California stand out as valuable markets textbook buyers who are predominately made up of the schooling classes, that is to say, white females led by white administrators (Department of Education, 2016; Lawrence, 2012).

In an Internet age of so-called urban myths, mis- and dis-information spread digitally, at minimum, if not exponentially, and multiple sources show that not only do many users pass along stories largely unread, or after only reading a headline (Gabielkov, Chaintreau, Ramachandran, & Legout, 2016), so, too, the endless half-life of urban myths is instantly visible to anyone with an Internet connection. Indeed, the late Roger Ailes might reasonably be credited with the rise of an agenda-driven media outlet cloaked in the trappings of dis-interested journalism (Alterman, 2014; Collum, 2016). In such an environment, potentially, the only remedy for contemporary urban myth-making and malicious or self-serving pseudoscience and mis- and dis-information—predictably—involves a better educated, more savvy populace. And to sum up, if belatedly, toward that end we propose the adoption of a critical literacy pedagogy—applied directly to *the word*—to offer writers and readers the skills needed to become critical creators and consumers of information.

Critical literacy pedagogy is an emancipatory practice that benefits students of all backgrounds. Critical literacy as defined by Lewison et al. (2002) "involves four dimensions: (1) disrupting the commonplace, (2) interrogating multiple viewpoints, (3) focusing on sociopolitical issues, and (4) taking action and promoting social justice" (p. 382). The goal of critical literacy pedagogy is emphatically *not* to validate or invalidate works of literature, but is instead to help students understand that any *truth* in a piece of writing does not have to be *their truth* (emphasis added) (Lankshear & Knobel, 1998; Comber, 1999; Luke, 2000).

When the importance of critical literacy is understood, it naturally follows that English Education educators above all others must consider how to assist preservice and in-service teachers in gaining the skills and experiences necessary to become critical literacy practitioners (Marshall & Klein, 2009). The proposition for this process is twofold: first, English educators must help their preservice and in-service teachers become critically literate themselves, and second, in so doing, those same English Education faculty must equip preservice and in-service teachers with the skills and strategies to negotiate any resistance, whether from students, administrations, colleagues, or parents, that they might encounter. And make no mistake about it, critical literacy is an emancipatory act, and history has shown that those in power are always reluctant to share that power.

Research in the usage of critical literacy is widespread and varied, although two commonalities have proven to exist. Critical literacy can be used in a wide array of educational pursuits, and critical literacy demands that instructors be willing to change and adapt their plans in relation to the growth of the students (Cohen, 2003; Lalik & Oliver, 2007; Morrell, 2008). As others have noted, a guiding tenet of critical literacy teaching and research is the goal of conscientization among the students. For this to become an authentic experience, then instructors must honor it by allowing students the freedom to direct their own praxis.

In a study conducted by Lalik and Oliver (2007), the researchers found that at times it was challenging to resist directing students toward predetermined goals and topics, rather than to follow the path created by mutual understanding and creation. This moment of release can prove to be quite difficult for even the best intentioned teachers. According to Cohen (2003), it was not uncommon for teachers trying to step beyond the bounds of tradition to have to battle back the oppressive traditions inherent in their standardized curriculum.

Critical literacy considers texts beyond the idea of inert collections of facts or ideas and engages in exploration of those collected words in relation to the political messages found within those texts. James Gee (2001) reminds his readers that all texts are inherently socially and culturally biased, and that such biases always work to either empower or oppress others. As Knoblauch and Brannon (1993) assert, "Literacy never stands alone…as a neutral denoting of skills: it is always literacy for something" (p. 17). Ultimately, critical literacy works to make the reader consider the position of self in relation to those messages (Ciardiello, 2004).

It was through the work of Paulo Freire that critical literacy emerged as a powerful tool for self-actualization, emancipation, and praxis—what he called conscientization. As a method of education, Freirian critical literacy offered the student and teacher an opportunity to come together to, not only acquire the dominant discourse, but also to question that discourse and its role in perpetuating the system of class divisions, both social and cultural. It was felt that those seeking to overturn a power structure must first understand how to function within that structure. That is not to say that they do function in that structure, but that they have an understanding of how others do (Freire, 1998).

Freire's groundbreaking work, *Pedagogy of the Oppressed* (1970), taught that the key to liberating oppressed people comes not from the educator, but from those who are oppressed. One cannot liberate another, but one can help another acquire the tools of liberation. For the educator, critical literacy is just such a tool. Freire also demonstrated that educators cannot merely deposit information into the minds of their students; they must give them the freedom to come to their own understandings, create their own world, and ultimately achieve conscientization.

Understanding that there is no *one truth* out there, but in fact there is an infinite variety of individual *truths—plural*, demands that teachers design lessons and consider assessments that take into account the role of cultural relativism in each student's learning process (Freire & Macedo, 1985). Yokota and Cai (2002) believed that "ignorance and prejudice are two main stumbling blocks to mutual understanding and appreciation among ethnic groups. To remove these blocks, we need more culturally specific books that give readers insights into cultures other than their own" (p. 25). Educating preservice teachers to approach their instruction in a manner that not only values each student's culture, but relies on it, will inevitably lead to more successful students. When considering such an undertaking, it is important to remember that by challenging hegemonic traditions we are challenging those people who have benefited most from those traditions (again, a group the majority of preservice teachers fall into). Caution must be taken, however: Research has demonstrated that there is a risk of alienating members of a group to the point that they become blindly defensive, and any chance at inspiring change is essentially lost (Apple, 2003; Jetton & Savage-Davis, 2005). Jetton and Savage-Davis (2005) found as Apple (2003) did that it is important that instructors not take an aggressive stance toward the injustices they may be far more aware of than most of their students. Teachers must instead model the teaching environment that they want their learners to aspire to. Bruna (2007) reminded her readers that the goal is not to make white kids feel guilty. She went so far as to tell her students that her multicultural teacher education classroom was not a place for studying Others, but was instead ultimately a space in which to "read the social meanings that shape our lives…as they relate to differences, similarity, and educational equity" (p. 115). This was a concern Apple (2003) expressed as well in considering the need to reeducate whites to a world in which *white* was also a race, and not the default for the human race, wherein all non-whites are viewed in relation to their lack of whiteness. Such an exploration needs to be approached in a supportive, non-combative manner if real change is to occur.

Critical literacy pedagogy further requires the use of multiple texts to analyze a situation, rather than taking one interpretation as being representative of the whole. Texts must likewise include a wide variety of representations meant to express meaning. These include, but are not limited to, books, magazines, newspapers, websites, e-zine's, movies, videos, graphic novels, advertisements, blogs, wikis, chat rooms, and so forth.

Another key component in the critical literacy classroom is the concept of psychological tools. These tools are inherent and unique to every culture (Berger & Luckmann, 1966; Moll, 1990; Vygotsky & Kozulin, 1986), and as such they encompass a vast array of expressionistic forms such as art, number systems, language and signs (explicit and inferred), and of course, literature. Smagorinsky, Pettis, and Reed (2004) believe that psychological tools work as a window into a culture, and understanding those tools allows one to act within a culture. Consequently, the nature of these tools and the acquisition, or *internalization*, and the usage, or *mediation*, of these tools and the manner in which they act as a scaffold between cognitive and metacognitive functions (Moll, 1990) is of great importance to the critical literacy practitioner.

Psychological tools such as signs (language) are the essence of any culture, and so any study of a culture and its practices must consider those signs in the context of the culture. From the very mundane and specific, such as recognizing and correctly interpreting traffic signs, to the more sophisticated skill of understanding gang tags, or being able to ascertain the level of seriousness of a No Trespassing sign (Berger & Luckmann, 1966; Moll, 1990; Vygotsky & Cole, 1978), one's understanding of a society's psychological tools is essential to understanding that society. Consequently, it is of the utmost importance that, when developing one's critical literacy, considerable effort be dedicated to the study of the sign systems (Semiotics) that govern the culture under consideration. Societies are full of signs that carry deeper meanings as ascribed by that society, and understanding that deeper meaning of a sign is part of being a member of a society (Vygotsky & Cole, 1978). The better one understands social and cultural signs of a society, the better one may understand that society.

Indeed, language is the most powerful of Vygotsky's psychological tools. One's ability to use language in its countless forms is often directly representative of the social status and level of success one may achieve within a society. As demonstrated by Mikail Bakhtin's (1981) concept of *heteroglossia*, societies are replete with set, specific codes—jargons, slangs, registers of lesser and greater formality, and even sociocultural and regional dialects—all reliant on shared meanings for mutual understanding. Whether it is the language of Wall Street or the language of Mean Street, one's ability to effectively communicate (internalization) within a certain skill set influences the status that one will be able to attain within their subset (Berger & Luckmann, 1966; Moll, 1990; Vygotsky & Kozulin, 1986).

Lastly, the social nature of learning (central to the theory of social constructivism) must guide considerations of developing critical literacy. Understanding the social and cultural influences involved in any individual student's learning process is crucial to understanding how the learner internalizes the reality that the outside world imposes upon that same learner's life (Moll, 1990). That is, in order to teach, learners and teachers alike must share a common discourse that understands and values the opinions and experiences of *both* (Berger & Luckmann, 1966). Most importantly, critical literacy pedagogy empowers writers and readers to express their opinions and experiences in a manner that is authentic and meaningful to them as individuals. In that pedagogy, teachers have a profound and lifelong effect on students, not only on how students see others, but even on how they see themselves. This influence dictates responsibility, and that responsibility is to equip students with the skills needed to experience this world in the manner in which they desire (Marshall & Klein, 2009). It is not the teacher's place to tell students what opportunities they should want out of life, but it is the teacher's responsibility to prepare learners to pursue the life they want. Critical literacy is essential to that pursuit.

CLOSE, BUT NOT QUITE THERE

While many teachers spend time critically analyzing the News, whether it comes from online posts and forums, or more traditional, dare one say *mainstream* sources, it is a mistake to assume that their readers experience and/or are exposed to that same level of information scrutiny when they are not in school. Consequently, teachers must design and implement lessons that specifically and directly address the modern mythologies and pseudoscience that are all too often mistaken for, or accepted as, fact.

As previously noted, understanding that there is no one truth out there, but in fact an infinite variety of individual truths, demands that teachers design lessons and consider assessments that take into account the role of cultural relativism in each student's learning process (Freire & Macedo, 1985). Yokota and Cai (2002) believed that "ignorance and prejudice are two main stumbling blocks to mutual understanding and appreciation among ethnic groups. To remove these blocks, we need more culturally specific books that give readers insights into cultures other than their own" (p. 25). Educating students in a manner that not only values each student's culture, but relies on it, will inevitably lead to more successful students.

One method of teaching critical literacy that is readily available and nearly free of emotional baggage inherent in engaging in real time critical analysis of political and social issues is to turn a critical literacy lens on the classics of canonical literature. To be clear, the goal is that students will learn to view *all* information through a critical lens, but students (especially culturally monolithic students) are better served if they first engage in critical literacy practices that include canonical texts that while still controversial, are far enough removed from modern life to be approached in a less emotional, more analytical manner. If students come to a topic already holding deep emotional beliefs, as is often the case with contemporary political and social issues, it is more difficult for them to set their biases aside and work through a critical lens. However, if they are able to hone their critical literacy skills in a less controversial or safer arena, those learners are more likely to be able to approach future issues, no matter how emotionally charged, with a more critical and clinical mind (Lewison & Heffernan, 2008).

However, before readers learn to view the world through a critical literacy lens, they must first turn that gaze upon themselves, and all while teachers remember that they cannot make any assumptions about the critical literacy skills the students do or do not already have. Teachers being prepared for classrooms of the future have had life experiences that are certain to be quite different from the experiences of the children they will teach (Au, 1998; Bruner, 1996; Delpit, 1991, 1995; Devine, 1994; Gee, 1992; Ladson-Billings, 1999) and are likely, through no fault of their own, to view education through what Freire (1973) called a "naïve and magical consciousness" (p. 39). This phenomenon is a Machiavellian mindset in which the world is perceived only in relation to one's own personal experience. Knowles and Holt-Reynolds (1991) asserted that "[p]reservice teachers use their experiences as students as if these were prototypical" (p. 104). If contemporary preservice teaching candidates—as homogenous members of a dominant culture—have empowering educational experiences, then they will likewise assume that the majority of their students will as well, and regardless of the fact that large numbers of those students do not belong to the same, dominant culture. Consequently, taking a critical literacy stance may not be a natural position for a teacher accustomed to viewing the world through the eyes of the dominant culture.

Of course, merely recognizing inequalities perpetuated through the written word is no more useful than recognizing that one is being charged by an angry bull. Recognition without action is of little value. Just as the angry bull should inspire one to take action, so should critical literacy pedagogy. One form of action English educators can take is through the process of conscientization. This is the Freirian concept that all learners, no matter their level, must come to recognize the personal and social components found within every aspect of learning, the emancipatory power of just such a realization, and then the inspiring of the learner to take action (Freire, 1998; Giroux, 2009). Conscientization comes from the Portuguese *consientizção*, meaning "learning to perceive social, political, and economic contradictions, and to take action against the oppressive elements of reality" (Freire, 1986, p. 35). For a student to become fully independent and self-determining should be the goal of all teachers.

For critical literacy scholars, the move to social action is of paramount importance if one is to be considered a true critical literacy practitioner (Apple, 1995; Freire & Macedo, 1987; Giroux, 1992; hooks, 1994; Janks, 2010; Morrell, 2008; Shor, 1996). Marshall and Klein (2009) noted that experts in the field believe that educators in the United States "are failing to prepare students to become active citizens in their neighborhoods, cities, states, nations, and world" (p. 218). Of course, it is not the job of the Secondary ELA teacher alone to prepare students to become active citizens, but the job of all teachers in all schools. Sleeter (1991) believed that "[e]mpowering education programs work with students and their home communities to build on what they bring; disabling programs ignore and attempt to eradicate knowledge and strengths students bring, and replace them with those of the dominant society" (p. 5). Using critical literacy to engage students in social action is one way to for Secondary ELA teachers to do their part.

Educators at all levels play a vital role in the shaping of society, and as such they should be active participants in that shaping rather than being relegated to the role of replicators of the status quo. As Freire (1986) wrote, "Those truly committed to liberation…must abandon the educational goal of deposit-making and replace it with the posing of the problems of human beings in their relations with the world" (p. 79). Teachers need to feel empowered to seek out injustice, work to expose it, and even eradicate it when possible (Marshall & Klein, 2009). As an English educator, my goal is for my students to leave my classroom as teachers who hold the rights of their students above all else, to know that democracy does not end at the doorway of the school or classroom, and that they ultimately as teachers have the strength to stand up for what is right and to have a say in just how our world is written.

Gee (2001) reminds us that all information is socially and culturally situated and that language and the study of communication, reflect deeply the social and cultural norms and values of authors and their cultural experiences. Critical literacy is one appropriate tool for such study, since it is a pedagogy that examines the sociopolitical factors that influence every work of human representation. The goal of critical literacy is to teach students to expose and subvert the oppressive literary traditions that much of our education system is built upon (Freire, 1998; Lankshear & McLaren, 1993; Shor, 1992, 1996). Teachers must work to expose those oppressive traditions and to empower their students to subvert that oppression through the same means by which it was originally delivered, in this case, the written word (Boyd et al., 2006). Lorde (1984) expressed the importance of members of a culture having their voices heard when she declared that "it is the responsibility of the oppressed to teach the oppressors their mistakes" (p. 114). To which Gerald Vizenor (1994) would add, "When the victims talk back, they stop being victims" (p. 85). In respect to his assertion, teachers at all levels must create the spaces that allow those voices to be heard (Boyd et al., 2006) and the Secondary ELA classroom is an excellent place to begin.

It is worth noting that the task of implementing wide-ranging critical literacy pedagogy faces several hurdles along the way, not the least of which is the fact that the vast majority of classroom teachers come from backgrounds that are privileged in traditional societal and classroom texts and are quite likely to be unaware that such injustices even occur. More than thirty years ago, Hanvey (1975) and Lortie (1975) each reported that most teachers in America were white, middle-class females. Entering a 21st century classroom, it is apparent that the demographics for teachers in the United States have changed little. As previously noted, current reports state that over 82 percent of teachers in the United States are white (Department of Education, 2016). What has changed, however, is the population of students inhabiting those classrooms. Recent predictions assert that by 2020 approximately 50% of the school-age population in the United States will consist of students from cultural backgrounds that are currently considered minorities (Weddington & Rhine, 2006). From then on, the numbers of students representing culturally diverse populations will increase and soon become the majority (Au, 2003; Ladson-Billings, 1999; Sapon-Shevin & Zollers, 1999). Additionally, as of 2015, 51% of public school students in the United States are eligible for free or reduced lunches (Southern Education Foundation, 2015). In other words, as the population of public school teachers in the United States continues to be overwhelmingly homogenous, the student body grows ever more diverse with, students coming from one-parent homes; two-parent, same sex homes; ethnically diverse homes, religiously diverse homes; and socio-economically diverse homes. Consequently, teachers must expand their literacy practices to include a more diverse and divergent classroom population.

HOW CRITICAL LITERACY? HOW IN PUBLIC SCHOOLS AND CLASSROOMS?

We have observed teachers who wish to develop their students' critical literacy skills, but who remain apprehensive about bringing controversial topics into their classrooms before their students have developed the critical thinking and social skills needed to engage thoughtfully in discussions that can be emotionally charged. Yet these same learners often live with emotionally charged issues, with family life that must be seen to be challenging to the most mature adults. Students of all ages experience injury, debilitating illness, and the loss of loved ones. Clearly, while we cannot expect such learners to be as critically literate as thoughtful adults, we can address those learners' critical literacy practices in a developmentally sensitive way, with full recognition of the learners' cognitive stature and status. By working with more accessible texts, whether canonical or not, and by additionally introducing more and more complex texts, teachers can support students' critical literacy development. Furthermore, by using canonical texts that are fully integrated into most school curricula—stamped with society's approval, as it were—we offer readers a potentially less threatening cognitive space in which to challenge the mores represented in those texts. Such a move in turn allows for exploration without the possibly less useful emotional connotations and energies surrounding more contemporary work. To be clear, there are no truly safe spaces (to borrow an overused term) in which to engage in critical literacy practices. Frankly, that is the point. The lack of safe places is the catalyst for examining the world through a critical literacy lens.

While the goal is always critical literacy for all, working with an accessible, popular text that contains readily observable flaws in the treatment of some cultures and groups may offer a more useful engagement, almost in a clinical sense, with literary analysis. And after all, for most readers the act of literary analysis—fraught with terminology such as *theme, motif, characterization, plot* and *conflict*—already smacks of voodoo, or magic, or impenetrably arcane cognitive gymnastics. At minimum, working with an established work may help in establishing a Vygotskian Zone of Proximal Development within which beginners may practice at disinterring the biases and cultural assumptions embedded in all texts.

To prepare classroom teachers, and their students, to engage in critical literacy practices we propose, and offer examples for, using a text that is widely available to classroom teachers nationwide; James Fenimore Cooper's *The Last of the Mohican.* Teachers can use this text to introduce students to critical literacy by to considering race relations and stereotypes rather than choosing a text that discusses modern race relations in America such as the treatment of African American citizens by police, or the Trump administration's hostile stance on immigration. Of course, this is not to imply that Native American race issues are a thing of the past; the protests and reactions to the Standing Rock protests are evidence of that.

One common example that demonstrates the role of critical literacy in exploring canonical texts in the Secondary ELA classroom is James Fennimore Cooper's *The Last of the Mohicans.* While the literary merit of this novel continues to be debated, its popularity continues more than 180 years after first publication. Cooper's most famous, or some would say infamous, work continues to be stocked in schools and libraries worldwide, as well as enjoying Hollywood success several times over. And because the offenses are so blatant and so obvious to the modern reader, this text is a perfect tool for introducing students to the central tenets of critical literacy practices.

After a brief introduction to the essential questions critical literacy asks of a text, students and teachers can explore the text through a literary lens.

To reiterate: Critical literacy as defined by Lewison et al. (2002) "involves four dimensions: (1) disrupting the commonplace, (2) interrogating multiple viewpoints, (3) focusing on sociopolitical issues, and (4) taking action and promoting social justice" (p. 382). As such, this is where classroom teachers may begin a critical literacy journey with their students.

While every classroom is unique, we do offer an overview of how a teacher might introduce a unit on critical literacy that begins with an exploration of *The Last of the Mohicans.*

Day One

Day one of exploring critical literacy through *The Last of the Mohicans* involves an exploration of what students already know, or think they know, about Native American culture as that culture has been represented in literature and other media (dimension 1 above). Teachers may want to create stations around the room with large post-it note or flip-chart sheets where students can record their existing ideas and knowledge (with those initial sheets preserved to be revisited later on). Once students have listed what they (think they) know about Native Americans the teacher can break the class into groups and have students discuss and record how they came to know these facts (dimension 2 above). Ideally, this latter discussion will help students realize that their sources of information may not be as reliable as one might prefer. Indeed, in the typical American classroom, the majority if not the entirety of what most teenagers in the dominant culture know about Native American people comes from romanticized works of literature and stereotypical Hollywood representations.

Day Two

In their second day, and concurrent to reading in the primary text if appropriate or necessary, learners can begin to engage in genuine research—online and/or library-based—about the reality of Native American life across multiple nations and cultures within the broader American population. This research must absolutely include ongoing comparisons between actual Native American cultures and the depictions of Native Americans still found in popular culture in a variety of media (dimension 3 above). This work can continue multiple days, and can include multiple tangents depending on the individual curriculum, class setting, and time available.

Day Three

In a move toward critical *literary* analysis, in the third or any subsequent day, or as outside reading, students may read Mark Twain's "Fenimore Cooper's Literary

Offenses" (1895), in which Twain critiques Cooper's characterization of Native Americans (and his writing) extensively. Equally valuably, students reading both Twain and Cooper must reconcile the two perspectives, one fiction, one satirical, and in that reconciliation begin to understand the mutability of perspective itself. As with a view of a die cast to rest with one facet showing one numerical value, but with five equally valid values on the other five faces, as we turn the literary work (or the media account, or the movie, or the blog) from side to side, from reader to reader, we encounter now this author's values, now that author's values.

Day Four and Beyond

With the reading at least partially contextualized by Twain, and by some sense of contemporary Native American cultures, students may begin to better understand why Cooper's romantic tale is in such need of revisiting and revisioning through the lens of *literary* analysis, and subsequently through the lens of critical *literacy* if we are to supplant images such as Cooper offers with more culturally accurate (and less offensive) ones. No student anywhere should be allowed to leave a reading of *Mohicans* without an extensive understanding of the nature of Cooper's misconceptions. Yet, for many years this book and others like it were considered nearly anthropological in their representations of Native Americans, just as some views of African American cultures continue to be influenced or driven by Harriet Beecher Stowe's *Uncle Tom's Cabin*. Stowe's work so deeply affected common impressions of African American culture that the term "Uncle Tom" is still used as a derogatory remark today.

These books and countless others (intentionally or not) have become the medium through which people believe they come to *know* another people. The romanticized image of the Native American as being somehow transcendent of humanity in a union with mother earth has been perpetuated to the point that the average American's image of Native Americans has become a caricature of a people represented through turquoise jewelry, feathered headdresses, and the greeting "How white man!" (Aldred, 2000). With Cooper, we can see the consequences of the power of the word when it is read (or taught) and accepted without question. Unequivocally, there is a need to teach our students to consider more than the text, to teach them to consider also the context, and to teach them to apply their own, critical lenses to *every* reading engagement.

To be sure, this is not to suggest an overhaul of the canon, or the public castigation of any authors, but merely a shift in the perception of literature and the word as the ultimate truth, to include considerations of culturally diverse learners (Boyd et al., 2006; Duffy, 2008; Giroux, 2009; Morrell & Duncan-Andrade, 2006). English educators need to impart an understanding that any text used in a classroom carries implied acceptance and validation by the school and school system (Doubek & Cooper, 2007). To study *The Last of the Mohicans* as a representation of a 17th–18th century white man's perception of native people does far more justice to those people (and to the book I would posit) than the continued perpetuation of the word as representing absolute truth.

CONCLUSION

The vaunted stature of texts as emblematic of *Truth*, as bastions of knowledge that is not to be challenged once in print seems to be most prominent in the ideology of school-based textbooks, and often manifests in a fevered defense of canonical literature (Apple, 2003). But it is difficult to ignore the fact that such perspectives actively promote and maintain social hierarchies as we continue to see traditional (middle-class white) values and norms represented in classrooms in which a large percentage of students arrive from outside of that dominant class (Apple, 2003; Hill-Jackson, 2007). Again the status quo is maintained as those students outside of the dominant social class are subjected to state approved curricula (Doubek & Cooper, 2007) in which they and their ways of life are often underrepresented, misrepresented, or worst of all, completely unrepresented in the literature of a state approved curriculum that strenuously resists revisioning or appropriating for critique works such as *Mohicans* (Morrison, 1993; Giroux, 1992; Shor, 1992).

This focus on conformity within education creates a hegemonic system designed to maintain current power structures rather than encourage democratic equality (Apple, 2003; Giroux, 1983). Yet, if we are ever to realize a more equitable or just republican democracy, this paradigm must be shifted further toward a pedagogy grounded in retaining individual cultures and considering the multitude of ways of knowing as expressed by those cultures (Apple, 1995; Banks & Banks, 1993; Boyd et al., 2006; Brice-Heath, 2006). Bishop (1992) maintains that "[i]f our society is to meet the challenges of demographic pluralism, all students need to recognize the diversity that defines this society, learn to respect it, and see it in a positive light" (p. 3). Very early on, John Dewey (1985), in considering the role of democracy in education, expressed a multicultural vision by stating that one of the guiding virtues of education should be "not only freer interaction between social groups (once isolated so far as intention could keep up a separation) but change in social habit—its continuous readjustment through meeting the new situations produced by varied intercourse" (p. 92). Adopting critical literacy pedagogy, we contend, is essential to that enterprise.

If we are to one day realize true equality of opportunity and some measure of social justice in our nation, today's classroom teachers must work to establish equity among students (Marshall & Klein, 2009). Toward that end, teachers can model and provide equality of opportunity, and equally importantly, provide a plethora of opportunities for those same learners to become more critically literately engaged with their own social situations and access to opportunity. Teachers can repeatedly model equity for all. Likewise, teachers can repeatedly model equality of opportunity. Teachers can repeatedly model their own critically literate acts in the social realm and as engaged citizens; mostly, though, teachers can model equal treatment for all people. Teachers can model how to respectfully interact with women, with members of all cultural and ethnic minorities, with people who belong or self-identify as members of different religions, or with varying sexual orientation, or with those who face any number of mental or physical challenges. Of course, accomplishing such a monumental, but worthwhile task is far beyond the scope of the Secondary ELA teacher, working (usually) alone in the classroom, but we argue that this tenet should be the guiding principle of public and private education at every level, in every content area.

REFERENCES

Aldred, L. (2000). Plastic shamans and Astroturf sun dances: New age commercialization of native American spirituality. *American Indian Quarterly, 24*(3), 329–352.

Alterman, E. (2014). What Ailes the media? *Nation, 298*(8), 6–8.

Apple, M. (2003, April). Freire and the politics of race in education. *International Journal of Leadership in Education, 6*(2), 107.

Apple, M. W. (1995). *Education and power*. New York, NY: Routledge.

Au, K. H. (1998). Social constructivism and the school literacy learning of students of diverse backgrounds. *Journal of Literacy Research, 30*(2), 297–319.

Banks, J. A., & Banks, C. A. M. (2003). *Multicultural education: Issues and perspectives* (4th ed.). New York, NY: John Wiley & Sons, Inc.

Baumeister, R. F., Zhang, L., & Vohs, K. D. (2004). Gossip as cultural learning. *Review of General Psychology, 8*(2), 111–121.

Bell, J. L. (2006). *Conspiracy theories of the revolution*. Retrieved from http://boston1775.blogspot.com/2006/07/conspiracy-theories-of-revolution.html

Berger, P. L., & Luckmann, T. (1966). *The social construction of reality*. New York, NY: Anchor.

Bishop, R. S. (1992). Multicultural literature for children: Making informed choices. In V. J. Harris (Ed.), *Teaching multicultural literature in grades K-8* (pp. 37–53). Norwood, MA: Christopher-Gordon.

Boyd, F. B., Ariail, M., Williams, R., Jocson, K., Sachs, G. T., & McNeal, K. (2006). Real teaching for real diversity: Preparing English language arts teachers for 21st-century classrooms. *English Education, 38*(4), 329–350.

Bruna, K. (2007, December). Manufacturing dissent: The new economy of power relations in multicultural teacher education. *International Journal of Multicultural Education, 9*(1), 1–17.

Bruner, J. (1996). *The culture of education*. Cambridge, MA: Harvard University Press.

Ciardiello, A.V. (2004). A democracy's young heroes: An instructional model of critical literacy practices. *The Reading Teacher, 58*(2), 138–147.

Cohen, P. (2003). Tricks of the trade: On teaching arts and 'race' in the classroom. In D. Buckingham (Ed.), *Teaching popular culture: Beyond radical pedagogy* (pp. 153–176). London: Routledge.

Collum, D. (2016). Fake news and real lies. *Sojourners Magazine, 45*(10), 42.

Comber, B. (1999, November 18–21). *Critical literacies: Negotiating powerful and pleasurable curricula: How do we foster critical literacy through English language arts?* Paper presented at the Annual Conference of the National Teachers of English, Denver, CO.

Delpit, L. (1991). The silenced dialogue: Power and pedagogy in the education of other people's children. In M. Minami & B. P. Kennedy (Eds.), *Language issues in literacy and bilingual/multicultural education* (pp. 483–502). Cambridge, MA: Harvard Educational Review.

Delpit, L. D. (1995). *Other people's children: Cultural conflict in the classroom*. New York, NY: New Press.

Department of Education. (2016, July). *The state of racial diversity in the educator workforce*. Retrieved from https://www2.ed.gov/rschstat/eval/highered/racial-diversity/state-racial-diversity-workforce.pdf

Devine, J. (1994). Literacy and social power. In B. M. Ferdman, R. M. Weber, & A. G. Ramirez (Eds.), *Literacy across languages and cultures* (pp. 221–237). Albany, NY: SUNY.

Dewey, J. (1985, c1916). *Democracy and education: An introduction to the philosophy of education.* New York, NY: Macmillan.

Doubek, M., & Cooper, E. (2007). Closing the gap through professional development: Implications for reading research. *Reading Research Quarterly, 42*(3), 411–415.

Duffy, J. (2008). Teaching for critical literacy and racial justice. *Democracy & Education, 17*(3), 38–45.

Foster, E. K. (2004). Research on gossip: Taxonomy, methods, and future directions. *Review of General Psychology, 8*(2), 78–99.

Foucault, M. (1980). *Power/knowledge: Selected interviews and other writings, 1972–1977.* New York, NY: Pantheon.

Freire, P. (1998). *Teachers as cultural workers: Letters to those who dare teach.* Boulder, CO: Westview Press.

Freire, P., & Macedo, D. P. (1987). *Literacy: Reading the word & the world.* South Hadley, MA: Bergin & Garvey.

Freire, P. (1986, c1970). *Pedagogy of the oppressed.* New York, NY: Continuum.

Freire, P. (1973). *Education for critical consciousness.* New York, NY: Seaburg.

Gee, J. (2001). Reading as situated language: A sociocognitive perspective. *Journal of Adolescent & Adult Literacy, 44*(8), 714.

Gee, J. P. (1992). *The social mind: Language, ideology, and social practice.* New York, NY: Bergin & Garvey.

Gabielkov, M., Chaintreau, A., Ramachandran, A., & Legout, A. (2016). Social clicks: What and who gets read on twitter? *Performance Evaluation Review, 44*(1), 179. doi:10.1145/2896377.2901462

Giroux, H. (2009). Education and the crisis of youth: Schooling and the promise of democracy. *Educational Forum, 73*(1), 8–18.

Giroux, H. A. (1983). *Theory and resistance in education: A pedagogy for the opposition.* South Hadley, MA: Bergin & Garvey.

Giroux, H. A. (1992). Post-colonial ruptures and democratic possibilities: Multiculturalism as anti-racist pedagogy. *Cultural Critique, 21*, 5–39.

Grochowski, S. (2016, December 7). Fourth grade textbook saying slaves were like 'family' pulled from Connecticut school district. *New York Daily News*. Retrieved from http://www.nydailynews.com/news/national/textbook-pulled-complaint-slaves-family-article-1.2902177

Hanvey, R. (1975). *An attainable global perspective.* New York, NY: Center for War/Peace study.

Hill-Jackson, V. (2007). Part III: Creating multicultural classrooms: Wrestling Whiteness: Three stages of shifting multicultural perspectives among White pre-service teachers. *Multicultural Perspectives, 9*(2), 29–35.

hooks, b. (1994). *Teaching to transgress: Education as the practice of freedom.* New York, NY: Routledge.

Hoover, D. W., & Milich, R. (1994, August). Effects of sugar ingestion expectancies on mother-child interactions. *Journal of Abnormal Child Psychology, 22*(4), 501–15.

Jetton, T. L., & Savage-Davis, E. M. (2005). Preservice teachers develop an understanding of diversity issues through multicultural literature. *Multicultural Perspectives,* 7(1), 30–38.

Knoblauch, C., & Brannon, L. (1989). *Teaching literature in high school: A teacher-research project* (Report Series 2.2). Albany, NY: Center for the Learning and Teaching of Literature.

Knowles, J., & Holt-Reynolds, D. (1991). Shaping pedagogies through personal histories in preservice teacher education. *Teachers College Record, 93*(1), 87–113.

Kovacs, P. (2008). Neointellectuals: Willing tools on a veritable crusade. *Journal for Critical Education Policy Studies, 6*(1).

Kutz, E., & Roskelly, H. (1991). *An unquiet pedagogy: Transforming practice in the English classroom.* Portsmouth, NH: Boynton/Cook.

Ladson-Billings, G. (1999). Preparing teachers for diversity: Historical perspectives, current trends, and future directions. In L. Darling-Hammond & G. Sykes (Eds.), *Teaching as a learning profession: Handbook of policy and practice.* San Francisco, CA: Jossey Bass.

Ladson-Billings, G. (2003). Foreword. In S. Greene & D. Abt-Perkins (Eds.), *Making race visible: Literacy research for cultural understanding* (pp. vii–xi). New York, NY: Teacher's College.
Lalik, R., & Oliver, K. (2007). Differences and tensions in implementing a pedagogy of critical literacy with adolescent girls. *Reading Research Quarterly, 42*(1), 46–70.
Lankshear, C., & McLaren, P. (1993). *Critical literacy: Politics, praxis, and the postmodern*. Albany, NY: State University of New York Press.
Lawrence, J. (2012, November 13). NCES teacher demographic data paints portrait of US teacher. *Education News*. Retrieved from http://www.educationnews.org/k-12-schools/nces-teacher-demographic-data-paints-portrait-of-us-teacher/
Lévi-Strauss, C. (1963). The structural study of myth. In C. Lévi-Strauss (Ed.), *Structural anthropology* (pp. 206–231). New York, NY: Basic Books.
Lewison, M., Flint, A., & Van Sluys, K. (2002). Taking on critical literacy: The journey of newcomers and novices. *Language Arts, 79*(5), 382–392.
Lewison, M., & Heffernan, L. (2008). Rewriting writers workshop: Creating safe spaces for disruptive stories. *Research in the Teaching of English, 42*(4), 435–465.
Lorde, A. (1984). *Sister outsider*. Freedom, CA: The Crossing Press.
Lortie, D. C. (1975). *Schoolteacher: A sociological study*. Chicago, IL: University of Chicago Press.
Macdonald, K., Germine, L., Anderson, A., Christodoulou, J., & McGrath, L. M. (2017). Dispelling the myth: Training in education or neuroscience decreases but does not eliminate beliefs in neuromyths. *Frontiers in Psychology, 8, Article 1314*. doi:10.3389/fpsyg.2017.01314
Marshall, J., & Klein, A. (2009). Lessons in social action: Equipping and inspiring students to improve their world. *Social Studies, 100*(5), 218–221.
Moll, L. C. (1990). *Vygotsky and education: Instructional implications and applications of sociohistorical psychology*. Cambridge: Cambridge University Press.
Morrell, E. (2008). *Critical literacy and urban youth: Pedagogies of access, dissent, and liberation*. New York, NY: Routledge.
Morrell, E., & Duncan-Andrade, J. (2006). Popular culture and critical media pedagogy in secondary literacy classrooms. *International Journal of Learning, 12*(9), 273–280.
Morrison, T. (1993). *Playing in the dark: Whiteness and the literary imagination*. New York, NY: Random House.
Pérez-Peña, R. (2017, January 26). Contrary to Trump's claims, immigrants are less likely to commit crimes. *New York Times*. Retrieved from https://www.nytimes.com/2017/01/26/us/trump-illegal-immigrants-crime.html
Sapon-Shevin, M., & Zollers, N. J. (1999). Multicultural and disability agendas in teacher education: Preparing teachers for diversity. *International Journal of Leadership in Education: Theory and Practice, 2*(3), 165–190.
Shor, I. (1992). *Empowering education: Critical teaching for social change*. Chicago, IL: University of Chicago Press.
Shor, I. (1996). *When students have power: Negotiating authority in a critical pedagogy*. Chicago, IL: University of Chicago Press.
Smagorinsky, P., Pettis, V., & Reed, P. (2004). High school students' compositions of ranch designs: Implications for academic and personal achievement. *Written Communication, 21*(4), 386–418.
Snopes. (n.d.). *Miracle Carburetor*. Retrieved from http://www.snopes.com/autos/business/carburetor.asp
Southern Education Foundation. (2015, January). *A new majority research bulletin: Low income students now a majority in the nation's public schools*. Retrieved from http://www.southerneducation.org/Our-Strategies/Research-and-Publications/New-Majority-Diverse-Majority-Report-Series/A-New-Majority-2015-Update-Low-Income-Students-Now
Twain, M. (1895). *Fenimore Cooper's literary offenses*. Retrieved from http://twain.lib.virginia.edu/projects/rissetto/offense.html
Valsiner, J. (n.d.). *Civility of basic distrust: A cultural-psychological view on persons-in-society*. Retrieved from https://semioticon.com/virtuals/risk/distrust.pdf

Vizenor, G. (1994). *Manifest manners: Postindian warriors of survivance*. Hanover, NH: Wesleyan University Press.

Vygotsky, L. S., & Cole, M. (1978). *Mind in society: The development of higher psychological processes*. Cambridge, MA: Harvard University Press.

Vygotsky, L. S., & Kozulin, A. (1986). *Thought and language*. Cambridge, MA: MIT Press.

Wang, Y. (2015, October 5). 'Workers' or slaves? Textbook maker backtracks after mother's online complaint. *The Washington Post*. Retrieved from https://www.washingtonpost.com/news/morning-mix/wp/2015/10/05/immigrant-workers-or-slaves-textbook-maker-backtracks-after-mothers-online-complaint/?utm_term=.75bcf3fc188a

Weddington, H., & Rhine, S. (2006). Comfort with chaos and complexity. *International Journal of Learning, 13*(2), 39–47.

Wines, M. (2017, July 19). Trump election commission, already under fire, holds first meeting. *New York Times*. Retrieved from https://www.nytimes.com/2017/07/19/us/trump-election-commission-already-under-fire-holds-first-meeting.html

Yokota, J., & Cai, M. (2002). Social justice and critical literacy. *Language Arts, 79*(5), 432–437.

Robert Williams
Radford University
Radford, Virginia

Daniel Woods
Radford University
Radford, Virginia

JOANNE ADDISON

7. TEACHING CRITICAL MEDIA LITERACY AS A SOCIAL PROCESS IN WRITING INTENSIVE CLASSROOMS

INTRODUCTION

A recent Pew Research Center survey (2016) sought to describe the pathways Americans take to news as well as their experience of various types of mass media. The results reveal that 50% of 18–29 years olds access news online. And, 7 out of 10 18–29 year olds prefer or only use mobile devices when consuming news. Further, approximately 1/3 of the people in this age group access news through social media sites. Importantly, younger people overall express a low level of trust in the information they access whether through mainstream mass media or social media. This high level of skepticism and high level of new media usage might suggest a critical turn away from the current propaganda function of much mainstream news media.[1] However, such a critical turn requires a level of media literacy that goes beyond skepticism. Early indications suggest that our youth may not be well-prepared to act as literate citizens in this environment.

For example, between January of 2015 and June of 2016, researchers at Stanford University collected and analyzed 7,804 student responses to an assessment designed to measure students' civic online reasoning or the ability to judge the credibility of information found on news media websites, photo sharing websites, and social media platforms such as Twitter and Facebook. In summarizing their study, the researchers' dismay is clear:

> By high school, we would hope that students reading about gun laws would notice that a chart came from a gun owners' political action committee. And, in 2016, we would hope college students, who spend hours each day online, would look beyond a .org URL and ask who's behind a site that presents only one side of a contentious issue. But in every case and at every level, we were taken aback by students' lack of preparation. (Wineburg et al., 2016, p. 4)

Given the turn of our youth toward fully digital platforms and today's proliferation in virtual spaces of fake news, advertising that mimics news, and social media automation such as Twitter bots, it is more important than ever that we develop pedagogical responses to what it means to be a literate citizen in today's media landscape.

 | DOI 10.1163/9789004365360_007

Literate citizenship depends upon active democratic participation. But, like the researchers from the Stanford study above, I worry that "democracy is threatened by the ease at which disinformation about civic issues is allowed to spread and flourish" (p. 5). More specifically, I worry about students' ability to access, analyze, and create online media in ways that counter the seeming chaos and distrust currently being sown. As students strive to determine what's "real," I do not want them to feel defeated but rather empowered, not to shrug their shoulders and say "what can you do?" but rather to roll up their sleeves and begin the work of active, literate citizens.

As a writing teacher committed to writing across the curriculum, I believe that one of the most important ways we can empower students is to provide them heuristics that can lead to critical analysis and writing, helping them to focus their attention in productive ways at a time when so many forces are vying for our inattention. Janice Lauer (2004) defines heuristics as a process of discovery involving "a series of questions, operations, and perspectives used to guide inquiry and knowledge creation" (p. 8). At this particular moment in time, students need heuristics that can help them understand the economic and ideological complexities of media literacy as played out in the relationship between audience, power, and information. Importantly, any heuristic that aims to help students analyze media literacy must do so within social contexts. In the rest of this chapter, I will show how Deborah Brandt's (2001) conception of sponsors and pathways alongside Noam Chomsky and Edward Herman's Propaganda Model (2002) can be used to scaffold the heuristic Bruce McComiskey (2000) invites readers to adopt for the own purposes in *Teaching Composition as a Social Process* to address gaps in critical media literacy. While none of these texts specifically address media literacy or online media literacy, all lay important foundations for the work required of teachers as we strive to help students embrace critical media literacy in digital environments.

THE COMMODIFICATION OF LITERACY AND MASS MEDIA

In 2001 Deborah Brandt published *Literacy in American Lives*. This was well before the public launch of social media and networking sites between 2004 and 2010 such as Facebook, Reddit, Twitter, Instagram, and many others. The analytical framework Brandt develops through this research now seems prescient as we strive to understand how media literacy works in the lives of our students. While it wasn't Brandt's goal to predict the critical media literacy needs of future students, she ends up doing so because during the time period that she studied, the 20th century, the groundwork was being laid for the situation in which we now find ourselves. Reminding ourselves of the economic and political landscape of literacy in the 20th century will help us chart a path forward.

Mass reading literacy emerged in America in the 19th century largely in response to nation building, evangelical Protestantism, and technological change. The common school reforms led to most children under 10 being provided with public education and cemented the strong association of literacy with schooling in ways that allowed for standardization and regulation of literacy. This, many at the time argued, would lead to a citizenry guided by reason and information, not superstition and magic. As Stevens (1987) points out, "The civic model for literacy was promulgated by a fervent evangelical Protestant tradition" (p. 107) aimed at developing a moral republic. In addition, the 19th century saw rapid changes in printing technology that allowed for the mass production of books and a significant increase in newspaper production (Stevens, 1987, p. 108). While literacy was largely an act in service to nation building, socialization, and religious observation of moral codes, these technological changes began to pave the way for commodifying literacy with all of the issues of access and control that commodification entails.

With this historical backdrop, Brandt embarked upon her study of 20th century writing literacy. Brandt's study remains unique in its use of direct evidence in the form of life histories that allowed her to explore writing as a lived experience. This study included 80 participants who ranged in age from 10 to 98, living in a geographically and economically diverse region of Wisconsin. Through an analysis of these life histories, Brandt worked to understand variations of literacy development within the context of large-scale economic forces that determined how that literacy was shaped as well as how it was valued by the culture at large. During the 20th century one of the defining functions of literacy remained its use as a tool to disseminate and reinforce existing and emerging social norms. But, the rapid capitalization of literacy revealed through these life histories highlights the ways in which literacy became tied less to notions of common good and social cohesion and more to competition and commerce.

These life histories of a group of people all living in the same geographic region teach us just how unequally written literacy is distributed across the economic spectrum. From Dwayne Lowery who was born in 1938 and in the 1970s "transitioned from a line working in an automobile manufacturing plant" to a union representative (p. 52) and Johnny Ames who was born in 1950 and spent "the late 1970s to the early 1990s" in prison, we learn about the importance of sponsors in literacy learning. From comparing four generations of the May family we come to understand "intergenerational strategies for literacy transmission" (p. 104). The written literacy experiences of 16 African Americans reveal that "African American-sponsored literacy has stayed more consciously connected to the original traditions of American literacy emphasizing collective faith, democracy, and citizenship" (p. 144). And contrasting the lives of Raymond Branch and Dora Lopez, both born in 1969, evidences the ways that economic inequality is manifest through the different values placed on the various literacies they acquired (p. 184).

In her conclusion Brandt details the implications of the changing nature of literacy development during the 20th century in America. Two of those implications are especially relevant to critical media literacy. First:

> literacy is being sponsored in much different ways than it was in the past. Through most of its history, literacy was affiliated with a few strong cultural

> agents—education, religion, local commerce … Now, sponsors of literacy are more prolific, diffused, and heterogeneous. Commercial sponsors abound … Schools are no longer the major disseminators of literacy. (pp. 197–198)

Relatedly, when literacy was affiliated with a few strong cultural agents, we relied on publishers, subject matter experts, teachers and other keepers of literacy to curate the information we received and to maintain boundaries between news information and advertising. And, importantly, since the publication of *Literacy in American Lives* (2001) public schools have been increasingly side-lined as major disseminators of literacy as the push for privately controlled, commercially sponsored charter schools intensifies.

Brandt's second implication focuses more specifically on the role of American public schools and universities:

> The insinuation of market forces into the meaning and methods by which literacy is learned pose crucial ethical and policy questions for public education. Especially dangerous are the ways that education is now being cast as a privatized and individualized commodity … American public schools and universities have not adequately confronted the tensions inherent in the recent transformation in literacy, especially the insatiable appetite of capitalism for more, better, faster, cheaper literates. (p. 204)

This implication illuminates Brandt's work as something of a microeconomic peek into the dramatic effects of the shift toward a neoliberal democracy on written literacy. Neoliberal policies have been a strong governing force in American lives since at least the 1970's, although certainly the framework for neoliberal democracy had been in place decades earlier.[2] While there is some debate as to all of the components of neoliberalism, its basic components are generally agreed upon to include:

- View of citizens as consumers and competitors, not creators and allies
- Focus on self-interest as opposed to community interest
- Value of free-markets, growth, and maximization of profit over regulation and socioeconomic security for the population as a whole (e.g., cuts to spending on social programs)
- Concentration of wealth in the hands of a few elites
- Privatization of historically social goods such as public school and written literacy to be driven by profit motives, not common good motives.

One of America's most prolific critics of neoliberalism is Noam Chomsky. In *Manufacturing Consent*, originally published in 1988 and updated in 2002, Chomsky and Edward S. Herman specifically critique neoliberalism within the context of mass media. Chomsky and Herman state that the mass media is essentially a system designed to amuse, entertain, and inform while also passing along values and codes of behavior that align with institutional structures. Similarly, as noted above, Brandt makes clear that one of the primary roles of written literacy remains the enculturation of citizens. And both show us how the commodification of literacy supports neoliberal policies, although neither focused specifically on digital media literacy.

What ties the work of Chomsky and Herman to Brandt is their emphasis on uncovering the pathways over which news media and written literacy travel and the ways that the commodification of both can lead to inequality. Chomsky, Herman, and Brandt end up offering us powerful analytical frameworks that can be used as heuristics in our classrooms to help students strengthen their civic online reasoning skills. As I mentioned earlier, using heuristics engages us in a process of discovery through "a series of questions, operations, and perspectives used to guide inquiry and knowledge creation" (Lauer, 2004, p. 8). An effective heuristic designed to increase critical media literacy would lead students through a process of discovering how and why a specific piece of communication works given a specific social context. Chomsky and Herman's Propaganda Model combined with Brandt's conceptualization of sponsors and pathways can be used to support valuable heuristics for students.

In designing their Propaganda Model, Chomsky and Herman argue that within the neoliberal framework mass media operates as systematic propaganda because powerful levers of money and power filter what is presented as news and marginalizes dissent (p. 2). Of course, the most powerful tool of mass media remains written literacy. Written literacy, as Deborah Brandt reminds us, is an especially "valuable" and "volatile" property because it is a material resource with economic and political value. "And, like other commodities with private and public value, it is grounds for potential exploitation, injustice, and struggle as well as potential hope, satisfaction, and reward" (2001, pp. 2–3). Chomsky and Herman identify 5 filters through which mass media passes on its way to becoming news distributed to the public at large, the three most important of which are spun from the implications of the commodification of information. Through this model they work to explain how audiences are influenced and how political consent is manufactured. "It traces the routes by which money and power are able to filter out the news fit to print, marginalize dissent, and allow the government and dominant private interests to get their messages across to the public" (Chomsky & Herman, p. 2). For example, in case studies presented in *Manufacturing Consent* and elsewhere, Chomsky and Herman show how corporate controlled U.S. news media treat people, countries, and events in very different ways depending on whether or not doing so is in the best interest of the U.S., especially in relation to our allies, not the facts of the situation.

In the 2002 update to the original version of their book, Chomsky and Herman argue that the model has grown even more useful between the first and second editions. I would argue that this model remains robust even in 2017 as major media outlets have consolidated even further. Chomsky and Herman's update does take a small turn toward digital awareness. While the internet may offer possibilities for strengthening participatory democracy and turning the neoliberal tide, Chomsky's concern about the ability of the internet to be employed as a critical tool seems to prove true: "The privatization of the Internet's hardware, the rapid commercialization and concentration of Internet portals … and the private and concentrated control of the new broadband technology, together threatened to limit any future prospects of the Internet as a democratic media vehicle" (p. xvi).[3] As Chomsky and Herman point out, the interactions and customization of online media made possible by new technologies mainly allow media firms to gather data in order to more effectively market goods and services (p. xvii). For example, Facebook makes billions of dollars by targeting ads to individual consumers based on first and third-party information Facebook has gathered and sells in partnership with other companies, usually without the user's explicit consent. This database marketing not only targets ads but also determines what media, whether fake or real, editorial or advertising, will appear in your feed. It is no wonder that students have a hard time distinguishing between a factual story and an ad given that the drive for profit has resulted in "the boundaries between editorial and advertising departments have[ing] weakened" (Chomsky & Herman, 2002, p. xvii).

The 5 filters Chomsky and Herman use to assess news media in terms of whether or not it serves a propaganda function include:

- The size, concentrated ownership, owner wealth, and profit orientation of the dominant mass-media forms
- Advertising as the primary income source of the mass media
- The reliance of the media on information provided by government, business, and "experts" funded and approved by these primary sources and agents of power
- "flak" as a means of disciplining the media (or negative responses to a media story that are often funded by corporations and government entities, such as a public relations firm being paid by energy companies to counter media reports of global warming)
- fear of some perceived global threat (e.g., anticommunism during the Cold War, terrorism today, etc.) as a national religion and control mechanism (Chomsky & Herman, 2002, p. 2).

Through a variety of case studies, Chomsky and Herman show how these five filters shape information in ways that result in what we often receive as news actually being experienced as propaganda. It is important to remember that there is at least one thing that may weaken mass media's ability to work through the propaganda model—public skepticism of the news and social media. As mentioned earlier, young people do express high levels of skepticism. However, skepticism is just a start, in and of itself it cannot lead to participatory democracy by media literate citizens. The ways in which new media technologies, and social media in particular, may weaken the propaganda model are unclear but intriguing.

As we return to Brandt's research we can see that she gives us more than an important historical account of literacy in the 20th century. From her analytical framework teachers can abstract heuristics that can be used in our classrooms to help students access and analyze media in critical ways. Her analytical framework was built on two concepts: sponsors and trade routes or pathways. Sponsors are agents "who enable support, teach, and model, as well as recruit, regulate, suppress, or withhold literacy—and gain advantage by it in some way" (p. 19). These sponsors control access to literacy and may possess powerful incentives that control the flow of literacy in both positive and negative ways. Sponsors might include parents, employers, teachers, political officials, social media networking sites, religious leaders, publishing companies and others. While Brandt's conceptualization of pathways or trade routes has received less attention than sponsors, it is no less important—especially when considering critical media literacy. We can visualize literacy trade routes as networks that allow media to move from places of production to places of consumption, encountering pathways and stoppages along the way that shape both producers and consumers. Toward the end of her book, Brandt asserts: "Basic literate ability requires the ability to position and reposition oneself among literacy's sponsoring agents as well as among competing forms of communication" (p. 98). In other words, moving beyond mere skepticism to participatory democracy requires helping our students to position themselves as agents empowered to analyze and even control the pathways along which media travels.

CRITICAL MEDIA LITERACY AS A SOCIAL PROCESS

As Thomas asserts in the foundational chapter for this collection, "we are experiencing a renaissance in examining how power and language are inseparable" (Chapter 2, this volume) that has been ignited by public discussions about fake news and post-truth. Writing intensive classrooms in all disciplines and at all levels of the curriculum may be uniquely well suited to addressing this situation through teaching critical media literacy as a social process. In other words, through an emphasis on the process of analyzing, composing and disseminating media-based texts in social contexts, with a focus on the relationship between audience, power, and information especially in the case of largely unregulated social media platforms such as Twitter, we can guide students toward a material understanding of media literacy through an awareness of the propaganda function of mass media and a developing ability to identify sponsors and navigate trade routes.

In his summary of social-process composition pedagogies, Bruce McComiskey (2000) makes clear that "composing is always situated within particular socio-political contexts rather than within autonomous individuals or structured minds" (p. 3). Relatedly, heuristic procedures that guide inquiry and knowledge creation should provide opportunities for discovery and knowledge generation on multiple levels within social contexts. The heuristic provided below guides students to view any written composition as the result of a process of social, economic, and political forces acting upon individuals in a society. And, in the case of critical media literacy, to identify the sponsors and pathways along which media travel with varying levels of success.

In *Teaching Composition as a Social Process* (2000), McComiskey offers a heuristic that works on three levels—textual, rhetorical, and discursive. All three levels draw attention to the ways that audience, power, and information act upon one another. In revising his heuristic as a way to draw upon the analytical power of Chomsky, Herman, and Brandt, I expand his definitions of these levels. Like McComiskey, I believe that all three levels need to be made overt in writing intensive classes, "even guiding students through peer review cycles and formative teacher comments that attend to each of the three levels of composing" (p. 7).

The textual level explores the role that conventions of linguistics and genre play in calling forth an audience. Following McComiskey's reliance on Walter Ong's (1975) "The Writer's Audience is Always a Fiction," the textual level of analysis focuses on the ways that linguistic and genre cues are used by a writer to fictionalize or characterize an audience based on the writer's past experiences of written texts. In other words, there is no monolithic knowable audience standing ready to receive a writer's communication in perfect unity. Instead, the writer uses linguistic and genre cues to imagine a certain type of audience and to support the rhetorical and discursive actions that the writer hopes will lead to some desired outcome.

While McComiskey and Ong consider the fictionalized role of audience they do not consider the possibility of a fictionalized role for the writer. A full consideration of what it might mean to consider that a writer is fictionalized is beyond the scope of this essay. However, developing heuristics for critical media literacy requires us to do so given the current reliance on anonymous sources, recognition of institutions as "individuals," and automated software such as Twitter bots that act like an autonomous individual in social media spaces. The construction of the writer, whether through the writer's own subjective assessment or the audience's fictionalization of the writer, acts on the rhetorical level. Here, too, we take into account the writer's position in relation to sponsors and pathways of media literacy. Finally, the discursive level focuses most explicitly on "the social composition of the writer and the institutional contexts in which composing takes place" (McComiskey, 2000, p. 10).

Textual Level

Format. What are the main ways these types of texts are formatted? How does the format of the text call the audience into a specific role? Has the writer effectively adopted the format of the text?

Style and tone. How does the style and tone of the text call the audience into a specific role? What cultural, social, or institutional values do the style and tone of the text reflect?

Genre. How does the genre of the text call the audience into a specific role?

Rhetorical Level

Writer's role. Who is the writer (an independent citizen, an employee/representative of an organization, an automated response (e.g., Twitter bot))? What credibility does the writer establish? How does the writer fit into the specific writing context? By what means does the writer gain access to this communication pathway? How does the writer define her role in relation to the audience?

Audience's attitudes. Does the writer view the audience as receptive, oppositional, or neutral? Given the writer's view of the audience, why does the writer choose the pathway through which the writer is communicating?

Writer's purpose. What is the writer's purpose for communicating to the audience? Is the pathway the writer has chosen the most effective pathway for communication? What sponsors (both individual people and larger entities like government bodies or corporations) along this pathway might support or obstruct the writer's purpose?

Desired action. What specific action(s) would the writer like the audience to take after reading the text?

Discursive Level

Institutions and forums. What institutions are involved in sanctioning the communication? What forum is used to distribute the communication (newspaper, social media site, etc.) How do these institutions and forums influence the communication at hand? What are the communication pathways these institutions travel in order to influence an audience? Who controls these pathways? How are these pathways supported (advertising, corporate sponsorship, independent development)? What are the sources of information used by the institution or forum?

Subjectivities. What aspects of subjectivity (class, ethnicity, gender, sexuality, age, etc.) does the writer invoke in reference to the audience? Does the writer invoke these aspects of subjectivity in positive, negative, or neutral ways? How are these subjectivities treated in the culture at large and why? How might cultural views of these subjectivities further or hinder the writer's communication? Are these subjectivities used to create fear of some type of global threat to one's nation or local community?

Cultural values. Who are the ideal citizens of the community to which the writer belongs? What are the beliefs, values, and norms the writer upholds? What sources of information does the writer use and how are they connected to the community to which the writer belongs? Who are the sponsors (both individual people and larger entities like government bodies or corporations) controlling the means of communication in this community?

Social values. Who are the ideal citizens of the world outside the writer's community? What values does the writer impose on these citizens? How might these values differ from the real values held by the citizens outside the writer's own community? What sources of information does the writer use and how are they connected to the community the writer wished to influence? Who are the sponsors (both individual people and larger entities like government bodies or corporations) controlling the means of communication in this community?

Students can use this heuristic in a number of ways as they engage in critical writing to analyze the validity of information being presented through social media and the news media. For example, students might be asked to choose among a few competing social media posts on a single issue, using the heuristic to uncover potential biases and the inequality inherent in those biases. Students might also be asked to choose paired examples of similar events to determine if the differences in how these similar events are reported are a result of social and economic biases. Or they might explore how coverage of a particular issue in the name of "neutrality" actually leads to bias if the neutrality washes away real material differences.[4] In short, the use of heuristics such as this one aims to create habits of mind that allow students to critically read the world.

I'll demonstrate in a bit more detail how this heuristic might be used through applying it to a NPR Story Corp episode and then to the recent removal, and at times destruction, of confederate monuments in the United States. On August 18, 2017, Francine Anderson's description of her experience at a "whites only" gas station aired on NPR. This story can be the foundation for a stand-alone assignment (perhaps at the high school level) or as a *critical media literacy raising* assignment in preparation for a more complex writing project at the college level. As Anderson explains, her father was driving her and her siblings home from a visit to her grandmother's:

> and my father did what no black man at the time was supposed to do—allowed his car to run out of gas," Anderson, now 65, says. "He ended up pushing the car, and the only place he could get to was a white truck stop with the 'White Only' signs up."
>
> When they got to the truck stop, Anderson says that despite the signs, her father went up and knocked on the door.
>
> "A guy came up, he said, 'What are you doing, nigger? Get away from here—can't you read?' And my dad, he took his hat and held it in his hand trying to make himself small, 'cause he was kind of a tall man," Anderson says. "He said to the guy, umm, 'I see your sign, sir. I'm sorry, I'm not trying to disturb you or your business. I just got my young kids in the car. Could I just buy a couple of gallons of gas?'"
>
> Anderson says the guy responded, "'I don't deal with your kind,' and he stepped back and he slammed the door."

> Her father then turned and walked back to the car—and Anderson says that, in that moment, she knew he was afraid.
>
> "He got in the car and I can remember asking him questions: 'Why can't we go? Why won't he give us any gas?' And he wasn't answering," she says. "It occurred to me as a little kid, 'we're in real trouble.'"
>
> But then the door to the gas station opened and another man came out. Immediately, her father stiffened up.
>
> Anderson says, "This guy got to the passenger window and said, 'I don't know what's wrong with that guy. I'm going to go get you some gas, OK?'" Anderson says. "I remember my dad was real grateful and saying, 'Let me give you these few dollars,' and the guy would say, 'No, no, it's OK.'"

At this point in the story I would stop the recording and ask students to draft a reaction to the events in this story. This might be an informal, in-class exercise or a more polished piece but should be completed relatively quickly after first hearing Francine Anderson's story. At the very least, these three prompts should be provided to students to guide their writing:

- What happened in the story?
- How do you feel about what happened in this story?
- Can you identify with this situation?

Once students have completed their reaction piece, play the rest of the recording for them:

> "If I talk to whites about that story, they focus on the man and how kind he was," Anderson says. "And he was kind, but at the same time when I talk to blacks about that story they're more focused on the fact that it wasn't illegal for him to deny us gas."

Some students will have responded more like the whites Anderson has shared her story with and some more like the blacks—for the purposes of this assignment it doesn't matter. What does matter is that students take their responses and interrogate them using the discursive level prompts. However a student responded, they should examine the institutions to which they belong, their subjectivities and their cultural and social values in understanding their response. They should also begin to develop a deeper understanding of the systemic forces at work that shape our reactions to such stories. None of this will be easy, but it is very important to ask students to begin to identify the lenses through which they read the world before they move on to a more formal critical media analysis.

As I write, the United States is experiencing a new level of turmoil that is partially being expressed through the removal and, at times, destruction of confederate monuments. Often, the removal of these monuments is occurring with little discussion and under the cover of night to avoid demonstrations and possibly violence. Despite what one thinks of these monuments, it is clear that their covert removal severely curtails opportunities for education, dialogue, and constructive activism. What we are left with in many cases, then, are media accounts. There is no shortage of competing media coverage of these events. In this context, students can be given the opportunity to use the heuristics to analyze different accounts of the same event in order to begin to make decisions about the veracity of each account. In doing so, they should pay close attention to whether or not certain types of media lend themselves to specific kinds of responses—in other words the extent to which the medium shapes the message. Or, students could be asked to choose one of the figures, such as Robert E. Lee, that these monuments represent and compare competing versions of these historical figures over time. This requires students to engage in historiography, or to write about the ways that others have framed a specific historical event or person. Students must go beyond summarizing the work of others to using the heuristics to help reveal the ways that audience, power, and information act upon one another over time.

Let's return to the students at the beginning of my chapter who lacked the most basic civic online reasoning abilities or, in other words, critical media literacy. As I noted, given the turn of our youth toward fully digital platforms, their inability to accurately judge the credibility of information found on the web, and today's proliferation in virtual spaces of fake news, advertising that mimics news, and social media automation such as Twitter bots, it is more important than ever that we develop pedagogical responses that empower students as agents in a participatory democracy. This can be achieved partly by helping students establish critical habits of mind that they carry from one context to the next. And one way to establish these critical habits of mind is through adopting heuristics that allow them to discover and generate knowledge through an awareness of the textual, rhetorical, and discursive levels of analyzing and composing texts.

NOTES

1. In *Manufactured Consent* (2002), Noam Chomsky and Edward Herman argue that American mainstream media operates largely as a form of propaganda due to overriding corporate interests. They suggest that skepticism is one of the main ways to counter this propaganda and that while the internet could have a democratizing effect on mass media it, too, is increasingly controlled by corporate interests.
2. For example, see Mirowski, P., & Plehwe, D. (2015). *The road from Mont Pèlerin: The making of the neoliberal thought collective, with a new preface.* Harvard University Press.
3. In 2012 Michael Corcoran sought to understand whether or not the growing popularity of social media was leading to a democratization of mass media. He concludes that the rise in social media usage does seem to correlate with a weakening of the propaganda function of American mainstream news media but isn't able to argue a direct causal link.
4. Noam Chomsky (2011) argues that climate change as caused by humans is viewed by a significant number of our population as a liberal hoax because in the name of neutrality mainstream media focuses on a simple dichotomy between those who believe in climate change and those who don't, giving them almost equal newsprint, even though only 1% of climate scientists don't believe in human-caused global warming.

REFERENCES

Brandt, D. (2001). *Literacy in American lives*. New York, NY: Cambridge University Press.

Chin, K., & David, G. (Producers). (2011, January 3). *Peak oil and a changing climate* [Video file]. Retrieved June 3, 2017, from https://www.youtube.com/watch?v=UUmwy0VTnqM

Corcoran, M., & Tafe, U. (2012). The propaganda model, class struggle and new media technology: An analysis of the propaganda model in an age of social uprising, and social media. Boston, MA: University of Massachusetts.

Herman, E. S., & Chomsky, N. (2010). *Manufacturing consent: The political economy of the mass media*. London: Random House.

Hillman, K. (Producer). (2017, August 18). *After 60 years, girl's experience at Whites-only gas station still hurts* (Morning Edition/Story Corps). Washington, DC: NPR. Retrieved from http://www.npr.org/2017/08/18/544264905/after-60-years-girls-experience-at-whites-only-gas-station-still-hurts

Lauer, J. M. (2004). *Invention in rhetoric and composition*. West Lafayette, IN: Parlor Press LLC.

McComiskey, B. (2000). *Teaching composition as a social process*. Logan, UT: Utah State University Press.

Mirowski, P., & Plehwe, D. (2015). *The road from Mont Pèlerin: The making of the neoliberal thought collective, with a new preface*. Cambridge, MA: Harvard University Press.

Mitchell, A., Gottfried, J., Barthel, M., & Shearer, E. (2016). *The modern news consumer: News attitudes and practices in the digital era*. Washington, DC: Pew Research Center's Journalism Project. Retrieved from http://www.journalism.org/2016/07/07/the-modern-news-consumer/

Ong, W. J. (1975). The writer's audience is always a fiction. *Publications of the Modern Language Association of America, 90*(1), 9–21.

Stevens, Jr., E. (1987). The anatomy of mass literacy in nineteenth-century United States. In R. F. Arnove & H. J. Graff (Eds.), *National literacy campaigns* (pp. 99–122). Boston, MA: Springer.

Wineburg, S., McGrew, S., Breakstone, J., & Ortega, T. (2016). *Evaluating information: The cornerstone of civic online reasoning*. Retrieved from https://sheg.stanford.edu/upload/V3LessonPlans/Executive%20Summary%2011.21.16.pdf

Joanne Addison
Department of English
University of Colorado – Denver
Boulder, Colorado

JASON L. ENDACOTT, MATTHEW L. DINGLER, SETH D. FRENCH AND JOHN P. BROOME

8. BEFORE YOU CLICK "SHARE"

Mindful Media Literacy as a Positive Civic Act

INTRODUCTION

In democratic societies, the onus of ruling is upon the citizens. Through deliberation and direct action, citizens create the discourses that morph into policy (Engle & Ochoa, 1998). One essential ingredient for effective dialogue is information, though valid and reliable information has not always been readily accessible, and the concealment of information has long been a threat to democratic action. The rapid evolution of technology has made information vastly more accessible, though the ease of sharing information through various social media channels has led to a new threat. The proliferation of purposefully false and provocative "fake news," has already played a role in disrupting the democratic process. The 2016 presidential election brought the issue of fake news to the forefront of public debate, but the continued propagation of fake news despite our awareness of it raises questions about the possibility of our living in a post-truth world. The purpose of this chapter is to provide educators with a guide for engaging students in a critical inquiry into the validity of source material, the credibility of information presented in source material, and sharing on social media as a positive civic action.

SHARING IN OUR SOCIAL WORLD

The tendency for humans to seek out information within their social networks is widely recognized (Boyd & Ellison, 2007) and seeking information from trusted others is not a phenomenon unique to the digital age. Social networks also accounted for the bulk of print media's "spreadability," though it was through a far less technologically advanced word-of-mouth circuit (Jenkins, Ford, & Green, 2013). This posed less of a threat because print journalists' credibility relied on source vetting and corroboration, resulting in the tendency for the most accessible information to also be the most accurate (Minkel, 2002).

However, the digital age has introduced social media platforms such as Facebook and Twitter that have made it possible to extend social networks into the cyber realm (Boyd, 2014). Credibility online is not always beholden to the journalistic standards we have grown accustomed to, leading to blurry distinction between credible news

 | DOI 10.1163/9789004365360_008

media, political blogs and citizen-generated content (Loader & Mercea, 2011). Unfortunately, as the sea of questionable news content has grown, our proclivity for trusting and sharing with those most like us has too. Social media sharing has become more politically polarized often within politically like-minded in-group/out-group affiliations on Twitter (Yardi & Boyd, 2010). Within this context, the quality of the news is trumped by the familiarity of its sharer, making the spread and acceptance of fake news all the more likely and disruptive.

What motivates people to share various content throughout their social networks? Gantz and Trenholm (1979) posited four motivations that constitute the tenets of Users and Gratifications Theory applied to sharing studies (Lee & Ma, 2012; Park, Kee, & Valenzeula, 2009; Ruggiero, 2000):

- Information—Users possess a desire to access and disseminate information they deem valuable.
- Socializing—Users view sharing as a means of social interaction.
  Entertainment—Users interact with content that provides personal enjoyment.
- Self-expression and status-seeking—Users incorporate various media into their identity and share it to increase their reputation.

We communicate for both social interaction and self-expression. Social media has vastly expanded our ability to share, and find the gratification that comes from it. However, our personal gratification should not be detrimental to society or even democracy. Our students must be mindful of what it means to share information as a positive civic action.

MINDFUL MEDIA LITERACY

Recent research has revealed how difficult it is for students to discern fake news from what is factual, with many students lacking knowledge of the basic conventions for verifying information online (Donald, 2016). Unfortunately, there are indications that these concerns are either stagnating or becoming worse over time (Considine et al., 2009). These limitations are not unique to our students, as adults fall prey to bias as well. Bias is powerful because it often corrupts truth, leading us to believe that information providers are untrustworthy, and leading us to wish-fulfilling beliefs that impact how we seek out evidence of the truth (Goldman, 1999). Those who perceive new information as a threat to their worldview often react by discrediting opposing arguments to protect their previously held beliefs (Nyhan & Reifler, 2010). Research has found that people with strongly held beliefs prefer to bolster their arguments by relying on previously learned information that aligns with their worldview rather than accept contradictory facts presented to them (Prasad et al., 2009). Even when presented with a balanced set of facts, those with strongly held beliefs will engage in "motivated skepticism"—preferring those that align with their beliefs and resisting those that do not (Taber & Lodge, 2006). Once false information is committed to memory it becomes stubbornly difficult, and sometimes even impossible, to remove

(Eucker, Lewandowsky, Swire, & Chang, 2011). In fact, efforts to correct false knowledge can backfire because they make the false information more familiar to the knower (Skurnik, Yoon, Park, & Schwartz, 2005; Weaver, Garcia, Schwarz, & Miller, 2007).

Promoting critical media literacy can be an important step towards ameliorating these problems. The National Association for Media Literacy Education (NAMLE) defines media literacy as, "the ability to access, analyze, evaluate, create, and act using all forms of communication" (2007, n.p.). Critical media literacy expands this concept to explicitly include popular culture, mass communication, and critical analysis of socially constructed meanings, political and economic contexts, as well as the relationships between media, audiences, information, and power (Kellner & Share, 2007; Morrell, 2002). Our students, as consumers of media, are an integral part of the context and power structure, and therefore should be mindful of that role. Media mindfulness (Serafin, 2009) emphasizes process over product when consuming mediated messages. When students practice media mindfulness they are constantly aware of what is seen, heard, or read while they negotiate meaning from source information. Students should be engaged with content, aware of context, and attentive to the various perspectives found within.

The introduction to this book highlights the unfortunate way in which the concept of "fake news" has almost lost its meaning as valid news and information becomes conflated with the purposefully fabricated. During the 2016 presidential election, fake news was created by fake news outlets to be shared by programmed bots and impressionable social media users. It rarely penetrated the traditional or mainstream news outlets, though its dominance of Twitter and Facebook more than made up for that. In our post-2016 Election world, we find specious claims regularly reported on by the mainstream media because they originate from authoritative sources. This problem is compounded by the discretionary use of the term "fake news" as a weapon to discredit legitimate news stories that are inconvenient for perpetuating certain narratives. Given our new reality, it is imperative that our approach to mindful media literacy includes a careful examination of the role that belief, truth and knowledge play in the consumption of mediated messages.

BELIEF + TRUTH = KNOWLEDGE

Knowledge depends upon the presence and acceptance of both truth and belief (Feldman, 2003). Truth is imperative because it is impossible to know something that is false. Likewise, acceptance of knowledge hinges on the knower's willingness to believe it. The presence of one of these conditions without the other does not constitute knowledge. It is possible to believe something that is false, and it is possible to withhold belief from something that is true. The conflation of knowledge with belief can have a powerfully detrimental effect on the truth. Belief is an easy concept to understand and employ but truth is far more complicated. Therefore, if our students are to unpack the concept of truth when consuming media, it is important for them to understand some basic ways in which truth is determined. With that in mind, we provide brief descriptions of the verification, utility, relative, and truthmaker approaches to determining truth that are utilized in the instructional component below.

Perhaps the most straightforward and well-known approach is the *verification* approach to truth, which relies upon the existence of evidence or justification to support a proposition as true (Feldman, 2003; Goldman, 1999). Of course, evidence can be misused, misconstrued, or even fabricated, which means that truth also depends upon the veracity of facts used to support it (Horwich, 2010). When using the *utility* approach to determining truth, we consider a proposition to be true if it leads to a desirable or workable outcome (Goldman, 1999). The utility approach is similar to the pragmatist approach in which something is considered true if it is useful or helpful for the believer to believe it (Horowich, 2010; James, 1975). The *relative* approach equates truth with what large and/or powerful groups of people believe to be true, regardless of evidence to the contrary (Horowich, 2010). The last approach presented here relies upon *truthmakers*, which are entities whose existence makes something true (Beebee & Dodd, 2005). We have adapted this concept to emphasize the important role that authoritative people play as truthmakers in the media. Under the truthmaker approach, we believe that something is true because a powerful or authoritative person or institution we trust told us it was true even if there is little or no evidence to support it.

Of the four approaches described here, the utility, relative, and truthmaker approaches are far less reliable because they are more subjective and susceptible to manipulation. They are also likely to be determined by our relationship with *how* things are rather than *whether* things are (Powell, 1999). The truthmaker approach is particularly problematic because authoritative figures or institutions often have facts or information that we do not possess, and this imbalance of power can be used to manipulate us into developing *apparent knowledge* in place of real knowledge of the truth (Feldman, 2003). Apparent knowledge is the assumption of truth based on authoritative claims and the unwillingness to accept, or lack of, contradictory evidence. Apparent knowledge is perhaps best understood by examining how it is used to promote self-interest. George Ross, the Executive Vice President of the Trump Organization and author of *Trump-Style Negotiation: Powerful Strategies and Tactics for Mastering Every Deal* (2006), describes how this works:

> If the other side *believes* that you are very knowledgeable about a subject, by reputation or even by your use of buzzwords, then they might come to the conclusion that you really know what you are talking about … This *apparent knowledge*—whether based on reality or only on perception—wins you some points because the other side's assumptions take over … Apparent knowledge can sometimes be more powerful than actual knowledge, but be aware that if the other side probes your apparent knowledge too deeply you may lose your credibility. (p. 197, emphasis in original)

It may seem unnecessary or overly complicated to delve into the Belief + Truth = Knowledge equation when examining media messages. However, the ways in which "fake news" has been defined, redefined, deployed and redeployed throughout the social media sphere have made such an analysis necessary. A critical analysis that focuses only on the source of the news or information is simply not enough anymore. We want our students to probe deeply into claims to dissect the truth and apparent knowledge so that those in power cannot manipulate them. With that in mind, we present the following framework for an inquiry-based instructional unit in which students critically examine information using media literacy strategies, explore the concept of "truth" while confronting their own biases and proclivities for trusting information, and reflect on sharing information on social media as a purposeful civic and democratic action.

CRITICAL INQUIRY FRAMEWORK

The inquiry presented here is guided by the four dimensions of the College, Career, and Civic Life (C3) Framework (NCSS, 2013), which include: (1) developing compelling questions and planning inquiries; (2) applying disciplinary concepts and tools; (3) evaluating sources and using evidence; and, (4) communicating questions and taking informed action.

D1: Developing Questions & Planning Inquiries

D1.1.6-8. Explain how a question represents key ideas in the field.

D2: Applying Disciplinary Concepts & Tools

D2.Civ.10.6-8. Explain the relevance of personal interests and perspectives, civic virtues, and democratic principles when people address issues and problems in government and civil society.

D3: Evaluating Sources & Using Evidence

D3.2.6-8. Evaluate the credibility of a source by determining its relevance and intended use.

D4: Communicating Conclusions & Taking Informed Action

D4.3.6-8. Present adaptations of arguments and explanations on topics of interest to others to reach audiences and venues outside the classroom using print and oral technologies (e.g., posters, essays, letters, debates, speeches, reports, and maps) and digital technologies (e.g., Internet, social media, and digital documentary).

D4.8.6-8. Apply a range of deliberative and democratic procedures to make decisions and take action in their classrooms and schools, and in out-of-school civic contexts.

Since critical media literacy is also an important component of this inquiry, we have incorporated key questions (Appendix A) for analyzing media sources from the National Association for Media Literacy Education (NAMLE, 2014). Using these questions as an entry point into critical analysis, students can examine information sharing as a civic action while reflecting on personal interests and democratic principles.

The outline below introduces each of the dimensions of the inquiry arc with some instructional considerations. This is followed by some suggested steps for classroom implementation. The outline is not divided into separate lessons due to the wide variation in class length (i.e., block vs. period scheduling). Instead, we provide an approximate and suggested time allocation for each phase of the inquiry.

DIMENSION 1: DEVELOPING QUESTIONS AND PLANNING INQUIRIES

Instructional Considerations

Inquiries guided by the C3 frameworks rely upon an overarching compelling question that students work to answer. Compelling questions focus on enduring issues, inspire curiosity, require application of disciplinary concepts, and promote student argumentation (NCSS, 2013). The compelling question is the driving force of the inquiry and should be central to performance tasks used for assessment later in the inquiry process.

When Is Sharing News or Information on Social Media a Positive Civic Action?

In the Classroom (Approximately 30 Minutes)

1. Pose the compelling question to the students as a writing prompt by displaying it on the board or screen.
2. Have students write down a 2–4 sentence response to the prompt in their journals or notebooks for later reflection.
3. With the class, discuss the idea of "positive civic action."
   A. What does this mean?
   B. Is it the same for everybody?
   C. What common ideas do we have about positive civic action?
   D. Where do we differ in our ideas or beliefs?
4. Inform the class that this question will be the focus of an inquiry that they will undertake. If time permits, invite students to share stories of a time in which they were not sure about sharing a piece of news or information on social media.

DIMENSION 2: APPLYING DISCIPLINARY CONCEPTS AND TOOLS

Instructional Considerations

Inquiries require structure in order to be effective, though they must also allow for multiple interpretations and conclusions. One way to provide balance between structure and flexibility is to create supporting questions that mutually reinforce the compelling question posed above. Supporting questions are more specific, and can be tied to disciplinary concepts or tools to promote students' construction of explanations and claims based on evidence (NCSS, 2013). Teachers might consider using the following supporting questions or creating similar questions of their own.

1. How do personal interests, perspectives, and biases impact the *creation and distribution* of news to the public?
2. How is the distribution of news affected by the power and influence held by those distributing it?
3. What role do personal interests, perspectives and biases play in the *messages* sent by a source of news or information?
4. How do personal interests, perspectives and biases impact the *meaning* that people make when they consume a source of news or information?
5. How do we know if a source of news or information is *credible* enough to be considered knowledge?

In the Classroom (Approximately 20–30 Minutes)

1. Discuss the importance of structure and flexibility during inquiry. It can be helpful to compare the students' inquiry with that of a police detective. Detectives have a process they follow when they try to solve a crime but they also have to be able to chase down an important lead when they think it might help their case.
2. Introduce the concept of supporting questions as the structure for the students' inquiry. Divide the students into groups of 4–5 and present each group with the list of supporting questions. Be sure to clarify the key concepts in italics before proceeding.
3. Ask each student to individually reflect on whether or not they have ever considered these questions when consuming a source of news or information. After an appropriate amount of time, allow each group to discuss the thoughts that occurred to them while they were reflecting on the questions.
4. If time permits, have each student write a brief reflection in their notebook or journal. This could also make an excellent "ticket out" and formative daily assessment.

DIMENSION 3: EVALUATING SOURCES AND USING EVIDENCE

Instructional Considerations

Establishing the credibility of sources is always important when engaging in inquiry. However, given the aforementioned grey area created when clearly false claims are published in legitimate news or information outlets, this inquiry also unpacks the concepts of truth, belief, and knowledge. These concepts are even more important when consuming news or information directly from a source on social media, where journalistic standards of evidence do not apply. The following activities are guided by the NAMLE key questions and the indicators from Dimension 3 of the C3 frameworks (Figure 1). The activities could be completed with any number of topics, and we provide articles covering the alleged connection between the 2016 Trump Presidential Campaign and Russian officials (Appendix A).

In the Classroom (Approximately 90 Minutes)

Activity 1: Determining source credibility. *The first of two activities, this exercise is designed to have students apply foundational media literacy skills to determine the credibility of source material.*

1. Divide students into pairs or groups of four (depending on class size) and give each group a different article so they can examine the topic from multiple perspectives.
2. Before reading the assigned articles, have the students review the NAMLE key questions for Authors & Audiences and Messages & Meanings. These questions will frame their reading, and they should underline, highlight or annotate their articles when they come across details that may help them answer the questions.
   A. For the sake of time, it is possible to have half of the students in each group answer the Authors & Audiences questions while the other half answers the Messages & Meanings questions.
3. Have students share their answers to the questions from their respective sections and discuss their thoughts of the validity of the source/information.
4. As a group, the students should identify any questions they were unable to answer and discuss possible avenues for collecting enough information to answer them.
5. After all of the groups have concluded their discussion of these sections of the NAMLE questions, bring the class together and have the students draft answers to the supporting questions 1–3. Draft responses could serve as a formative assessment and opportunity for students to reflect on their personal perspectives.
6. With the class, discuss the similarities and differences found between each of the articles on the same topic in light of the NAMLE key questions covered.

Activity 2: Seeking knowledge. *In this activity, students will go beyond the foundational task of determining source credibility to critically examine the ways in which "truth" is manipulated by those in power to spread misinformation in support of an agenda or to maintain status quo conditions.*

1. Pose the following questions to the class: "Is the Earth round or flat? How do you know?"
   A. These might seem like silly questions today but they were not always silly. Knowledge can be a tricky thing and it raises the question, "How do we know something?"
2. Discuss the complexity of "truth" as a concept that philosophers continue to debate, and introduce the knowledge equation: *Truth + Belief = Knowledge*

3. In order for something to be considered "knowledge" it must have both truth and belief. Just having one or the other won't cut it. Present the following, or similar, examples:
   A. Example 1: Belief without truth does not equal knowledge:
      i. Bob believes that the Earth is flat, but in truth there is extremely credible evidence (e.g., satellite images) that shows the Earth is not flat. Therefore, Bob does not "know" the shape of the Earth.
   B. Example 2: Truth without belief does not equal knowledge:
      i. There is overwhelming credible evidence that the Earth's climate is getting warmer; however, Sally does not believe that the Earth's climate is changing. Therefore, Sally does not "know" the status of Earth's climate.
4. If time permits, encourage the students to come up with other examples. Emphasize the importance of critically analyzing information sources for *knowledge* rather than just truth or belief.
5. Discuss the impact that belief without truth can have in real life. Consider using the example of the 2016 Presidential election when fake news sources presented a lot of information that was not *true*, but when people *believed* these stories, they thought they had *knowledge*.
6. Introduce the approaches to determining truth that the students will be using with their media sources:
   A. Verification Approach
      i. Claim is true because there are credible and reliable facts that support it. This is the most reliable approach.
   B. Utility Approach
      i. Claim is true because it works, it is in our best interest for it to be true, and/or it is useful for the knower to believe it.
   C. Relative Approach
      i. Claim is true because a lot of people believe that it is true even if there is evidence that it is not true.
   D. Truthmaker Approach
      i. Claim is true because an authoritative or powerful source said that it is true even if there is evidence that it is not true.
7. Have the students return to their groups to answer the NAMLE key questions in the Representations & Reality section. Here is where it is again necessary to go beyond foundational media literacy skills and incorporate critical analysis.
   A. Inform the students that now they will need to look deeper than just evaluating the source in front of them to critically analyze the credibility of the assertions, claims, and arguments made by sources within the story.
8. Have the groups divide a piece of paper into 2 columns. In one column, they will evaluate the article using the Representations & Reality questions. In the other column, they will evaluate the assertions, claims and arguments made by the people within the story itself.

9. When answering the NAMLE questions "How credible is this source?" and "Can I trust this source to tell me the truth?" have the students refer to the four approaches listed above.
10. Have each group discuss the results of their analysis by asking:
    A. How is truth represented by this source?
    B. Should we consider this credible?
    C. How do our perspectives, values, and beliefs affect our judgment of its credibility?
    D. How could we investigate on our own to verify the truth of these claims?
    E. Which of these approaches (verification, utility, relative, truthmaker) is most susceptible to manipulation by powerful or influential figures?
    F. When should we be skeptical of a claim even if it is presented in a credible media source?
11. Conclude the activity with a class discussion or journal entry that addresses the fourth supporting question: "How do we know if a source of news or information is *credible* enough to be considered knowledge?"

DIMENSION4:COMMUNICATIONCONCLUSIONS&TAKINGINFORMEDACTION

Instructional Considerations

Dimension 4 includes both communicating conclusions as well as taking informed action. Since the focus of this inquiry is on the civic act of sharing information, both of these aspects of Dimension 4 are very important. Once the students have answered all four of the supporting questions, they should be positioned to answer the compelling question. This often takes the form of a performance task that emphasizes the compelling question and serves as a summative assessment.

In the Classroom (Approximately 45 Minutes)

Critical media literacy emphasizes the important role that mass forms of communication can have on our knowledge and beliefs. A Boolean Google search for "media influencer" returns just over a million results (1,090,000). The classroom does not replicate the exponential reach of a social media feed, but it is a good place to introduce the concept of responsible sharing in larger spheres. This begins by communicating conclusions using a whole class S-P-A-C-E discussion.

1. Arrange students in a large circle where everyone can see each other and discuss as a whole class.
2. Pose the compelling question to the group: "*How do I know when sharing news or information on social media is a positive civic action?*"
3. Teacher role: facilitate discussion and record students' progress toward S-P-A-C-E completion

S = Support your ideas with evidence
P = Paraphrase/build on others' ideas
A = Ask questions
C = Comment with depth and respect
E = Encourage participation in others

4. As students discuss, have a roster with all students' names handy so you can mark students' progress toward S-P-A-C-E during the discussion.
   A. E.g., When a student asks another student a question, mark "A" next to their name, and when he supports his ideas with evidence, he will earn an "S" as well, and so on.
   B. It could be helpful to have students write "S-P-A-C-E" on a piece of paper and cross out each letter as they complete it.
5. Encourage the students to use examples from the articles they read and to be mindful of how their perspectives will differ from others.

Taking Informed Action: Sharing as a Positive Civic Action

1. Present the students with the following "rating scale" for sharing information and ask them to rate each of the sources they read:

0	*1*	*2*	*3*	*4*	*5*	*6*	*7*	*8*	*9*
Definitely Not OK to Share				Not Sure—More Investigation Needed					Definitely OK to Share

2. Since sharing on social media often happens in the spur-of-the-moment, challenge the students to rate Facebook posts or tweets such as those provided in Appendix A.
3. Have students discuss their ratings as a group. Remind them to refer back to the process they followed for analyzing sources to provide support for their ratings.
4. Wrap up the discussion by having students critically reflect by posing the following questions to themselves: "What might somebody else have to gain if I share this? Who might be hurt if this information is commonly believed to be true?"

INQUIRY CONCLUSION/DEBRIEFING

The purpose of this critical inquiry was to help students develop the analysis skills needed to promote information sharing as a positive civic action. One possible way to determine whether this purpose was achieved is to have the students complete one final journal entry on the topic. The students should reflect on how this inquiry changed the way they think about sharing news or information on social media, how they will approach the news differently in the future, and how they will decipher "truth" in the information they consume.

The development of media mindfulness is an iterative process that relies upon continued engagement with various forms of media that challenge students' media literacy skills. The inquiry framework presented here could be modified to work with many different media sources. Beyond the development of those skills, it is also important for students to return to the notion of sharing information as a positive civic action. Information sharing is a political act, and it is not always benign. Students should be encouraged to confront their biases, understand the perspectives of others, and judge for themselves whether clicking "share" is serving not just their own self-interest, but also the common good.

REFERENCES

Beebee, H., & Dodd, J. (Eds.). (2005). *Truthmakers: The contemporary debate* (pp. 1–16). New York, NY: Oxford University Press.

Boyd, D. (2014). *It's complicated: The social lives of networked teens*. New Haven, CT: Yale University Press.

Boyd, D., & Ellison, N. (2010). Social network sites: Definition, history, and scholarship. *IEEE Engineering Management Review, 38*(3), 16–31.

Considine, D., Horton, J., & Moorman, G. (2009). Teaching and reading the millennial generation through media literacy. *Journal of Adolescent & Adult Literacy, 52*(6), 471–481.

Considine, D. M., & Haley, G. (1999). *Visual messages: Integrating imagery into instruction*. Englewood, CO: Libraries Unlimited.

Donald, B. (2016, November 22). *Stanford researchers find students have trouble judging the credibility of information online*. Retrieved from https://ed.stanford.edu/news/stanford-researchers-find-students-have-trouble-judging-credibility-information-online

Ecker, U. K., Lewandowsky, S., Swire, B., & Chang, D. (2011). Correcting false information in memory: Manipulating the strength of misinformation encoding and its retraction. *Psychonomic Bulletin & Review, 18*(3), 570–578.

Feldman, R. (2003). *Epistemology*. Upper Saddle River, NJ: Prentice Hall.

Gantz, W., & Trenholm, S. (1979). Why people pass on news: Motivations for diffusion. *Journalism Quarterly, 56*(2), 365–370.

Horowich, P. (2010). *Truth-meaning-reality*. New York, NY: Oxford University Press.

James, W. (1975). *Pragmatism*. Cambridge, MA: Harvard University Press.

Jenkins, H., Ford, S., & Green, J. (2013). *Spreadable media: Creating value and meaning in a networked culture*. New York, NY: New York University press.

Kellner, D., & Share, J. (2007). Critical media literacy is not an option. *Learning Inquiry, 1*(1), 59–69.

Lee, C. S., & Ma, L. (2012). News sharing in social media: The effect of gratifications and prior experience. *Computers in Human Behavior, 28*(2), 331–339.

Loader, B. D., & Mercea, D. (2011). Networking democracy? Social media innovations and participatory politics. *Information, Communication & Society, 14*(6), 757–769.

Minkel, W. (2002). Web of deceit. *School Library Journal, 48*(4), 50–53.

Morrell, E. (2002). Toward a critical pedagogy of popular culture: Literacy development among urban youth. *Journal of Adolescent & Adult Literacy, 46*(1), 72–77.

National Association for Media Literacy Education. (2007, November). *Core principles of media literacy education in the United States*. Retrieved May 3, 2017, from https://namle.net/publications/core-principles

National Council for the Social Studies. (2013). *The college, career, and civic life (C3) framework for social studies state standards: Guidance for enhancing the rigor of K-12 civics, economics, geography, and history*. Silver Spring, MD: National Council for the Social Studies.

Nyhan, B., & Reifler, J. (2010). When corrections fail: The persistence of political misperceptions. *Political Behavior, 32*(2), 303–330.

Park, N., Kee, K. F., & Valenzuela, S. (2009). Being immersed in social networking environment: Facebook groups, uses and gratifications, and social outcomes. *CyberPsychology & Behavior, 12*(6), 729–733.

Prasad, M., Perrin, A. J., Bezila, K., Hoffman, S. G., Kindleberger, K., Manturuk, K., & Powers, A. S. (2009). "There must be a reason": Osama, Saddam, and inferred justification. *Sociological Inquiry, 79*(2), 142–162.

Ross, G. H. (2006). *Trump-style negotiation: Powerful strategies and tactics for mastering every deal.* Hoboken, NJ: John Wiley & Sons.

Ruggiero, T. E. (2000). Uses and gratifications theory in the 21st century. *Mass Communication & Society, 3*(1), 3–37.

Serafin, G. M. (2009). Media mindfulness. In D. Macedo & S. R. Steinberg (Eds.), *Media literacy* (pp. 178–186). New York, NY: Peter Lang Publishing.

Skurnik, I., Yoon, C., Park, D., & Schwarz, N. (2005). How warnings about false claims become recommendations. *Journal of Consumer Research, 31*(4), 713–724.

Taber, C. S., & Lodge, M. (2006). Motivated skepticism in the evaluation of political beliefs. *American Journal of Political Science, 50*(3), 755–769.

Weaver, K., Garcia, S. M., Schwarz, N., & Miller, D. T. (2007). Inferring the popularity of an opinion from its familiarity: A repetitive voice sounds like a Chorus. *Journal of Personality and Social Psychology, 92*(5), 821–833.

Yardi, S., & Boyd, D. (2010). Dynamic debates: An analysis of group polarization over time on twitter. *Bulletin of Science, Technology & Society, 30*(5), 316–327.

Jason L. Endacott
Curriculum & Instruction
University of Arkansas
Fayetteville, Arkansas

Matthew L. Dingler
Social Studies Curriculum & Instruction
University of Arkansas
Fayetteville, Arkansas

Seth D. French
English Curriculum & Instruction
University of Arkansas
Fayetteville, Arkansas

John P. Broome
College of Education
University of Mary Washington
Fredericksburg, Virginia

APPENDIX: INSTRUCTIONAL RESOURCES

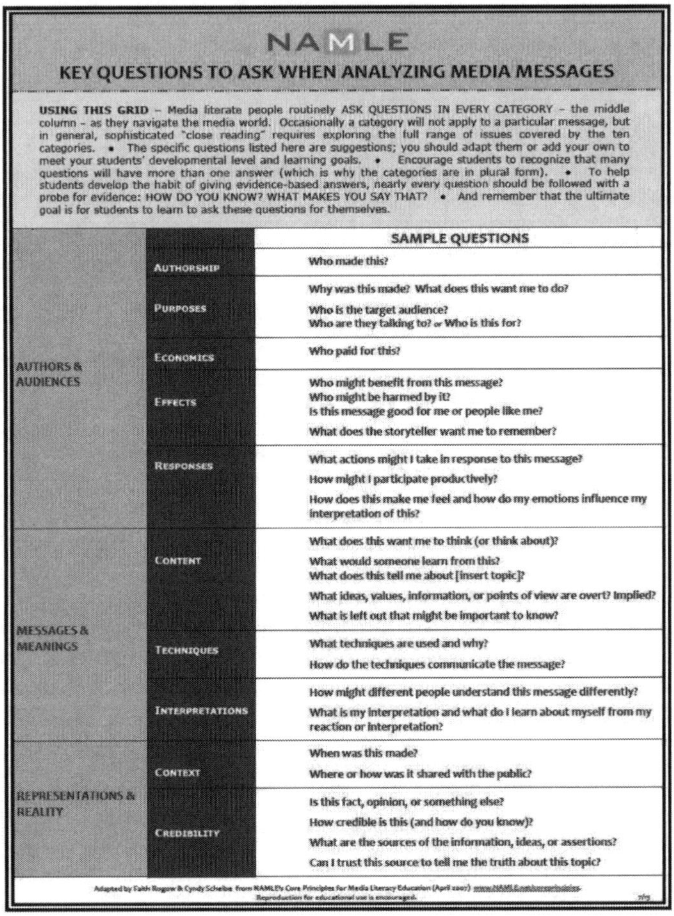

NAMLE

KEY QUESTIONS TO ASK WHEN ANALYZING MEDIA MESSAGES

USING THIS GRID – Media literate people routinely ASK QUESTIONS IN EVERY CATEGORY – the middle column – as they navigate the media world. Occasionally a category will not apply to a particular message, but in general, sophisticated "close reading" requires exploring the full range of issues covered by the ten categories. • The specific questions listed here are suggestions; you should adapt them or add your own to meet your students' developmental level and learning goals. • Encourage students to recognize that many questions will have more than one answer (which is why the categories are in plural form). • To help students develop the habit of giving evidence-based answers, nearly every question should be followed with a probe for evidence: HOW DO YOU KNOW? WHAT MAKES YOU SAY THAT? • And remember that the ultimate goal is for students to learn to ask these questions for themselves.

		SAMPLE QUESTIONS
AUTHORS & AUDIENCES	AUTHORSHIP	Who made this?
	PURPOSES	Why was this made? What does this want me to do? Who is the target audience? Who are they talking to? *or* Who is this for?
	ECONOMICS	Who paid for this?
	EFFECTS	Who might benefit from this message? Who might be harmed by it? Is this message good for me or people like me? What does the storyteller want me to remember?
	RESPONSES	What actions might I take in response to this message? How might I participate productively? How does this make me feel and how do my emotions influence my interpretation of this?
MESSAGES & MEANINGS	CONTENT	What does this want me to think (or think about)? What would someone learn from this? What does this tell me about [insert topic]? What ideas, values, information, or points of view are overt? Implied? What is left out that might be important to know?
	TECHNIQUES	What techniques are used and why? How do the techniques communicate the message?
	INTERPRETATIONS	How might different people understand this message differently? What is my interpretation and what do I learn about myself from my reaction or interpretation?
REPRESENTATIONS & REALITY	CONTEXT	When was this made? Where or how was it shared with the public?
	CREDIBILITY	Is this fact, opinion, or something else? How credible is this (and how do you know)? What are the sources of the information, ideas, or assertions? Can I trust this source to tell me the truth about this topic?

Adapted by Faith Rogow & Cyndy Scheibe from NAMLE's Core Principles for Media Literacy Education (April 2007) www.NAMLE.net/coreprinciples.
Reproduction for educational use is encouraged.

Figure 1. NAMLE key questions to ask when analyzing media messages

Sample News Articles

ABC News Article: Information Trump shared with Russians came from Israel, official says. http://abcnews.go.com/Politics/information-trump-shared-russians-israel-official/story?id=47446314

NBC News Article: *Trump gave russians secrets news orgs are being asked to withhold.* http://www.nbcnews.com/storyline/isis-uncovered/trump-gave-russians-secrets-news-orgs-are-being-asked-withhold-n760811

New York Times Article: *Israel said to be source of secret intelligence trump gave to russians.* https://www.nytimes.com/2017/05/16/world/middleeast/israel-trump-classified-intelligence-russia.html?_r=1

Reuters Article: *Putin offers transcript to prove Trump did not pass Russia secrets.* http://www.reuters.com/article/us-usa-trump-putin-idUSKCN18D1EA

Sample Social Media Sources

Figure 2. Trump tweet from Riyadh

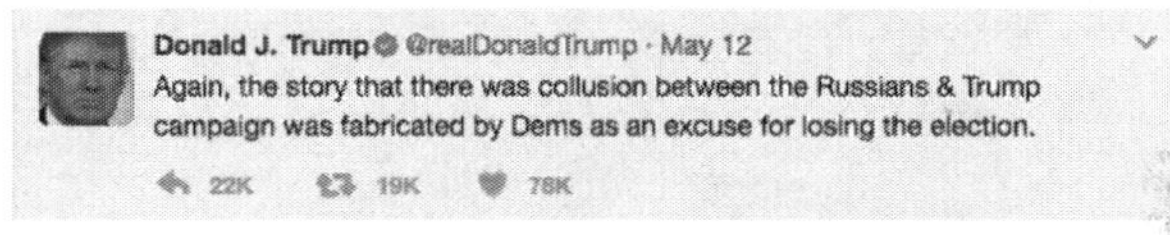

Figure 3. Trump collusion tweet

Figure 4. Trump industrial production tweet

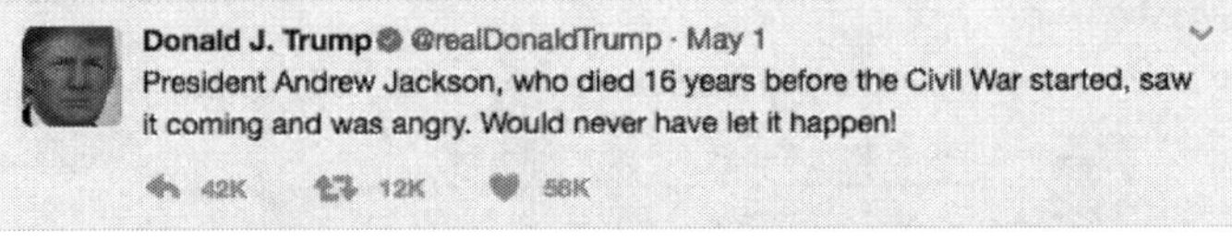

Figure 5. Trump Andrew Jackson tweet

ERIN O'NEILL ARMENDAREZ

9. ENGAGING THE STORIED MIND

Teaching Critical Media Literacy through Narrative

It was the best of times, it was the worst of times,
it was the age of wisdom, it was the age of foolishness.
– Charles Dickens, *A Tale of Two Cities*, 1859

INTRODUCTION

Given the unfortunate chaos surrounding fake news and "alternate facts" (Kellyanne Conway in Todd, 2017) educators must decide: how should critical media literacy be taught? What's the best way to turn the worst of times into a teachable moment? It seems obvious at this point that students can't truly be educated without learning to distinguish actual facts and logical conclusions from false claims and propaganda. Simply ignoring the current information crisis will only make the problem worse. But how do educators broach the subject of contemporary media without appearing to take sides? Clearly, students must learn to find verifiable facts on their own. Likewise, they must be encouraged to question authority and to reason logically for themselves.

Among the many approaches to teaching critical media literacy, narrative analysis seems one of the most neutral and engaging strategies. Students enter classrooms already familiar with hundreds, maybe even thousands of stories. They are already aware that stories are used to push ideology, moral values. They've heard their fair share of cautionary tales and so should be eager to question, to analyze, and to learn to use narrative as a powerful form of rhetoric for their own purposes. Middle, high school, and college-level students, once taught, should actually enjoy learning to recognize elements of narrative in songs, TV shows, movies, YouTube videos, in political speeches, newscasts, and feature articles in newspapers and magazines. While students may initially find analysis a challenge, with some prompting, they will quickly learn. Instructors can develop level-appropriate units or can teach entire courses themed on narrative analysis. Before delving into the basic principles for teaching narrative analysis, an overview of youth media consumption and of how narrative functions in human cognition to reinforce ideology and propaganda should prove helpful.

 | DOI 10.1163/9789004365360_009

AMERICAN YOUTH AND MEDIA

In order to engage kids in critical media literacy conversations and activities, it's important to know how the youth in U.S. schools actually consume media. According to a Common Sense Media study (2015), teenagers between 13 and 18 use about nine hours of media a day beyond their school work, media consumed primarily for entertainment purposes. Tweens ages 8 through 12 consume about six hours a day. The study revealed that music and TV are still the most common media for tweens and teens, with boys spending a bit more time playing games and girls spending more time using social media. Findings indicated that kids from low-income families have less media access, but when they do have access, they spend more time using digital devices than their wealthier peers (p. 1). Other studies offer disturbing conclusions on the inability of teens and college students to distinguish fake news from real news and advertisements from legitimate news stories on their digital devices. According to a recent study, students at Northwestern University assumed the best sources of information would appear at the top of a list of search results; consequently, they didn't bother to check for the reliability of sources when looking for information (Wineburg & McGrew, 2016, p. 1). A recent Stanford University study (2016) showed that students from middle school to college too often accepted content without going beyond the surface features of a website to analyze its reliability. Researchers caution, "At present, we worry that democracy is threatened by the ease at which disinformation about civic issues is allowed to spread and flourish" (p. 5) Unfortunately, students aren't as wise in their media consumption as their teachers might have hoped: "Many assume that because young people are fluent in social media they are equally savvy about what they find there. Our work shows the opposite" (Stanford History Education Group, 2016, p. 7).

In a 2016 article published in *Social Education*, Alan C. Miller pointed out that humans have a tendency to seek information that validates their own biases; most people don't naturally go looking for alternative or opposing facts. Consequently, educators should give students the tools to recognize their own biases. Miller explained the concept of "confirmation bias," where people are more likely to believe claims that align with their own biases, even when they're false, and "disconfirmation bias," where people assume that information conflicting with their biases must automatically be wrong. Miller drew from Daniel J. Levitin's 2016 book *A Field Guide to Lies: Critical Thinking in the Information Age* to emphasize the importance of developing an awareness of and an antidote for personal bias.

A recent Gallup survey revealed that 59% of college students don't trust the press and many don't trust major news organizations to present an accurate picture of important events (Miller, 2016). Many consumers aren't aware of the algorithms used by Facebook and other social media; they just assume that whatever is pushed at them is "the news." Students should be taught to seek information across a wide range of sources, deliberately following some media outside their ordinary comfort zones so that they'll be less likely to make hasty assumptions as news breaks on social media. The fuller, more accurate picture often evolves slowly over weeks and months. "Facing Ferguson: News Literacy in a Digital Age" is an online unit that includes videos, learning outcomes, and lesson plans designed to engage students in the development of critical media literacy skills (facinghistory.org).

If schools and educators fail to adequately teach critical media literacy, students may be quickly pulled into false narratives during those years when identity is being developed. In an article in the *Washington Post* (2015), Arno Michaelis, former white supremacist and author of *My Life After Hate,* described how his attraction to the Greek and Norse warrior/hero ideology gradually led him to be "very comfortable with hate and violence." Michaelis, raised in an alcoholic home, became an alcoholic himself at the age of 16 and, alienated from the teachers and kids in his school, gravitated toward racist skinhead music. His hatred and paranoia soon consumed him, and he formed a racist group called Hammerskin Nation. Michaelis explained, "When everything is going wrong in your life, it's much easier to blame Jews/Muslims/blacks/Mexicans/gays/anyone-but-yourself than it is to face your flaws and begin the hard work to account for them." White supremacists adeptly recruit such kids, offering them a sense of belonging and a mission in life. Having learned empathy from those who refused to hate, Michaelis echoed the ideas of Martin Luther King, Jr.: "We cannot hate violent extremism out of existence … This is not a problem that we can punish our way out of."

Michaelis mentions Dylann Roof, the young man responsible for the murders in the Emanuel AME Church. It is widely known that Roof's racist beliefs were developed through web searches where sophisticated algorithms kept feeding him more and more lies and mistruths. His manifestos, available online, tell a story of American history quite different from the one currently taught in American schools. Powerless and alienated, Roof sought "alternative facts." He found the answer to his lack of meaning and power in the contemporary world. He found the propaganda and ideology packaged especially for young men in his situation. It gave him all the answers he needed.

Roof's original manifesto, available via the *New York Times* online, is an interesting artifact in the hands of an educator. The kid could write beyond the ability of many freshmen enrolling in open admissions universities and community colleges. He apologized for the sentence-level error in his handiwork; a high school dropout, he nevertheless considered his audience. Imagine Roof's impulse to *write*, to attempt to justify himself in a communicative act, fully aware that his pages would be universally available.

Roof's epiphany toward racist violence evolved thus:

> The event that truly awakened me was the Trayvon Martin case. I kept seeing and hearing his name, and eventually I decided to look him up. I read the Wikipedia article and right away I was unable to understand what the big deal was. It was obvious that Zimmerman was in the right. But more importantly this prompted me to type in the words "black on White crime" into Google,

> and I have never been the same since that day. The first website I came to was the Council of Conservative Citizens. There were pages upon pages of these brutal black on White murders. I was in disbelief. At this moment, I realized something was very wrong. (Roof, 2016)

It's obvious here that Roof was capable of writing—and reading. All the factors contributing to his fascination with Trayvon Martin and his decision to commit mass murder may never be known. But in Roof's manifesto, and in ISIS' publication *Dabiq*, which is sophisticated propaganda meant to recruit Westerners, we must realize that depraved extremism isn't aimed at the illiterate. *Dabiq*'s pages are written by someone who has achieved a high level of rhetorical sophistication in English. The magazine contains articles on warriors rescuing kittens, only eventually getting to how Allah would require followers to hate "sodomites" gunned down in the mass shooting in Orlando. The problem is not illiteracy but an inability to recognize narrative used as propaganda, narrative that transforms the powerless and the alienated into deluded heroes of all-too-often violent tales.

NARRATIVE AND HUMAN COGNITION

White supremacists aren't the only ones interested in the powerful connections between narrative and ideology for untrained, susceptible minds. In 2011, the Defense Advanced Research Projects Agency (DARPA) announced a call for research into narrative as it convinces humans not only to think and to believe but also to act, sometimes violently. The U.S. military and governments worldwide have been awakened to what narratologists who specialize in the relationships between human cognition and narrative have known for decades: extremists may effectively use narrative to recruit disillusioned global youth into utopic fantasy worlds, ultimately inciting some of them to murder.

In their 2013 article entitled "The Military Interest in Narrative," Mark A. Finlayson and Steven R. Corman discussed propaganda involving the use of what they call level II narratives in various media, including audio, images, video or a combination of two or more. Level II narratives employ stereotypical characters, conflict, drama, emotional intensity, and also may use cultural symbols, metaphors, or images to invoke viewer or reader empathy and to establish an emotional connection that bypasses ordinary human reason (pp. 176–179). The power of narrative to control human action is confirmed in the autobiography of the late American Jihadist Omar Hammami: "The war of narratives has become even more important than the war of navies, napalms [sic], and knives" (quoted in Finlayson & Corman, 2013, p. 176).

To date, ISIS has been horrifyingly successful in using social media to recruit young people from around the globe using false narratives on the topics of victimhood, belonging, and utopianism (Glavin, 2015, p. 1). Governments around the globe recognize the power of social media to mobilize disenfranchised youth toward false utopias and false justification for barbaric violence. DARPA researchers admit the possibility of unethical use of new knowledge gained about the connections between neurobiology, human cognition, and narrative. Educators have a unique and extended opportunity to teach the critical media literacy skills necessary for recognizing narrative propaganda, which is particularly insidious as it bypasses ordinary reason and may be used in a variety of media, sometimes in ways that aren't recognizable as narrative to those who have not yet learned to identify its features and uses.

ADJUSTMENT NARRATIVE AND IDEOLOGY

Since students are daily consuming hours' worth of media messages, many of which distort the truth and propagandize, what is the best way to engage them in developing critical media literacy skills so that they will immediately recognize strong bias and false or distorted fact before succumbing to sophisticated appeals to their vulnerabilities? Since narrative is already such a powerful mediator of human cognition, and since students are consuming narrative in a variety of forms, including movie and TV plots, song lyrics, YouTube videos, advertisements, and print media such as magazines, books, and newspapers, it makes sense to approach the subject of critical media literacy first through the lens of narrative. By the time students reaches middle school, indeed even before, they have been exposed to common narratives perpetuated by society's strongest institutions, family, school, church, government, and the media. Many educators are already familiar with the concept of the "grand narrative" or "master narrative" first named by Jean-François Lyotard in *The Postmodern Condition: A Report on Knowledge* (1979). Lyotard's grand narratives codified social norms and expectations in any given society; however, they were inevitably distortions of the truth, as there were always alternate narratives to contest them. Even after deconstructionists and postmodernists have done their best to elevate the importance of alternatives to the "grand narratives," pointing out their oversimplifications and flaws, many grand narratives are still alive and well in the United States today, available for analysis as a means of teaching critical media literacy.

At this point, it is only fair to credit the originator of the term "adjustment narrative." In *On Teaching Literature* (1972), critic Northrop Frye, admittedly considered obsolete by most contemporary scholars, first used the term. Possibly, Frye's adjustment narrative predates the concept of the grand narrative, offering educators a very practical approach to analyzing the rhetoric of narrative and its potential abuse as it excludes and marginalizes in its oft-oversimplified version of reality. Frye discussed the archetypes encountered in many stories, pointing out the similarity in treatment of archetypal characters and situations across world literature. He stated, "Every belief or doctrine which can be expressed as a general statement or proposition is also the moral of a possible story" (p. 14). Frye identified reading and writing as "passive skills" (p. 15). Simmering beneath the surface of American social mythology codified in narrative, he warned, is the tendency to "treat it as a body of established social principles, to be imposed on everyone without criticism. This produces a mythology which aims at conditioning all citizens in habits of docility and obedience, or, as it is called, adjustment" (p. 16).

Frye argued that many classroom materials, when analyzed for adjustment mythology, seem to presume that "the main function of education is to produce docile citizens" (p. 16). He disparaged the use of American literature to mythologize the American past, propagandizing students toward a "nostalgic version" of history. The goal of such curriculum and pedagogy was "all too often to train the student in stock response, not imagination, and the end of the process to get him in adult life to repeat the liturgy of the adjustment myth, in a series of cliché notions…" (p. 17). Recognizing the possible harms, Frye called for a study of "the rhetorical devices of advertising, propaganda, official releases, news media…" (p. 18). He assured educators that teaching students to recognize the rhetorical strategies common in media should not be difficult. Without that awareness and ability, students would become adults susceptible to the delusions of totalitarianism. He hoped students would be taught about the constructed nature of "social vision" (p. 19).

In this aspect of his work, Frye predicted the importance of critical media literacy. His concept of "adjustment narrative" is relatively easy for teachers and students alike to grasp. Adjustment narratives are (and always have been) constructed simply to "adjust" human thought and behavior. Once students are able to see how common narratives not only reinforce certain social beliefs and norms but also inevitably exclude or marginalize those who cannot or will not "adjust," they will begin to automatically notice these same stories everywhere they look. Where formerly they would have been taken in by these narratives as benign reinforcement of unquestioned truths, they will realize the oversimplified nature of adjustment narrative and its true basis in implicit assumption. Since much propaganda is related through story, including that which reinforces biases deliberately encouraged by those who conflate American mythology with American history, students will be able to unpack much of the false rhetoric in the public sphere by automatically recognizing it as "story." They'll be able to see what ideals a particular story reinforces, who it serves, and who it excludes.

SUGGESTIONS FOR CLASSROOM PRACTICE

In order to teach students to analyze adjustment narrative, educators should first familiarize them with the most common narrative lines repeated in American media. Many of these narrative lines occur in stories across cultures as they serve to reify cultural and social norms in many civilizations, not just ours.

These stories typically involve one or more of the following:

- The American hero
- The American family

- True love
- Science and technology
- Coming of age (high school and college)
- Crime, justice, and the trial
- Success and prosperity
- Human equality and diversity.

Many young people already feel constrained by some of these oft-repeated, oversimplified storylines, yet they do not realize how powerfully adjustment narrative works to create assumptions, expectations and biases that remain unquestioned if no alter-narrative is ever considered. In order to analyze media critically for adjustment narrative, students must first be able to identify it. Once they recognize it, they can learn to analyze it to determine which social ideas and beliefs are taught and reinforced by each narrative pattern. Since students are already so familiar with narrative in a variety of media, instructors don't have to get "political." Once students have learned the basic process for analysis, they will be able to successfully analyze narratives in songs, TV programs, videos, news releases, biography, advertisements—as one student exclaimed after a semester of adjustment narrative analysis, "I will never look at the world the same way again. Ever."

Instructors can teach adjustment narrative in the classroom simply by selecting some sample narratives for model, individual, and/or group analysis. The beauty of this approach is that instructors don't *have* to address the power structures that are deliberately perpetuating the narratives. Eventually, students will recognize them all on their own. Students will quickly see how each story reinforces some virtue, value, or social norm. After that, they should be prompted to consider who the story as told marginalizes or excludes—with adjustment narrative, it will undoubtedly be someone whose experience doesn't fit the story. Finally, students can reflect upon why the story is so commonly told. What purpose does it serve? How does it attempt to "adjust" behavior? Who could it hurt? Who does it ignore? How might that exclusion or assumed judgment cause problems for people? What are the alternative narratives that exist outside of the predominately accepted story?

In teaching students to analyze adjustment narrative, it seems important to acknowledge its partial truth and social function. Adjustment narrative is often used to teach core values; it becomes problematic when alter-narratives are not allowed, when marginalized groups are oppressed, and when someone is ignored or "other"-ized. This may be difficult for students to see, as those excluded or harmed may not be specifically mentioned at all in the story. Initially, concrete thinkers (many students are) will not realize the implicit messages in many of the adjustment narratives they consume daily. With time and practice, they will get better and better at making those connections. It is best to begin with stories where the exclusions are relatively obvious. Before attempting to analyze stories, students might be encouraged to explore their own biases and how those biases might make it more difficult for them to see multiple sides of a story. They can be cautioned: stories with which they easily identify will seem quite benign. Those that obviously challenge their own experience will be much easier for them to analyze. It takes a lifetime to develop bias; gaining a less myopic vision will also take some time.

One safe, simple narrative that can be used in class to open the conversation on adjustment narrative is the Horatio Alger story. The Horatio Alger Society has a website that features some short stories written by the author. A good story for discussion might be "John Stevenson's Good Fortune" (1867). In this story, readers are introduced to the family of John Stevenson, who is employed by a Mr. Green. Stevenson is hopelessly underpaid; he and his wife do all they can to stretch a dollar, but prices are high. Initially, when Stevenson asks for a raise, Green assumes he is paying enough. Later, Green visits the Stevenson home, where he discovers that the family cannot afford to purchase overcoats for basic human warmth. He has visited the home to ask Stevenson to do some extra work after hours, which Stevenson gladly does. Shortly thereafter, Green awards him with a generous raise, even more than he had hoped for.

The message here is clear: work hard, be assertive but don't complain, and eventually your employer will recognize your initiative and you'll be rewarded with appropriate compensation and prosperity. In analyzing this narrative, students will first recognize that the value in this story is in its encouragement of hard work, honesty, and integrity. When asked who the narrative excludes or marginalizes, students would probably say, lazy people. Right? Certainly, that's true. But there's more to it. To encourage a deeper analysis, instructors might ask, "Who works hard, is honest, has integrity, and doesn't get appropriate compensation?" It shouldn't take students long to realize that there are many people who fall into this category. Some of them may have parents who are working hard, yet still struggling to make ends meet. Students can do research on the number of people who work full-time and still live below the poverty level. In addition, they can look for statistics on which workers are most marginalized in the U.S.'s current pay system. Students may realize how the story may be used to implicitly blame those who fail to prosper. When the poor are blamed for their poverty, economic equity is much less likely to become possible in the future.

An entire unit could be developed to explore this pervasive narrative and its social consequences. Instructors can use movies like "The Pursuit of Happiness" and stories like Nikolai Gogol's "The Overcoat" to see how the adjustment narrative of the Horatio Alger-type American dream is used to inspire workers, while other narratives may be questioning and challenging it. Instructors might play political speeches (using a variety of political affiliations) so students can see how the Horatio Alger story is evoked to cause constituents and voters to rely on certain assumptions about our society that may not always be true.

Perhaps the most pervasive, over-arching adjustment narrative, one used powerfully to socialize males, is the adjustment narrative of the American hero. This hero is seen over and over again in television programs and movies. The American hero possesses an inordinate strength, Samson-like, in fact. He (not always, but usually "he") is able to overcome impossible odds to destroy (and of course, destruction is necessary) evil foes who threaten the American way of life. Ultimately, he is willing to put himself into harm's way. He is fearless, mentally, spiritually and physically epic in his stature. He is independent and can think for himself, capable of working with and through various agencies to achieve his goal but also completely willing and able to go it on his own. No monster, army, or corrupt politician can bring him down. Movies depicting this hero often include extended battle scenes. Of course, such stories have been told since the beginning of civilization. Students can learn to recognize the oversimplification in many of the iterations of the hero adjustment narrative, the glorification of the often unnecessary use of violence, and the repression of other, better solutions to personal and social problems. The hero narrative often surfaces in the narrative of the kid who has to stand up to a bully. This narrative is repeated over and over again in movies and in sitcoms, until every kid must conclude that he or she is hopelessly flawed when unable to confront or overcome a bully.

Television channels repeat ad nauseam old Westerns and war movies. Stephen Crane's *Red Badge of Courage*, Tim O'Brien's *The Things They Carried*, and Ernest Hemingway's short stories on war, some of which are available for free online, offer an alternative perspective on this adjustment narrative, as does the story of NFL football player Pat Tillman, who gave up the dream of playing pro-football to enlist after 9/11 (Tillman was tragically killed by friendly fire, which was initially hidden). *Hacksaw Ridge* (2016), a movie about conscientious objector Desmond T. Doss, who survived the Battle of Okinawa without firing a shot, offers another good example. Doss's story is also presented in the award-winning documentary *The Conscientious Objector* (2004) and in recently published books. Much information on both Tillman and Doss is available for free online for students wishing to fully explore their stories. Students can examine the rhetoric of national defense, both written and spoken, for features of the American hero story to see how it can be used to propagandize and to beg the question of whether or not a particular war is justifiable or whether or not all heroes must use violence to achieve their ends. Certainly, it would be appropriate to explore the narratives of heroes (male and otherwise) who fought oppression without resorting to violence.

American adjustment narrative on crime and punishment has the potential to do as much social damage as any by perpetuating the idea that the good guys always get the bad guys—and they often need or deserve killing, prison at the very least. The crime and punishment narrative is often associated with the American hero narrative, and sometimes the heroes can be women. Heroes make sure crime is punished, regardless of personal consequence. They always find the right perpetrators of crimes and bring those criminals to justice. This plot is repeated over and over and over again on American TV. Crime drama appears to be one of the most popular TV genres. Kids are often exposed to an untold number of iterations of this plot. In their attempts to be politically correct but also to attract viewers from all demographic groups, contemporary crime dramas like *NCIS* (there are several spin offs), *Rookie Blue*, *Blue Bloods*, and *Hawaii Five-0* all feature very diverse casts of hot detectives and cops risking their lives to stop the criminals who want to destroy the safety of ordinary citizens. They chase and kill drug dealers, terrorists with nuclear bombs, serial killers, a healthy list of the usual suspects all of whom are evil and many of whom end up dead without a trial in front of a jury of their peers. The message here is clear: good guys need guns, much bigger guns than the cops of the '50's. Without them, they couldn't stop bad guys, and bad guys need to be stopped because—they're just bad. On occasion, a plot line might include some complications on *why* a particular criminal is bad, but basically, they are bad and need to be brought to justice. Of course, there are also corrupt police, judges, and etc.—but—these also are caught and brought to justice.

Crime and justice movies and shows wouldn't be very interesting if they portrayed the actual process of how the criminal justice system works. The accused often wait years for a trial. Sometimes, they are never apprehended. Sometimes, it's difficult, even impossible to know whodunit, and of course the laws on the books, the judges, and the lawyers are often not as dependable or as predictable as those portrayed in the oversimplified plots. In these programs and movies, suspects do have rights, and good cops follow the law, but they often show obvious resentment, even hatred, toward the criminals they apprehend. These cops *know* who's responsible for what, and they make sure just desserts are meted out. Programs like *Dateline NBC* titillate viewers with hard questions during interviews of suspected killers or those incarcerated for crimes they claim not to have committed. In these true crime programs, murder is presented as infotainment: In the sleepy town of X, all was well, until loved-by-all cheerleader Betty Boop went to a football game…unfortunately, she never made it home that night. Look, here's her distraught mother and sister with the family dog. Could the murderer have been Colonel Mustard in the library with a candlestick? Or was it Professor Plum with a wrench in the conservatory? There's *us*, viewers who are ordinary citizens (read, not criminals), and *them*, the ruthless *other* who need to be caught and put away.

Who does this repeated narrative exclude, marginalize or harm? There are movies and news stories featuring people who were wrongfully incarcerated, sometimes even wrongfully executed. Students can do research to find out how many people are in prison in the U.S. as opposed to other parts of the world, and for what. They can research the socio-economic differences in the way justice is meted out in the contemporary U.S. to begin to understand the complexity but also to some degree the injustice that may be extant and perpetuated by current assumption and propaganda as politicians on the stump assure us: the right people are going to jail so the rest of us can live idyllic lives. But who are the most dangerous criminals overall? Students can watch documentaries like the one on the BP Deepwater Horizon oil spill—and draw their own conclusions. They can watch documentaries by filmmaker Michael Moore, who is famous for presenting alternative narratives against the status quo, read about the death threats against him, and without any prompting whatsoever, students will understand that inevitably, any story of human good and evil they read or hear in the news is probably way more complicated than it seems.

Finally, contemporary narrative on science and technology can also be considered, as it drives powerful, potentially disastrous assumption in the U.S. This narrative pushes the common assumption that no matter *what* the impending disaster—striking meteors, invading aliens, apocalyptic doomsday scenarios—scientists and those skilled with technology will right at the last minute MacGyver a solution to save the day. *Whew*! Good old American ingenuity. It'll cure cancer, solve global warming, and bring on the utopia we've all been expecting. Before the turn of the twentieth century, writers were already anticipating the destructive capabilities of science, industrialization, automation, and overconfidence in human technology. Poems like Whitman's "When I Heard the Learn'd Astronomer" and stories like Nathaniel Hawthorne's "Rappaccini's Daughter" illustrate the dehumanizing effects of a preoccupation with "progress" divorced from human emotion and spirit. Henry Adams' famous "The Dynamo and the Virgin" (1900) worried that human spirit would be diminished by the coming age of machines. While science and technology have undoubtedly improved the quality of life for many on planet Earth and have solved some of our most horrific problems—i.e., smallpox—they are human activities that have undeniably also brought much misery to the planet.

Students given the opportunity to read about the scientific motivation, experimentation and achievement associated with Operation Paperclip or the Tuskegee Experiment, for example, will come to see the oversimplified assumptions pushed at them in American adjustment narrative related to science and technology. Students exposed to the ideas of the Victorian writer William Morris, Native American environmental activists, or "Professor Dumpster" (Jeff Wilson, an Austin professor who lives in a dumpster) might be able to imagine another kind of reality, gaining a constructively critical view of their own. Reading about the evolution of superbugs, factory farming, and global warming might help them to realize that unfortunately science may not be able to solve all of the problems it creates. Articles on these problems, as they contain narrative structure complete with characters and causation, offer counter narratives to adjustment narrative on the totalitarian power exercised by advances in science and technology, in some cases Pandora's boxes we can never close again. Hope can be mighty difficult to summon in the full realization of damage already done. Such realizations are sobering, sometimes even depressing, but if the developing minds of our youth are not allowed to contemplate them, there may never be sufficient time or space for actual truth or for reparation before it's too late.

Interested instructors can prepare level-appropriate units that meet grade-level outcomes while teaching kids to recognize and to analyze adjustment narratives. Beginning with the most obvious examples of these narratives embedded in contemporary song, video, TV, advertisement, social media, news, and political rhetoric, instructors can lead students through an engaging intellectual journey as they reconsider the narratives as common to them—and as unnoticed—as the air they breathe. They can consider the social value of such narratives but also learn to shift perspectives, to see the social harm implicit in repeating overly simplified stories to reinforce assumptions that are not true. Students can learn to recognize common adjustment narrative everywhere and to see the complexity of communities within their schools, their towns or cities, and the nation. During a unit or a course, students individually or in groups can track a particular narrative line through a variety of media. Further, they can track a particular event through various media over time to see how the "stories" unfold. They can even fashion their own songs, videos, stories, scripts, and press releases using adjustment narrative to counter common propaganda. They can then learn to shift perspectives, offering the same stories from different vantage points. In so doing, if their learning is reinforced throughout their educational experience, students will become literate in the use of narrative to spread or to counter propaganda. This will serve them well in their critical analysis of media messages. Once taught, they will never forget.

REFERENCES

Common Sense Media. (2015, November 3). *Landmark report: U.S. teens use an average of nine hours of media per day, tweens use six hours*. Retrieved from https://www.commonsensemedia.org/about-us/news/press-releases/landmark-report-us-teens-use-an-average-of-nine-hours-of-media-per-day

Finlayson, M. A., & Corman, S. R. (2013). The military interest in narrative. *Sprache und Datenverarbeitung/International Journal of Language Data Processing, 37*(1–2), 173–191.

Frye, N. (1972). *On teaching literature*. New York, NY: Harcourt, Brace, Jovanovich, Inc.

Glavin, N. A. (2015, December 7). Counter ISIS' narratives on social media. *The New York Times*. Retrieved from https://www.nytimes.com/roomfordebate/2015/12/06/how-can-america-counter-the-appeal-of-isis/counter-isis-narratives-on-social-media

Michaelis, A. (2015, June 25). This is how you become a White supremacist. *Washington Post*. Retrieved from https://www.washingtonpost.com/posteverything/wp/2015/06/25/this-is-how-you-become-a-white-supremacist/?utm_term=.4e5b5c1f4b00

Miller, A. (2016). Confronting confirmation bias: Giving truth a fighting chance in the information age. *Social Education Week, 80*(5), 276–279. Retrieved from http://www.thenewsliteracyproject.org/sites/default/files/media/Confronting%20Confirmation%20Bias.pdf

Roof, D. (2016, December 13). Dylan Roof manifesto. *New York Times*. Retrieved from https://www.nytimes.com/interactive/2016/12/13/universal/document-Dylann-Roof-manifesto.html

Sanchez, J. (n.d.). *Narrative networks (archived)*. Arlington County, VA: Defense Advanced Research Projects Agency. Retrieved from http://www.darpa.mil/program/narrative-Networks

Stanford History Education Group. (2016, November 22). *Evaluating information: The cornerstone of civic online reasoning* [Executive Summary]. Retrieved from https://sheg.stanford.edu/upload/V3LessonPlans/Executive%20Summary%2011.21.16.pdf

Todd, C. (Host). (2017, January 22). Meet the press [Television series]. *Conway: Press secretary gave "alternative facts"* [Video File]. Retrieved from http://www.nbcnews.com/meet-the-press/video/conway-press-secretary-gave-alternative-facts-860142147643

Wineburg, S., & McGrew, S. (2016, November 2). What students don't know about fact-checking. *Education Week, 36*(11), 22, 28. Retrieved from http://www.edweek.org/ew/articles/2016/11/02/why-students-cant-google-their-way-to.html

Erin O'Neill Armendarez
English Department
New Mexico State University – Alamogordo
Las Cruces, New Mexico

MARK A. LEWIS

10. SUPPORTING MEDIA-SAVVY YOUTH-ACTIVISTS

The Case of Marcus Yallow

INTRODUCTION

Adolescents constantly face criticism from an unforgiving public for their actions inside and outside of school. They are repeatedly described as self-centered, hormone- and adrenaline-driven, and immature (cf. Lesko, 2012). These characterizations, as stereotypes often do, work to generalize anyone aged between 12 and 18. However, cultural artifacts—such as literature, movies, and television shows—can function to disrupt and complicate how adolescents are understood by the public (Messner & Leggo, 2014; Lewis, 2016; Lewis & Renga, 2016). For example, in the classic young adult novel *I Am the Cheese* by Robert Cormier (1977), the adolescent protagonist is portrayed as a passive, impotent ward of the State, and, therefore, his story has been criticized for possibly leading youth toward disenfranchisement attitudes (Walsh, 2012). However, if one perceives adolescent readers as active critics of social and political movements, then *I Am the Cheese* becomes a particularly useful novel in "inciting both young readers' critiques of institutional power and behavior, and youths' own actions toward building a more socially just society" (Lewis, 2014, p. 12). Moreover, from the student movements of the 1960s through the "Battle in Seattle" in 1999 through the "Jena 6" movement, youth have played central roles at key activist moments in U.S. history (Anderson, 2012). In other words, not all young people are socio-politically disengaged, passive media consumers, and burgeoning citizens; rather, many are engaged, active, productive citizens using their complex and savvy understanding of technology and media exactly because of their age.

With the aim to support such engaged youth, I employ Cory Doctorow's award-winning young adult novels *Little Brother* (2008) and *Homeland* (2013), a highly-entertaining, techno-thriller duology that tells the story of the hacktivist Marcus Yallow and his friends, in order to both highlight positive portrayals of youth and illustrate how fiction can be used to discuss critical media literacy (CML) in the secondary classroom. I begin this chapter with a brief overview of my critical youth studies framework, particularly how this perspective problematizes youths' engagement with digital literacies and new media. I then introduce Doctorow and his novels before turning to a theme-based analysis of Marcus's story. Classroom instructional ideas are included for each theme, and then I close with larger implications for our youth and our society.

 | DOI 10.1163/9789004365360_010

"...WE MAY BE YOUNG, BUT WE'RE NOT SCUM": AN ASSET-BASED PERSPECTIVE OF ADOLESCENCE AND YOUTH

The overarching framework of my analysis follows a critical youth studies agenda that begins with a sustained consideration of the complexities of young people's lives, and a deep understanding of how power and knowledge build certain realities and understandings of adolescence and youth (cf. Best, 2007). This agenda also involves challenging the adult gaze that excessively worries over the becoming of youth toward adulthood, rather than attempting to value the ideas, beliefs, and interests of adolescents in the moment of being young. This deficit- and surveillance-based perspective stems from a pervasive developmentalist paradigm, often propagated through current educational practices that employ standardized and statistical ways of describing youth (Tilleczek, 2014). Since these standards are set by adults, rarely with young people's input, if a young person does not meet such standards, then adults determine them to be "delayed, aberrant, deviant, or simply queer" (O'Loughlin & Van Zile, 2014, p. 48) and, therefore, decide upon interventions to ensure that they return to the "correct" path toward adulthood. Youth feel the adult gaze acutely, as one of the protagonists in *Little Brother* proclaims, "We may be dumb, we may be young, but we're not scum" (p. 166). Her opening phrase is meant ironically, as she and her friends are very talented computer geeks and hackers, yet it, along with the closing phrase, also illustrate how youth both internalize and intuitively understand how adults view them. A critical youth studies framework, however, contends that these damaging standards and perspectives are inherently influenced by outside socio-cultural-political contexts, which need to be examined in conjunction with other internally-based developmentalist descriptors, in order to more fully understand how ideas of youth are fabricated (Popkewitz, 2012). I believe this framework provides a more discerning perspective for any examination of youths' lives and digital literacy practices.

Digital literacies have become central in all our lives, but particularly in the lives of youth. The Pew Research Center (Lenhart, 2015) reports in a 2015 survey that 92% of teens go online daily, and only 12% of teens report that they do not have access to a phone. Further, 91% of teens use their phones to go online, so they are literally carrying Internet and social media access with them everywhere they go. With this level of online engagement, it is imperative that youth have a keen understanding of CML concepts, especially in this current era of news media corporate conglomerates controlling the content and types of stories presented in local outlets (for example, see Zurawik, 2017, reporting on the Sinclair Broadcast Group). I ground my understanding of CML in Kellner and Share's (2005) explanation of five conceptual concepts from The Center for Media Literacy (http://medialit.org/). First, one must understand that all media messages are constructed to present a particular message, also known as the principle of non-transparency. Second, media uses particular signs and symbols to communicate views of socially constructed categories, such as age, race, gender and class. Third, each consumer interprets media messages disparately based on personal backgrounds. Fourth, media messages have agendas, both positive and negative, that make social, cultural and political statements. Fifth, almost all media messages have the primary aim of profit and power, whether they hope the consumer makes a purchase or watch a television program or believe in a certain political platform. These concepts remain central to how youth consume and produce technology and media through digital literacies.

A critical youth studies framework begins with the notion that youth are *both* producers and consumers of media, and use digital literacies to play with online personas and position themselves intentionally and politically in online spaces. In other words, more recent generations, who have grown up with new media, have a nuanced relationship with digital and social media platforms, and use these public spaces to "trace intimate patterns of who they are as part of the larger exploratory terrain of youthful becoming and quest for belonging" (MacIntosh, Poyntz, & Bryson, 2012, p. 213). Further, critical youth studies argue that young people strive to build their own created spaces, their own content, and adapt gaming spaces for their own needs, in ways that demonstrate their distinctive knowledge of media literacy to communicate messages about both themselves and their views of the world (Jones, 2014; Roseboro, 2014). However, two important cautions to consider include how corporate interests in controlling consumer behavior often use youth-created spaces to inform their advertising practices, and that personalized technology can lead to individual worldviews and convictions, yet not necessarily toward group action on social justice issues (MacIntosh et al., 2012). That being said, in my own interactions with youth, both as a teacher and a researcher, I attempt to start with the idea that youth are productive and critical actors in media engagements, rather than passive consumers of technology and media.

Finally, I am employing a *youth lens* (Petrone, Sarigianides, & Lewis, 2014) in my textual analysis. The first essential question of this lens asks the audience to identify ways cultural artifacts, particularly narrative texts, represent both the stage of life commonly labeled adolescence, and the people identified as living within that stage, usually youth aged 12 to 18. Then, the second essential question of this lens asks the audience to analyze how those identified representations reify and/or subvert commonsensical and stereotypical understandings about adolescence and youth. For the purpose of this chapter, in addition to these broad analytical questions, I also focused on ways youth characters employed and engaged with technology and media in order to answer questions about their relative success and failure with critical media literacies.

"I BELIEVE THAT THE INTERNET CAN CHANGE POLITICS FOR THE BETTER": CORY DOCTOROW'S LITTLE BROTHER AND HOMELAND

Cory Doctorow is a self-described technology activist, blogger, novelist, and professor. He also consults for the Electronic Frontier Foundation, a non-profit civil liberties group that supports technology freedom (http://craphound.com/bio/).

Despite being a college dropout (or, maybe, thankfully a college dropout), he is a talented computer programmer and has a keen understanding of how technology and media intersect (Pond, 2004). He has particular views on network freedom—the Internet should be free and open so that everyone has access in order to campaign on issues—copyrighting—it is an issue of freedom of speech, due process, and the right to education—and privacy—technology has changed from a "liberating force" of access to ideas toward a tool of surveillance, such as using cellphones to track youth "like they're a felon" (Tucker, 2010, p. 23). These views are highly present in his fiction, particularly his concerns over open access (he offers much of his fiction for free online), which is a major part of the plot of the *Little Brother* and *Homeland* duology (Fletcher, 2010). For example, Marcus Yallow in *Homeland* parrots Doctorow's views when trying to obtain a webmaster job with a local politician, "…I believe that the Internet can change politics for the better—make it more accountable, more transparent. That's why I want to work here" (p. 94). These two novels have received positive critical acclaim and several awards, including both receiving a Prometheus Award for best libertarian science fiction, and *Little Brother* earning a John W. Campbell Memorial Award for Best Science Fiction Novel, a Sunburst Award for Excellence in Canadian Literature of the Fantastic, and a White Pine Award for best Canadian young adult novel.

Little Brother

The first book of Doctorow's duology begins with Marcus—also known by his online handle, w1n5t0n—and his three friends—Jolu, Van and Darryl—being detained in the immediate aftermath of a terrorist attack on San Francisco's Bay Bridge. Marcus resists answering the questions of his interrogators, which leads to his relocation to an undisclosed prison and a more torturous interrogation. He eventually succumbs and reveals the information his interrogators want—a passcode to his phone—and once they establish his and his friends' complete innocence in the attack, he is released. However, one of his friends is not released, and it is unclear what happened to him. This injustice, along with an ever-increasing and intrusive surveillance by the Department of Homeland Security (DHS), leads Marcus to decide to use his deep knowledge of technology and media to build a network to support like-minded youth—which become an anonymous online and real-world hacktivist group named the Xnetters—to disrupt the legally questionable tactics the government is using to identify terrorists and supposed terrorist-sympathizers. However, the more Marcus, now known by his new online handle, M1k3y, by his fellow hacktivists, along with his new girlfriend, Ange, work to get the general public to understand the societal (and Constitutional) ramifications of allowing the government to invade personal privacy in the name of national security, the more rigorous and intrusive the strategies DHS employs to identify the Xnetters. As well, in reaction to their activism, the more strident the opinions from certain media outlets become on how the Xnetters support and embolden terrorists. As DHS tightens its circle on identifying Marcus and other

Xnetters, he is forced to make riskier and riskier decisions on how to proceed with his activism and resistance.

Homeland

The sequel continues Marcus and his friends' story a couple years after the end of *Little Brother.* Marcus and Ange have solidified their relationship, Darryl and Van are dating, and Jolu has begun a tech start-up. Ange is a communications major at a local college, but Marcus had to quit school because both his parents have lost their jobs and he cannot afford the costs. Marcus and Ange run into an old enemy while at Burning Man, who gives them access to a secret set of files—approximately 800,000—that provide evidence of the illegal and immoral activities of DHS and other corporations. She asks them to make the files public if anything happens to her. Shortly afterwards, Marcus witnesses her kidnapping by corporate security forces, so he must decide what to do with the files. He enlists Jolu, Darryl, and Van to help him create a darknet site for cataloging the files while he decides what to do; he wants to know what exactly he would be releasing. Meanwhile, he gets a job as a webmaster for a local politician, and the citizens of San Francisco are continually protesting social, political, and economic conditions of the city. Marcus attempts to balance the demands of his new job, exploring the files, and navigating the activism happening in the city. People continually ask him to participate due to the relative fame he earned in the aftermath of the Bay Bridge bombing, yet he worries over being detained again by those in power that do not want the information in the files to become public.

MEDIA-SAVVY YOUTH-ACTIVISTS

From the perspective of a youth lens, with ideas of CML in mind, I determined four major themes in Doctorow's duology: youth activism and adult complacency, privacy rights, security versus surveillance, and the changing press. In what follows, I discuss each theme as presented in the stories, and weave throughout possible classroom ideas for employing the novels to explore CML aspects.

"Don't Trust Any Bastard Over 25": Youth Activism, Adult Complacency

In *Little Brother,* the DHS employs several strategies to monitor, detain, and arrest San Francisco citizens in the name of national security. Marcus, his friends, and a growing network of youth—the Xnetters—find ways to disrupt the agenda of the DHS by "jamming" their surveillance, essentially using their savviness with technology to outwit the DHS. A rallying call of these youth becomes, "Don't trust any bastard over 25" (p. 166), which is based upon a similar slogan from 1960s student movements. Essentially, the youth protagonists are angry and simply will not accept the government's media messaging that national security trumps their rights as citizens. As a way to build upon the characters' actions to discuss the principle of non-transparency, teachers could bring in historical or contemporary news clips—such as the political rhetoric surrounding the "discovery of weapons of mass destruction" prior to the Iraq War—and ask students to analyze how different political players used the media to communicate a certain message in order to curry the public's favor.

For example, many of the adults in *Little Brother* remain complacent and accept media stories about what is occurring in the bombing aftermath. Such as, the DHS continues to describe the actions of the Xnetters as terrorist and the members as terrorist-sympathizers, and many of the adults believe that narrative, rather than the possibility that the hacktivists are trying to get the public to understand that the DHS is overstepping citizens' Constitutional rights. Marcus's father, despite being detained himself on the way home from work, argues that the DHS tactics are necessary to "catch the terrorists" (p. 137). Marcus argues the other side, but the complacency of his father to accept the media messaging of the government erodes his ability to consider Marcus's views. Moreover, he takes on the role of a dominating adult that dismisses youth as incomplete people who cannot fully understand the world. For example, he starts calling Marcus "son," which Marcus views pejoratively because it makes him feel that his father had stopped thinking of him as a "person and switched to thinking of me as a kind of half-formed larva that needed to be guided out of adolescence" (p. 217). In this way, youth activism tends to lose to adult complacency due to deficit-based views of adolescence.

Such deficit-based views are reiterated in *Homeland.* On Marcus's first day at his new job as webmaster for the local politician, Joseph Noss, the campaign manager explicitly explains her views of young people. She tells Marcus that "bright young men" like himself need supervision in order to ensure that they understand the difference between what they want and what is actually needed. This perspective is put in a stark comparison with stories on how youth hacktivists use media to "d0x" individuals or groups that should be exposed due to illegal and/or immoral behavior (p. 159; "d0xxing" involves mining someone's online history for evidence of their behavior and then publicly posting it to social media sites, although it should be noted that "d0xxing" can also involve its own invasion of privacy, as hackers often illegally enter the target's computer). On one hand, Doctorow presents an adult who does not believe that youth have the ability for discernment, and, on the other hand, he includes several anecdotes that illustrate youths' clear moralistic views of the world. Further, in *Homeland,* youth demonstrate their keen grasp on how emerging technology and media spaces provides them a power to organize that previous generations do not. Yet, they also realize that older generations are using the same technology and media spaces as "power to spy on us more than ever before, to control us and find us and snatch us" (p. 122). By definition, youth hacktivists employ CML concepts because they remain skeptical of the messages and agendas of corporations and governments, and then use their own youth-created media spaces to resist and disrupt those messages and agendas, naming them propaganda. In Doctorow's duology, the youth-activists use the Xnet and the darknet in productive ways to meet their goal of ending the control and surveillance being employed by the DHS and other immoral corporate actors.

As Roseboro (2014) explains, interactions within cyberspace involve both the visible and the invisible. Politicians and corporations present through the media certain visible messages, but CML demands that the consumer mine those messages for the invisible. The youth in Doctorow's novels constantly look for the invisible, thereby providing role models for readers to take up similar practices within their own interactions within cyberspace. Secondary teachers could ask students to mark all instances in which Marcus and his friends engage in such critical reading of the Internet and mainstream media as they search for the truth as discussion starting points for engaging in such critical reading. Then, ask students to find examples of invisible messages in the visible media produced by corporations and politicians in their own lives. Teachers could also ask students in investigate how different generations engage in social media practices, asking questions such as how do their grandparents' and parents' media use differ from their own, what can they learn from older generations about productive and negative media usage, and what can they teach older generations about productive and negative media usage.

"It's about Your Life Belonging to You": Privacy Rights

Marcus and his friends spend much of their time worrying over the privacy of their technology and online presence, especially after their detainment by DHS after the Bay Bridge bombing. In *Little Brother,* the Xnet was created for the sole purpose of having a private online space that only like-minded activists could discuss problems with DHS's actions and plans to fight against those actions. Essentially, Marcus built the space by using an Xbox and then distributing other Xboxes to interested youth to connect with the network. It worked perfectly until the DHS caught on to the system—by turning a few youth to their side through threats and intimidation—and infiltrated Xnet to identify its members. On all of their devices, Marcus and his friends use operating systems with names like ParanoidLinux, for their laptops, and ParanoidAndroid, for their cellphones, which reveal their perspective on privacy. Marcus even builds a virtual machine onto his laptop hard drive where he stores all data he wants to remain private that is invisible to anyone snooping his computer, unless they have a particular password to access it. Much of their concern over privacy stems from the extreme surveillance of the DHS and other corporations, and their hacktivist practices, but it also reflects their views of the right for people to have privacy in their personal lives. As Marcus explains early in *Little Brother*:

> There's something really liberating about having some corner of your life that's *yours,* that no one gets to see except you … It's not about doing something shameful. It's about doing something *private.* It's about your life belonging to you. (p. 57, emphasis in original)

It is clear that Marcus equates privacy rights with the opportunity to remain an individual with personalized beliefs and practices. The common belief of adults is that youth do not worry over what they post publicly online, yet these youth care much about their privacy rights and are judicious on what they put in social media and other public platforms, primarily due to the nature of their political situation, but it is not improbable to believe they would have similar views if they did not live under such intense surveillance. In other words, these fictional youth are practicing strong CML skills. Teachers could leverage this part of the story to encourage students to consider their own social media practices, both in terms of what they post and how they comprehend others' posts—especially from entities that have a particular agenda. One idea would be to ask students to track their social media usage for one week, and report on their practices as well as critique themselves on how they employ social media to present themselves and consume information.

They participate in similar practices as their story moves into *Homeland.* They use the darknet to house the compendium of files describing the illegal and immoral activity of DHS and other corporations in order to hide them from probing eyes. Marcus remains silently worried about privacy as he considers cataloguing the files, which manifests in how he discusses security with the campaign manager of Joe Noss, "…as soon as you start looking into security, you discover that there's always more you could be doing" (p. 93). However, a leak occurs from Marcus's team of hacktivists cataloguing the data. The leakers use Reddit to share some information present in the files. First, they want to remain anonymous due to the nature of the information—police departments were using a "lawful intercept" network appliance that downloads spyware onto phones by sending fake app updates—and for fear of retaliation and arrest. Second, they understand that spaces like Reddit provide a reliable space for sharing truth in the face of powerful entities that do not want the public to know or even think about practices that invade personal privacy. In this way, these fictional youth are positioned as experts on how to effectively employ CML practices. Teachers should similarly position their students as experts (Garcia, Mirra, Morrell, Martinez, & Scorza, 2015) as they ask them to analyze media messages for their underlying aims of profit and power, such as focusing on a contemporary controversy like climate change and structuring classroom activities that afford youth opportunities to not only discover and discuss the complexities of social and political issues, but also how "expertise" is characterized by divergent media outlets.

The use of apps and social media is increasing exponentially in our society, yet the existence of privacy settings and practices by users seems to indicate a simultaneous need for contact and a need for personalized privacy (Roseboro, 2014). Therefore, a possible CML project could include asking secondary students to research how their peers use privacy settings in their apps and social media. They could also research the technology behind why phone apps need access to a user's contact list, photos, and other data in order operate effectively. Although perhaps not a real possibility for classroom curriculum, it could be interesting to encourage interested youth to hack the code behind these apps to understand (and, dare I say, disrupt) the need for these settings. Using Reddit and similar sites, like Marcus and his friends, they could also see if others have discussed this topic in online spaces.

"Oh, They Understand Computers": Security versus Surveillance

Returning to the nature of the intense surveillance present in Doctorow's duology, the youth protagonists have rich discussions about the relationship between security and surveillance. Youth are constantly under surveillance while in school, from the constant presence of adults in the hallways and public areas to the use of metal detectors and closed-circuit cameras to random locker searches. Marcus outlines such practices at his high school, including a no-phone policy, firewalls on all computers, and gait-recognition cameras—technology that records all students' unique walking patterns so they can be tracked throughout the school. Some of his first forays in hacktivism involved subverting school security, and posting online—as w1n5t0n—how to replicate his practices for other youth. He also faces increased surveillance in public arenas, such as the San Francisco Police Department tracking his BART travels through his subway pass. He and his fellow Xnetters resisted such practices by "jamming" the system by finding a way to send false readings through the arphid (or RFID) scanners. Yet, as Marcus and his friends' story evolves into hosting and examining the documents they were given on the darknet, they discuss how "messed up" the current society is over security versus surveillance, as well as who has power and what they are doing with that power. Marcus wonders if current society has more problems than past generations, but his friend, Jolu, points to how technology and media have changed those problems because of access, and how they need to continue being activist until everyone realizes that there should be limits to surveillance because such practices mostly do not actually increase security. He responds to Marcus's question:

> Oh, they understand computers. And they're doing everything they can to invent new ways to mess you up with them. But if we leave the field, it'll just be *them.* People who want everything, want to be in charge of everyone. (*Homeland*, p. 123, emphasis in original)

Again, these youth understand how they need to use technology and media to broadcast truth to combat the misinformation presented by those who hold powerful positions in society.

Teachers could use this aspect of Doctorow's story as a model for how counterstories can complicate how different groups are presented in the media (Kesler, Tinio, & Nolan, 2016). For example, divergent media outlets characterize movements and peoples in our society—such as Black Lives Matter, immigrants, Antifa, "misguided" youth—in different ways depending on the stories they choose to tell about such groups. Students could collect several of these stories and then craft their own digital counterstory in response to a trend they find in the media broadcasts. Then, they could post their counterstories to online spaces like YouTube and ask for viewer comments. The comments they receive could then be used to analyze and critique the nature of online commentary and its relative productivity.

"Now I Do Journalism": The Changing Press

Little Brother was published in 2008, a short decade ago, and, yet the way Doctorow describes the use and power of print journalism sounds incredibly anachronistic. Marcus's parents have the daily paper delivered, he stops to read headlines at newsstands regularly, and when it comes time to go public with his story of un-Constitutional detainment, torture, and surveillance, he meets with an investigative print journalist, Barbara Stratford. After relating what happened to him, she explains the next steps, "Now I do journalism. You go away and I research all the things you've told me and try to confirm them to the extent that I can" (p. 269). Much of today's media lacks such criticality and caution; rather, it is full of talking heads spouting biased opinion either without thought or worry about the repercussions of their statements, or with exact purpose to influence the electorate with unsubstantiated claims about social and political issues. Doctorow also includes media anecdotes that reflect this side of mainstream media in *Little Brother*, but Barbara Stratford still becomes Marcus's savior. Building upon Kellner and Share's (2007) fifth principle of CML, teachers could ask students to compare the Stratford character with contemporary "opinion journalists" who rarely research the topic upon which they are commenting, and even deliberately use sophistry to convince their audience the "truth" of a certain political stance.

Move forward five years to 2013, when *Homeland* is published, and the role of the print, traditional media has shifted in Doctorow's duology. When Marcus considers his options on what to do with the darknet documents, he mentions giving the files to Stratford as an option. His friend, Jolu, immediately dismisses that idea because it would be "too slow" since she would have to research the content and prove to an editor that the content was publishable, which could take a week or longer. His sentiment clearly reveals a particular view of how media should function to these youth—it should be immediate and unedited. Therefore, it is no surprise that after the San Francisco police shut down a peaceful protest with riot gear, tear gas, and a HERF (an electronic pulse to shut down cell phones), Marcus uses new media to post footage of the event:

> I posted the video to the Internet Archive, YouTube, and popped a torrent on The Pirate Bay for good measure, wrote a paragraph explaining that I'd shot this at the demonstration after the HERF event, pasted it in, tweeted it, and crawled beneath the covers. (*Homeland*, p. 339)

He accomplished this media blitz from the comfort of his own bedroom. Soon after, mainstream media outlets were contacting him to get permission for them to broadcast the video on their programs and websites. The way the press works has fundamentally changed, and these youth understand that they have the ability to broadcast their own voices within new media outlets, and that they no longer have to passively hear the news read to them by anchors on mainstream media.

This changing press indicates how both the media and the public views what is publishable. In English language arts classrooms, teachers often ask students to work through the writing process until they have a finished product to submit, usually for a grade. However, current media practices have created a debate over what is finished versus publishable (Roseboro, 2014). These practices illustrate the notion that no writing is ever complete, but under constant revision. Marcus does not take the time to edit his video for time or content, similar to how traditional, mainstream media outlets might, he simply takes the raw data and posts to multiple Internet sites. Then, others take that video and create something new, even if it is by simply adding comments to the site, as every comment changes the product. In this way, no product is ever finished, but that product does need to get to a place where it is publishable. In Marcus's case, he needed to get the video public due to the drastic nature of the event. For secondary students working on a writing project, however, they would need to craft their work until it is publishable—whether that means completing a blog entry or a video—but then they would also want to keep revising that product as they get feedback from peers, teachers, and, possibly, the public. Teachers helping students use new media to show students how a disposition of constant reflection on whether their work is publishable, and deciding when it is finished, would support their growth as writers.

ACTIVISM AND PATRIOTISM

> Governments are instituted among men, deriving their just powers from the consent of the governed, that whenever any form of government becomes destructive of these ends, it is the right of the people to alter or to abolish it, and to institute new government, laying its foundation on such principles and organizing its powers in such form, as to them shall seem most likely to effect their safety and happiness. (Declaration of Independence, 1776)

Marcus refers to this quotation several times in *Little Brother* to justify his views and actions resisting the ever-increasing surveillance being employed by DHS. He understands activism as a form of patriotism in that he is striving to alter government practices in order to maintain individual freedom. He does not assume that because the state is taking actions in the name of national security, then those actions must not only be just but also aimed at the "safety and happiness" of the people. Rather, he views those government practices to impede upon that safety and happiness, and, therefore, unjust and destructive. Due to these views, the state through the DHS attempts to silence him and his friends, and is only thwarted in that endeavor by outrage from the larger public. Further, youth are particularly positioned to resist adult media practices because they have hacktivist mentalities. They constantly question the messages communicated by media and corporations, and they have the technology and media savviness to show how these messages are not completely based on truth. As Marcus says, "Never underestimate the determination of a kid who is time-rich and cash-poor" (*Little Brother*, p. 87). Of course, youth also need support from adults who advocate for and with young people because activism is hard. Teaching youth about CML can be an effective way to meet this goal.

Both Jolu and Van discuss at different moments in *Homeland* the tension and cost related to a constant state of activism. Marcus has trouble sleeping throughout much of the novel due to the pressure of having the information stored on the darknet and not knowing the best way to use that information to better society and bring the most egregious of perpetrators to justice. Jolu points out that he also has to take care of himself if he wants to be productive:

> I've noticed that you spend a lot of time trying to change the outside world, but not much energy on changing how the outside world makes your inside world feel. I'm not saying you should give up on changing the world, but you might try doing a little of both for a while. (p. 162)

Van also worries over Marcus, but due to her fear of trouble and her sense of the futility of activism. She explains her view on why Marcus should simply not pursue making the darknet documents public:

> He's going to walk away from this. He's right: this is too risky for him. It's not his fight … And why does it *need* to come out? Is it going to solve anything? Don't you think everyone already knows that the whole system is rotten? (p. 214, emphasis in original)

Jolu and Van voice valid concerns about being activists and participating in hacktivism, especially for youth who lack agency in an adult world. So, yes, activism is hard and comes at a high cost, yet, change is needed and the truth needs to be heard, particularly in the face of the constant biased rhetoric voiced on mainstream media outlets. Therefore, youth-activists deserve space and support inside and outside of schools to voice their views of the world and their hopes for change.

TRADE BOOKS

Cormier, R. (1977). *I am the cheese.* New York, NY: Random House.
Doctorow, C. (2008). *Little brother.* New York, NY: Tor Teen.
Doctorow, C. (2013). *Homeland.* New York, NY: Tor Teen.

REFERENCES

Anderson, N. S. (2012). Youth activism. In N. Lesko & S. Talburt (Eds.), *Keywords in youth studies: Tracing affects, movements, knowledges* (pp. 314–318). New York, NY: Routledge.
Best, A. L. (2007). Introduction. In A. L. Best (Ed.), *Representing youth: Methodological issues in critical youth studies* (pp. 1–36). New York, NY: New York University Press.

Fletcher, R. P. (2010). The hacker and the hawker: Networked identity in the science fiction and blogging of Cory Doctorow. *Science Fiction Studies, 37*(1), 81–99.

Garcia, A., Mirra, N., Morrell, E., Martinez, A., & Scorza, D. (2015). The council of youth research: Critical literacy and civic agency in the digital age. *Reading & Writing Quarterly, 31*(2), 151–167.

Jones, R. (2014). Machinima: Gamers start playing director. In A. Ibrahim & S. R. Steinberg (Eds.), *Critical youth studies reader* (pp. 380–384). New York, NY: Peter Lang Publishing.

Kellner, D., & Share, J. (2005). Toward critical media literacy: Core concepts, debates, organizations, and policy. *Discourse: Studies in the Cultural Politics of Education, 26*(3), 369–386.

Kesler, T., Tinio, P. P. L., & Nolan, B. T. (2016). What's our position? A critical media literacy study of popular culture websites with eighth-grade special education students. *Reading & Writing Quarterly, 32*(1), 1–26.

Lenhart, A. (2015). *Teens, social media & technology overview 2015.* Retrieved from http://www.pewinternet.org/2015/04/09/teens-social-media-technology-2015/

Lesko, N. (2012). *Act your age! A cultural construction of adolescence* (2nd ed.). New York, NY: Routledge.

Lewis, M. A. (2014). Questioning governmental surveillance: The enduring political commentary of Robert Cormier's I am the cheese. *First Opinions, Second Reactions, 7*(1), 10–12.

Lewis, M. A. (2016). Illustrating youth: A critical examination of the artful depictions of adolescent characters in comics. In C. Hill (Ed.), *Teaching comics through multiple lenses: Critical perspectives* (pp. 49–61). New York, NY: Routledge.

Lewis, M. A., & Renga, I. (2016). (Re)imagining life in the classroom: Inciting dialogue through an examination of teacher-student relationships in film. In M. Shoffner (Ed.), *Exploring teachers in fiction and film: Saviors, scapegoats, and schoolmarms* (pp. 65–75). New York, NY: Routledge.

MacIntosh, L. B., Poyntz, S., & Bryson, M. K. (2012). Internet. In N. Lesko & S. Talburt (Eds.), *Keywords in youth studies: Tracing affects, movements, knowledges* (pp. 213–218). New York, NY: Routledge.

Messner, K., & Leggo, C. (2014). Surprising representations of youth in saved! and loving Annabelle. In A. Ibrahim & S. R. Steinberg (Eds.), *Critical youth studies reader* (pp. 304–314). New York, NY: Peter Lang Publishing.

O'Loughlin, M., & Van Zile IV, P. T. (2014). Becoming revolutionaries: Toward non-teleological and non-normative notions of youth growth. In A. Ibrahim & S. R. Steinberg (Eds.), *Critical youth studies reader* (pp. 47–57). New York, NY: Peter Lang Publishing.

Petrone, R., Sarigianides, S. T., & Lewis, M. A. (2014). The youth lens: Analyzing adolescence/ts in literary texts. *Journal of Literacy Research, 46*(4), 506–533.

Pond, D. (2004). Interview with Cory Doctorow. *The Massachusetts Review, 45*, 742–754.

Popkewitz, T. S. (2012). Research and regulation of knowledge. In N. Lesko & S. Talburt (Eds.), *Keywords in youth studies: Tracing affects, movements, knowledges* (pp. 59–71). New York, NY: Routledge.

Roseboro, D. L. (2014). Mediated youth, curriculum, and cyberspace: Pivoting the in-between. In A. Ibrahim & S. R. Steinberg (Eds.), *Critical youth studies reader* (pp. 360–369). New York, NY: Peter Lang Publishing.

Tilleczek, K. (2014). Theorizing young lives: Biography, society, and time. In A. Ibrahim & S. R. Steinberg (Eds.), *Critical youth studies reader* (pp. 15–25). New York, NY: Peter Lang Publishing.

Tucker, P. (2010). Cory Doctorow meets the public. *The Futurist, 44*(6), 22–25.

Walsh, C. (2012). Inducing despair? A study of Robert Cormier's young adult fiction. In A. E. Gavin (Ed.), *Robert Cormier* (pp. 113–128). New York, NY: Palgrave Macmillan.

Zurawik, D. (2017, July 7). Sinclair Broadcast Group is finding out how harsh the national spotlight can be. *The Baltimore Sun.* Retrieved from http://www.baltimoresun.com/

Mark A. Lewis
School of Education
Loyola University Maryland
Baltimore, Maryland

SARAH BONNER, ROBYN SEGLEM AND ANTERO GARCIA

11. CREATING WOBBLE IN A WORLD OF SPIN

Positioning Students to Challenge Media Poses

INTRODUCTION

In today's participatory information age, the blurring of lines between fact and fiction has become a reality. As recent political outcomes have demonstrated, adults can be easily swayed by fiction and half-truths simply because a story emerged on their Facebook feed. Comment boxes reveal a mass confusion about what constitutes facts, with many buying into the concept promoted by Kellyanne Conway that opinions can form "alternative facts." Thus, in our work with middle school students, it comes as no surprise that these adolescents mirror their adult counterparts, struggling in deciphering credible sources, authentic news, and forgery. Snippets of conversations overheard in hallways and while working on class projects demonstrate a naivety toward the motives authors of multimedia texts might possess. In fact, many are completely unaware that what is often called "spin" even exists. This can be seen not only in the parroting of political rhetoric heard within homes and on TV, but also in the unquestioning embrace of what it means to be beautiful and popular as defined by the capital forces that exist all around us. Leaving these forces unchecked only perpetuates the greed that continues to motivate those in positions of power. As we've argued elsewhere (Garcia, Seglem, & Share, 2013), critical media literacy in today's participatory culture is an important stance on which classroom learning must be shaped. As experts in the use of language, English teachers have the opportunity to disrupt these forces by helping to illuminate instances of language used to manipulate others toward goals that are not necessarily in larger society's best interests. Through critical literacy, ELA teachers can help students differentiate between truths, examining whose truth lies in the lines, codes, and images that make up each text.

ELA educators can demonstrate to students how misinformation can impact their stances—or poses—toward the larger world. This is about not only building intentionality around media literacy but also proactivity and resilience in pushing against false narratives, language and multimodal images that reinforce a current climate of racism, sexism, xenophobia, heterosexism, and other forms of dehumanization. In particular, we see this as being framed through using the concept of Pose, Wobble, and Flow in work with preservice teachers, as described by Antero in his work with Cindy O'Donnell-Allen (2015). This chapter illustrates how Sarah used the model to help her eighth-grade students in a small, rural school begin to wobble and unpack the multiple facets of "post-truth" America. We begin by defining the Pose, Wobble, Flow framework and situating it within the ELA classroom. Next, we describe how Sarah introduced the framework to her students, preparing them with the language needed to describe their experiences with the upcoming unit on misinformation. After detailing how Sarah helped her students uncover their poses, we detail how she used the book *unSpun: Finding Facts in a World of Disinformation* (Jackson & Jamieson, 2007) as a guide to helping them examine the ways language can be used to distort the truth. Further, we explore how students applied their understanding of reliable sources by designing and participating in a series of student-led debate discussions and by constructing a series of reflections that correlated with their belief systems. Finally, we discuss instances of Wobble and Flow achieved in this unit and the implications this approach has for the language arts classroom.

POSE, WOBBLE, FLOW FRAMEWORK

Recognizing that teaching—like the media Sarah's students explored in her classroom—is never built on a neutral premise, Garcia and O'Donnell-Allen (2015) describe Pose, Wobble, and Flow (PWF) as a cyclical means to grounding a "culturally proactive" approach to ELA teaching and professional development. Written to describe how teachers sustain their work across a career, it is important to recognize that PWF is "not about an endpoint; it is a framework to help acknowledge how one's practice changes over time and requires constant adaptation" (p. 5).

As the name implies, PWF is built around three concepts that synergistically guide teachers in self-sustaining critical practice. First, educators name and adopt a pose that they want to intentionally address in their practice. This is "a stance or mindset you willingly take on as a teacher for well-considered reasons" (p. 5). While several initial poses are suggested by Garcia and O'Donnell-Allen, their work intentionally focuses on educators shaping poses around the needs of educators wherever they are located geographically and across their careers. While one teacher may need support in a pose on classroom spatial design as a new teacher, another may want to focus on better integrating the civic dimensions of English language arts that guides her practice. As such, poses, we want to emphasize, are grounded in intentionality, need, and current clarity of the learning environment and one's positionality within it.

Following a "pose," the PWF's central concept of wobble is built on the work of Fecho (2011). In his work, Fecho explains that wobble is "a liminal state, a state of transition. Where there is wobble, change is occurring. … That which was once this is moving slowly—at least at first—toward becoming that" (p. 53). It is important to recognize that wobble is not *bad*; it is *necessary*. We grow and learn through and from wobble. We highlight it in this chapter—as do Garcia and

O'Donnell-Allen—in order to build mindfulness and awareness of the needs of individuals and their own wobble.

Finally, flow is "both the moments of psychological well-being one experiences in singular moments during the everyday course of teaching, and the larger overall project of linking complementary poses together over the span of one's teaching career" (p. 7). Flow is never a lasting state; it too is liminal. Likewise, it is not a *good* state to be in as if contrasted with wobble; it is also simply necessary over time. Achieving moments of flow reflect how growth and realization occur over time to help strengthen practice. Moving between moments of wobble and of flow, educators gain a new sense of their practice by seeding a vision for certain kinds of poses to be enacted in their classrooms and apprising their progress across a school year.

Taken collectively, it is important to recognize that PWF is not a linear model of first adopting a pose, momentarily struggling with it, and then achieving mastery evermore. That is not how teaching works. As classrooms are fixed in sociocultural spaces that are constantly in flux and that teachers and students are not robots that are programmed for replicability, flow and wobble *change meaning* over the course of one's career. What was once counterintuitive and confusing about culturally-sustaining discourse in one's classroom, for example becomes a more solid grounding to identify new areas of wobble in one's critical pedagogy.

Further, as a model to initially support current and pre-service teachers across a critically-engaged classroom career, we want to highlight that PWF describes how educators must adjust to the shifting climates of fear, oppression, and nationalism that cloud what happens in classrooms daily. Considering the increase in incidents of hate in the current post-Obama era (Southern Poverty Law Center, 2016), and the intersecting role of echo-chamber like processes of disseminating information (Barbera, Jost, Nagler, Tucker, & Bonneau, 2015; Colleoni, Rozza, & Arvidsson, 2014), PWF as a model offers possibilities for shaping critical resiliency amongst the students and teachers that ensure that classroom learning ecologies thrive.

While this model is developed for teachers, we highlight how encouraging youth to develop critically-proactive stances—informed by notions of privilege, power, and agency—is an important first step toward sustaining metacognitive understanding of wobble and flow across one's civically engaged life within classrooms and beyond. In particular, when considering the complex media landscape in which kids are saturated, we believe that identifying critical framing of media as a pose for students is crucial. As youth today read, write, and produce media as part of a complex "connected learning" ecology (Garcia, 2014; Ito et al., 2013), understanding the purposes of media within students' individual interests, being able to understand the sources that they are exposed to, and developing skills for critique are important aspects of instituting critical poses for youth engagement with media today. At the time that we write this, national policy concerns are tweeted—typos and all—regularly from a highly divisive president, often grounding language within racism, sexism, transphobia, and xenophobia. If we cannot look toward current national leaders for highlighting critical and "humanizing" (Winn & Paris, 2014) approaches to language and media, we believe we must then ground such practices in the classrooms for our posterity.

INCORPORATING POSE, WOBBLE, AND FLOW IN THE MIDDLE LEVEL ELA CLASSROOM

In engaging in the PWF process with students, most of the poses the students took related to their relationships with media were not surprising; they were, in fact, the very reason we designed the unit. Like many around the country, we were disturbed by what we were hearing not just in the halls of this small school, but in the halls and classrooms spanning the United States. Sarah, in her work with 8th graders, directly heard students uttering derogatory phrases aimed at specific populations. Robyn, in her work with preservice teachers, listened as many of her student teachers shared similar stories from their school placements. And Antero, in his conversations about PWF with educators across the country heard too regularly the kinds of fractured climates of partisan bickering filtering into classroom spaces. We knew students used the poses familiar to them to unconsciously react to the world around them and that the poses were primarily reproductions of the messages they were exposed to through their home contexts, peer groups, and media choices. We also knew that middle school was a crucial time to examine their beliefs or poses as adolescents are in the crux of identify formation. Thus, we reasoned that the ELA classroom would be a safe place for students to not only examine their poses, but also explore *why* the held the poses they did.

Our goal was to help students wobble in their poses, which required them to not only delve into their beliefs but to also explore the poses they take when encountering texts or when tasked with learning something new. Not surprisingly, our students—like many students and adults around the world—simply turned to Google and typed in a question. The first results were most often the ones they read (or skimmed) and used. They possessed little understanding of how those results were determined, not recognizing that some of the listings were sponsored by companies that paid to be featured at the top of the list. Similarly, many turned to *Wikipedia* without understanding how the crowdsourced creation of this text helped frame the information they were receiving. And few, if any, recognized the importance of understanding domains such as .org, .gov., and .com. Recognizing the development of these research skills, as well as the development of a critical mindset when approaching texts, is vital to an informed society, we set about designing a unit that intentionally pushed students away from their initial inclinations. We wanted them to wobble, not because we wanted each of them to share our personal beliefs, but because we wanted our students to be more mindful of the poses they take, helping them to not just blindly follow family, friends—and perhaps most importantly, the media messages they encounter daily.

The Project

For any educator, the beginning of the 2016 school year became significantly unique due to the nature and influence of the highly media-driven presidential election. The media storm surrounding the election created a whirlwind that blurred fiction and truth. Regardless which side Americans supported, the media posed a challenge to consumers making it harder to understand where truth could actually be examined. As many adults struggled—and, continue to struggle—with skepticism, the media also shaped students' abilities to "read the word and the world" (Freire & Macedo, 1987).

In a Midwest rural junior high school that serves predominantly Caucasian students and is rooted in both tradition and conservatism, these blurred lines became evident as the population returned to school that fall. Within the ELA classroom at the beginning of the year, Sarah observed the growing influence it took on the student population in connection to both conversation as well as the growth of election paraphernalia. After the Electoral College determined President Trump to the be the winner of the 2016 presidential election, many students entered the school hallways and the ELA classroom chanting such lines as "build that wall" and "lock her up." While all students deserve the right to voice their beliefs, this type of language created an unsafe school culture. It became clear that the need to address text-impacting ideas such as fake news and post-truth America became necessary in efforts to positively impact school culture and beyond.

The unit began by posing a problem to the ELA students in regards to "fake news" and how media trends highlight the manipulation of partial truths in efforts to make headlines valuing speed over accuracy. Initially, students viewed *The Washington Post* interview featuring actor Denzel Washington commenting on his recent experience with fake news and how several media outlets reported his death even though the report was false (Samuels, 2016). In efforts to facilitate discussion after watching the interview, students examined the impact on media when thinking about the consequences of reporting news first or not presenting news accurately. This discussion led to a series of thoughts related to skepticism and questioning what students currently know by what the media tends to tell them.

Using the Pose, Wobble, and Flow framework, Sarah channeled the energy of the election aftermath along with student reaction and started a journey to unpack the facets of the post-truth America problem. In order for students to understand the term pose and its connection to the framework, Sarah used a series of yoga poses with her ELA students. At the beginning, the physical poses seemed achievable by the general student population; however, as the poses increased in flexibility and rigor, students could not maintain balance and often fell out of place. This served as a metaphor for students in moving forward in the framework. As discussed with students, the easily achievable poses acted like our own personal truths and the increasingly harder poses—which created student bodies to wobble for balance—represent the actions taken that would force one to think differently about our beliefs and; therefore, change the stance or position that once had been created.

Periodically throughout the unit, this metaphor served as a foundation in both questioning and response as it brought common language and experience into context. In efforts to help facilitate the unpacking of post-truth America and fake news, it became evident that additional resources were needed to achieve this goal. To understand how to wobble in a climate of posing, Sarah facilitated a book study with her ELA students centered around the text *unSpun: Finding Facts in a World of Disinformation* (Jackson & Jamieson, 2007).

Overview of UnSpun. Jackson and Jamieson founded the accredited website FactCheck.org and addressed the concept of spin in our media as a form of deception. Throughout the beginning, the text introduced the concept by simply stating that "we live in a world of spin—'spin' is a polite word for deception" (Jackson & Jamieson, 2007, p. 1). In continuation, it posed the problem of how Americans continue to be bombarded with daily mixed messages, partial truths, and fabricated facts as they interact with media. In addition to addressing the problem with spin, it also painted a historical picture of how the news media—once vigilantes of the truth—have morphed into timid or distracted entities that often overlook deception.

Jackson and Jamieson (2007) continued by saying "spin comes at us today in ways that didn't even exist a decade or so ago—on cable news talk shows, advocates issue torrents of factual claims daily; seldom challenged by their amiable hosts—and, the internet has enabled a potent new weapon of deception…viral marketing" (p. 8). As a means to unlock the deceptions of 21st century news media, major themes threaded throughout the text included: (1) the warning signs of 'spin' and bogus news; (2) identifying common deception 'tricks' used on the public and how to defend against those tricks; and, (3) in a world of deception, how to find trustworthy and objective sources of information that can be used to determine truth and impact belief. The heart of the *unSpun* text spoke to the development of the skepticism readers should have with today's news media and how telling fact from fiction should not be a difficult task. Jackson and Jamieson presented a tool that would ultimately strengthen the consumer to become a better-informed citizen.

Making the decision to use the book *unSpun: Finding Facts in a World of Disinformation* did not come easy. When thinking about text to use with middle school students, teachers often shy away from advanced material because of the rich vocabulary and content that pose major comprehension barriers. However, due to the nature of student interest, the Jackson and Jamieson text ultimately proved to meet the needs of the learners. Sarah implemented this text in the form of a book study along with reading supports such as reading guides, mini lessons, and class discussions to insure student comprehension success.

Student work on book. At the beginning of the book study, Sarah introduced the text structure to her ELA students by modeling annotation strategies and the introductory prologue. In addition to this direct instruction, Sarah provided a reading guide that would help support student comprehension by breaking down the text into manageable chunks. The reading guide consisted of a pre-reading section containing both a word cloud emphasizing key vocabulary and questions that promoted prediction strategies. Students utilized the keywords in the word cloud and their own prior knowledge to collaboratively construct answer to the prediction-based questions.

Once students had a foundational idea of the material, Sarah proceeded to use the introductory prologue to model during reading strategies that included vocabulary identification and periodic annotated summaries (to students, it was known as chunking). Sarah used a read aloud method to students while periodically stopping in subtitled sections to annotate and interject short personalized summaries of the text to encourage both main ideas as well as overall comprehension. The ELA students proceeded to work with Sarah and the introductory chapter to interact with after reading strategies. After Sarah and her students completed the annotations, Sarah encouraged her students to revisit the predictions once created prior to reading the chapter. Students confirmed and adjusted their predictions together as a group—engaging in small group discussions. From there, students personally reflected on the material in efforts to facilitate connections, questions, and overall comprehension of the text. After modeling the introductory prologue, Sarah assigned chapters to student reading groups along with specific chapter reading guides to facilitate student group processing.

Although this ELA classroom supports student interest and thrives in student choice when connecting to reading, chapter division and assigning was necessary due to factors such as reader readiness and mature content. In some chapters throughout the text, the content, vocabulary and the amount of reading varied and, for those students who struggled in reading, Sarah selected chapters that would challenge, but not completely overwhelm, students. In contrast, other chapters spoke to more rich adult-like content that deemed suitable for more mature readers; therefore, Sarah assigned these chapters to readers whose readiness toward reading and mature content could manipulate the text both effectively and purposefully.

As student groups collaborated on the *unSpun* chapters and reading guides, Sarah threaded a series of mini lessons that impacted the processing and connecting to the reading. These lessons facilitated whole-class discussion in examining student wobble moments and exploring gullibility among consumers by analyzing advertisements. After students became mantled experts of their assigned chapters, Sarah prompted students to collaborate in designing a presentation of the assigned chapter to their classroom peers. In addition to connecting text content to class discussion, mini lessons also addressed effective presentation methods as well as how to engage in questioning and feedback strategies. Student presentations not only filtered chapter material, but they also included a visual metaphor to support student understanding of the main ideas or themes threaded within the chapter. An example of a visual metaphor constructed by a student group connected to the game “Headbandz.” The student group studied a chapter in the *unSpun* text that spoke directly to the importance of credible evidence. According to the student group, they explained that in “Headbandz”—the game where one player wears a headband holding an unknown word while depending on other players, who can see the word, to give clues in order to guess the word correctly—one cannot win without the correct information. Students translated the concept of this game to how it factors into searching, finding, and processing credible text. Without the right clues, one cannot win the game; and, one without the right facts cannot formulate the truth. By viewing credible sources from this perspective, students cultivated value to the source finding process because they could understand the consequences of having deficient information.

Translating to student debates. Jackson and Jamieson (2007) state that when presented with a claim, it becomes essential to “keep an open mind, ask questions, cross check, look for the best information, and then weigh the evidence” (p. 179). In addition, *unSpun* calls for citizens to “respect the facts” as they continue to interact and process information in today’s media-driven climate. Working with the *unSpun* text served as a precursor to exploring argumentative learning standards in the form of classroom debates. Knowing that students needed credible sources in developing their positions, Sarah used the major themes of the student chapter presentations to create parameters students could use when searching for sources. Leading up to the classroom debates, a series of mini lessons needed to be put into place to ensure the success of the debate process. These mini lessons included: (1) reviewing persuasive strategies such as stating opinion and supporting opinions with reason and evidence; (2) analyzing the difference between persuasion and argumentation; (3) exploring the parts of an argument (claims, counterclaims, reason, and evidence); and, (4) modeling the understanding of the Whole-Group Triangle debate forum. As students selected topics, the Whole-Group Triangle debate structure allowed for the entire class to participate in the debate process all at once in an organized and productive manner. Sarah used this structure to formulate groups that identified as “pro,” “con,” and “fact checkers.”

Once students understood the components of the debate structure, it became time to select a debate topic. Using the Middle School Public Debate Program (MSPDP) topic list, students collaboratively selected potential debate topics for the class. Once students chose a series of topics, Sarah used a classroom dry erase board to write the topics in order for students to visually see all of the potential choices. After selecting a series of potential topics, students participated in a dot democracy activity to narrow down the topics to the one that would be integrated into class discussion. From the ten to twelve topics written on the board, each student took a dry erase marker and placed a dot next to the debate topic they favored. Students in this voting process were allowed to place three dots next to their top three debate topic choices. The topic with the highest amount of dots generated by student input ultimately became the next debate topic for the following week.

Utilizing the triangular structure for the debate process allowed Sarah to not only engage all of her students both collaboratively and collectively, but it also provided an experience that reiterated the major themes of the *unSpun* material. Debate topics selected at the beginning of the week would then transition to collaboration time throughout the week in effort to prepare for the whole group discussion. Sarah continued to position herself as an overall facilitator throughout this process and mantled the fact-checking group as debate moderators by allowing them to meet

Table 1. Unit overview

Reading supports	*Read the prologue together to prepare students for the book* • Model annotation strategies/chunking of the text • Use think-aloud strategies to emphasize predicting, summarizing, connecting, and inferring • Review vocabulary strategies for understanding complex words *Provide reading guides for each chapter* • Create word clouds to emphasize key vocabulary • Include questions that encourage students to make predictions • Encourage students to return to their predictions once they have read the chapter
Collaborative book study	• Students work collaboratively to unpack their assigned book chapter, completing reading guide together. • Teacher facilitates mini lessons and whole-group discussions revolving around student needs and the concept of wobble. • Collaborative groups create a visual metaphor to capture the main ideas of their chapter and present to the class.
Student-led classroom debates	*Incorporate mini-lessons to prepare for debate* • Review persuasive strategies • Contrast persuasion and argumentation • Examine parts of an argument • Model the Whole-Group Triangle debate forum *Divide students into three groups: for, against, and fact checkers* *Select potential debate topics through the dot democracy process* *Assign tasks according to roles* • For and against groups research credible sources for information to support assigned positions • Fact checking group analyzes the sources being used by both sides while constructing arguments • Fact checking group designs debate questions for both sides and share them throughout the week so that discussion is student-driven and student-managed *Conduct debate* *Reflect over process* • Student participation • Moments of wobble • Individual performance

with both sides, review the credibility of research, and pose questions for each side to answer. After the debate process, Sarah engaged students in a post-debate reflection writing that addressed student participation, potential "wobble" moments, and overall individual performance.

BOOK STUDY OVERVIEW USING *UNSPUN*: FINDING FACTS IN A WORLD OF DISINFORMATION

Instances of Wobble

In their work with teachers, Garcia and O'Donnell-Allen (2015) assert, "Identifying the realities of our students' lives confirms the need to alter and refine that [teaching] practice on an ongoing basis" (p. 134). As Sarah observed in watching the poses presented by her 8th grade students, there was a need to refine her own practice in order to address her students' needs. These seemed to echo the "cultural, social crisis" (p. 133) identified by Garcia and O'Donnell-Allen. Through this unit, Sarah's intent was to help her students *feel* and work through their individual wobbles, to help them change their approach to consuming and presenting information. Looking across her students' work and discussions, it is evident that she was successful in helping her students wobble in at least six ways: (1) verifying sources, (2) backing ideas with evidence, not opinions, (3) asking good questions, (4) understanding the importance of current information, (5) recognizing "twisted truths," and (6) identifying and empathizing with the other side. The following sections elaborate more on each of these instances of wobble.

Verifying sources. On the surface, the verification of sources seems pretty basic and intuitive. Yet, as the larger world is witnessing—sometimes to our great peril—this is a practice that is often neglected. The Internet provides quick information. It's easy to find "facts" in an instant, and it's just as easy to create and spread those facts in an instant. While immersed in this unit, Sarah witnessed her students checking their sources, often double checking the domain address to ascertain whether or not they were more likely to be reliable, and overheard them discussing the importance of using at least two websites to verify information. Not only did students learn about the role of credible sources in terms of how they can be verified, but they also embodied the role of the source moderator that continuously verified sources throughout the debate process. She also watched them begin to question *who* the information was coming from, chuckling over one student's exit slip comment which stated, "No 8th grader can prove a scientist wrong."

Backing ideas with evidence, not opinions. Building upon their skills of verifying sources, students were also seen wobbling when it came to the importance of using evidence to support their sides. This is where the debates became the most valuable. When given the task to argue a side—regardless of whether they agreed with the side—students quickly learned that debates required more research than opinion.

Further, at times when students found themselves faltering in their arguments, they were often able to recognize when they hadn't found enough evidence to support their reasoning. And even more encouraging, was one student's reminder to not say things if you don't know whether they're true.

Asking good questions. Savvy students began to recognize the key to finding reliable evidence was the ability to ask good questions. Plugging in simple keywords or phrases was more likely to lead to less reliable evidence. Conversely, asking more precise questions tended to lead to more accurate information. Under the whole-group triangle debate process, being both the debater and the fact-moderator played a significant role in how students viewed the research process. Students kept each other accountable by asking source-related questions because either it became their "job" (the moderator) or they knew they wanted to avoid questioning (the debaters). Sarah facilitated an environment where it made questioning part of the process in an attempt to turn process into habit.

Understanding the importance of current information. Students also discovered that the world of information itself can wobble. What was true years ago may no longer be true, therefore students began to pay closer attention to the dates of publication. One student established three years as a rule of thumb. Anything older was disregarded.

Recognizing "twisted truths." A term coined by a student, twisted truths refer to finding sources that support the other side's facts but changing a few words to ensure the "facts" support the side being argued. This understanding echoes the idea of "alternative facts" promoted by the current administration. Fortunately, this group of 8th graders saw past the alternative reality seen by some of our government officials, recognizing the twisted nature of disregarding evidence provided by experts in the field. In our eyes, the skepticism that an overwhelming majority of the class developed was one of the most rewarding wobbles in the unit. Students began to look carefully at the aesthetics of a website, using these as a clue to the reliability of information. One student quipped that a website "looks like a 12-year old designed it," and then moved on to find a more reliable source. The idea of truth resounded in their conversations, debates, and physical documents. Students began to recognize the different approaches to spin that were outlined in their study of *unSpun*, and they began to consciously look deeper at information, searching for clues that would indicate truthfulness. They recognized, as one student took the time to articulate, that social media has made it easier to find an audience that is skewed toward a particular stance, an audience that doesn't always care if the information has been fact-checked or is true.

Identifying and empathizing with the other side. The final point of wobble that we found encouraging was the students' ability to recognize the merit or at least the reasoning of the share of the population that did not necessarily share their own beliefs. They began to see that even if you don't agree with a viewpoint, there are elements of "good" to the other side. Further, they realized that when topics are personal, it can be difficult to understand the other side, but that there are reasons people think and do what they do.

Glimpses of Flow

At the end of the *unSpun* unit, it became clear that lessons permeated from this unit into others as students continued to work with research and credible sources. By participating in both the book study as well as the series of debates, many wobbles evolved from these experiences that became a natural part of student processing. Threaded throughout the semester, Sarah continued to facilitate student-driven inquiry projects called 20% Time or Genius Hour. These projects started at the beginning of the semester and students dedicated one day per week toward its progress. Not only did the 20% Time projects engage in student interest and promote civic engagement, but they were also supported by research. As a result, students were required to present their findings in the form of a TED-Ed-style talk. Throughout their presentations, it became evident that speaking with facts over opinions emerged as a major flow. In a platform so easily susceptible to opinion-based discussion, students readily accessed their research, referred to evidence periodically to support their experiences, and provided the audience with references at the end of their presentations. Connecting back to the argumentative unit in regards to the debate process, students understood that stronger debates had stronger research; therefore, the need to provide research throughout their own inquiry-based projects morphed into instinct based on prior experience.

In addition to inquiry projects, Sarah extended students' critical engagement by facilitating a design unit that allowed students to rethink reading. Derived from an overall negative student outlook on reading, Sarah wanted to create a means to where students could be engaged in authentic change that could impact students, teachers, and school policy in regards to reading as well as potentially increase the value of reading among her students. At the beginning of the unit, students discussed their issues with reading and participated in a whole-group discussion around 21st century learning. From this discussion, four major rethinking themes emerged: (1) physical spaces; (2) the integration of technology; (3) community involvement; and (4) motivation and focus strategies for students. Students chose a theme that related to their personal interests and collaborated with other students who shared their interest. With that in mind, collaborative student groups collected research related to their specific theme in efforts to formulate a solution-based proposal connected to the theme.

Evidence of flow throughout this unit became clear in the form of searching, finding and utilizing credible sources. The sources generated as a result of facilitating this unit were chosen in contrast to sources cultivated by students at the beginning of the school year. Collaborative student groups formulated research banks—which consisted of a Google document table and a collection of research themes, main ideas and annotations, and source citations. Using the research bank, student groups created a checks and balance system of utilizing high quality sources to make sure they found credible information. It became evident that students participating in this culture of finding credible sources—including verifying steps, understanding the importance of quality sources, and recognizing twisted truths—created a flow in their long term learning. Student groups utilized their research by formulating authentic solutions using a proposal writing format. Many solutions proposed by students as a result of this research included prototypes for redesigning the school library and hallways mirroring college campuses, creating and maintaining Little Free Libraries for the community, and creating a student-managed social media campaign that would promote student reading choices.

In addition to 20% Time and the design framework addressing the concept of rethinking reading, Sarah also observed flow in her students as they presented their epiphany projects at the end of the school year. The epiphany project challenged the students to individually reflect on the time spent in the ELA class and create a product that demonstrates the big ideas learned throughout the course of the year. Throughout the course of the epiphany project presentations, instances of flow became evident in connection to credible sources as students made this one of their central talking points. Many students claimed that finding sources throughout the school year could not just be any source, but that they had to find "good sources." In addition to the quality of sources, students also formulated ideas that correlated to expressing information, personal beliefs, and the damaging impact of not having all of the facts. Students bridged these concepts together to comment on how formulating a belief system is not only essential, but it also requires the support of credible information.

The student epiphanies brought light to the intersection of student voice and instances of flow. Students often connected their experiences with the debate process to the idea of being prepared with what to say in regards to speaking about a position, taking a stance, and supporting a stance with plausible evidence. Student voices became strengthened by implementing a flow of credible sources. Many students alluded to the idea that they were not scared to share their opinion if they knew they "had all of the facts."

Sarah's students highlight a diverse set of wobbles with wrangling meaning and understanding across today's complicated media landscape. Like the teachers that PWF was developed for, these students highlight the need to revisit poses over time and to understand that culture *changes* over time. A stance that was once successful may not be what is most helpful for students or for teachers in a different sociopolitical climate, geographic location, or temporal context. As the world changes, so too do the poses we must take to interpret and meaningfully participate in the world. As these poses shift, so do the feelings of wobble, and the moment-to-moment experiences of flow. As media proliferates and as fake news grows in serpentine ways of occluding truth, the media literacy opportunities for young people, their engagement with the broader world, and the role of ELA classrooms must adapt.

REFERENCES

Barbera, P., Jost, J., Nagler, J., Tucker, J., & Bonneau, R. (2015, August 21). Tweeting from left to right: Is online political communication more than an echo chamber? *Psychological Science, 26*(10), 1531–1542.

Colleoni, E., Rozza, A., & Arvidsson, A. (2014). Echo chamber or public sphere? Predicting political orientation and measuring political homophily in Twitter using big data. *Journal of Communication, 64*(2), 317–332.

Fecho, B. (2011). *Teaching for the students: Habits of heart, mind, and practice in the engaged classroom.* New York, NY: Teachers College Press.

Freire, P., & Macedo, D. (1987). *Literacy: Reading the word and the world.* Westport, CT: Bergin and Garvey.

Garcia, A. (Ed.). (2014). *Teaching in the connected learning classroom.* Irvine, CA: Digital Media and Learning Research Hub.

Garcia, A., & O'Donnell-Allen, C. (2015). *Pose, wobble, flow: A culturally proactive approach to literacy instruction.* New York, NY: Teachers College Press.

Garcia, A., Seglem, R., & Share, J. (2013). Transforming teaching and learning through critical media literacy pedagogy. *Learning Landscapes, 6*(2), 109–124. Retrieved from http://www.learninglandscapes.ca/images/documents/ll-no12/garcia.pdf

Ito, M., Gutiérrez, K., Livingstone, S., Penuel, B., Rhodes, J., Salen, K., Schor, J., Sefton-Green, J., & Watkins, S. C. (2013). *Connected learning: An agenda for research and design.* Irvine, CA: Digital Media and Learning Research Hub.

Jackson, B., & Jamieson, K. H. (2007). *unSpun: Finding facts in a world of disinformation.* New York, NY: Random House.

Samuels, E. (2016, December 14). *Denzel Washington calls upon journalists to tell the truth* [Video file]. Retrieved from https://www.washingtonpost.com/video/entertainment/denzel-washington-calls-upon-journalists-to-tell-the-truth/2016/12/14/b218db8e-c248-11e6-92e8-c07f4f671da4_video.html

Sarah Bonner
School of Teaching & Learning
Illinois State University
Normal, Illinois

Robyn Seglem
School of Teaching and Learning
Illinois State University
Normal, Illinois

Antero Garcia
Graduate School of Education
Stanford University
Stanford, California

AUTHOR BIOGRAPHIES

Joanne Addison is a professor of English at the University of Colorado Denver, where she primarily teaches Rhetoric and Multimedia Writing courses. Her work focuses on literacy acquisition and digital education, emphasizing the articulation between high school, college, and our everyday lives.

Sarah Bonner is a veteran Language Arts teacher at Heyworth Junior High School in Heyworth, Illinois as well as a current doctoral candidate in the School of Teaching and Learning at Illinois State University. Her work focuses on inquiry-based learning in the middle school. You can learn more about her work with students at www.languagearts301.pbworks.com or follow her on Twitter at MrsBonner301.

John P. Broome is an Associate Professor of Education at the University of Mary Washington in Fredericksburg, Virginia. His research interests focus on the intersection of civic learning and social justice in schools with a focus on race, equity, and privilege. Before joining UMW, Dr. Broome completed his Ph.D. at the University of Virginia and taught secondary social studies in public and private schools in the Commonwealth of Virginia.

Matt Dingler is a graduate assistant at the University of Arkansas, where he is earning a Ph.D. in Curriculum & Instruction. His research interests lie within the many realms of critical theory and pedagogy, specifically applied to social studies education. He may be reached at mldingle@uark.edu.

Jason L. Endacott is enjoying his eleventh year in higher education. Before beginning his career in higher education, Dr. Endacott taught middle school social studies at New Mark Middle School in the North Kansas City, Missouri, school district. He enjoys working with secondary students in social studies classrooms to uncover and explore ways in which they think about history and historical figures.

Seth French is doctoral fellow studying Curriculum and Instruction at the University of Arkansas, where he primarily teaches English Education courses. His work focuses on student engagement and new literacies, with special emphasis on critical media literacy and gamification. You can follow him on Twitter at gamesethmatch.

Antero Garcia is an Assistant Professor in the Graduate School of Education at Stanford University where he studies how technology and gaming shape both youth and adult learning, literacy practices, and civic identities. Prior to completing his Ph.D., Antero was an English teacher at a public high school in South Central

Los Angeles and co-designed the Critical Design and Gaming School. Antero's most recent book is *Good Reception: Teens, Teachers, and Mobile Media in a Los Angeles High School*. He received his Ph.D. in the Urban Schooling division of the Graduate School of Education and Information Studies at the University of California, Los Angeles.

Christian Z. Goering is an associate professor of English Education at the University of Arkansas where he directs the Northwest Arkansas Writing Project and works with the licensure programs in English Education and Theatre/Communications. Goering taught high school English in Topeka, KS and is a nationally board certified teacher. In 2016 he co-edited *Recontextualized: A Framework Teaching English with Music* (Sense) and co-authored *The Arkansas Delta Oral History Project: Culture, Place, and Authenticity* (Syracuse UP). He's a singer-songwriter in his spare time and organizes a monthly Songs in Progress event in the community.

Troy Hicks is a professor of English and education at Central Michigan University. He directs both the Chippewa River Writing Project and the Master of Arts in Educational Technology degree program. He can be followed on Twitter: @hickstro

Mark Lewis is associate professor of literacy education at Loyola University Maryland, where he teaches courses in children's and young adult literature, disciplinary literacy, and English methods. His research interests include examining representations of adolescence and youth in young adult literature, and the literacy practices of linguistically diverse learners. You can follow him on Twitter @ MarkLewisLUM.

Sharon Murchie (@smurchies) teaches English at Bath High School in Bath, Michigan and is a teacher consultant for Red Cedar Writing Project and Chippewa River Writing Project. She is currently working on her Doctorate in Educational Technology and is driven to promote and support critical thinking, advocating for the integration of technology in thoughtful and deliberate ways. She blogs personally at mandatoryamusings.blogspot.com and academically at sharonmurchie.wordpress.com.

Janet Neyer (@janetneyer) teaches English at Cadillac High School in Cadillac, Michigan, where she is passionate about incorporating authentic reading, writing, and research experiences into her classes. She is a co-director of the Chippewa River Writing Project in mid-Michigan. She blogs about teaching, learning, reading, and writing at upnorthlearning.org.

Erin O'Neill Armendarez is associate professor of English at New Mexico State University Alamogordo, where she teaches freshman and sophomore level writing courses. From 2013–2017, she served as New Mexico Higher Education Policy

Analyst for the National Council of Teachers of English. She has published numerous book reviews, book chapters, and articles.

William M. Reynolds teaches at Georgia Southern University. He has authored, co-edited and co-authored several books most recently. *Forgotten Places: Critical Studies in Rural Education* (2017), *Practicing Critical Pedagogy: The Influences of Joe L. Kincheloe* (2016), *Expanding Curriculum Theory: Dis/positions and Lines of Flight* (2016) and *Critical Studies of Southern Place: A Reader* (2014). He is editor of a series with Intellect Books entitled, *Critical Cultural Studies: Toward Transformative Curriculum and Pedagogy*, co-editor with Brad Porfilio of a series with Lexington Books entitled, *Youth Culture and Pedagogy in the 21st Century* and editor of the new series *Critical Media Literacies* with Brill | Sense.

Robyn Seglem is an Associate Professor in the School of Teaching and Learning at Illinois State University where she teaches content literacy and language arts courses to middle-level preservice teachers, as well as graduate level literacy and educational technology courses. She has served as a co-director of the Flint Hills Writing Project, an affiliate with the National Writing Project, and is a nationally board certified teacher. Robyn worked with a team of ELA educators to recently revise and update the standards for English and Language Arts for the National Board for Professional Teaching Standards. She taught for nine years in middle school and high school language arts classrooms.

P. L. Thomas, Professor of Education (Furman University), taught high school English in South Carolina before moving to teacher education. He is currently a column co-editor for *English Journal* (National Council of Teachers of English) and author of *Trumplandia* and *Beware the Roadbuilders* (Garn Press). Follow his work at http://radicalscholarship.wordpress.com/ and @plthomasEdD.

Kristen Hawley Turner is an associate professor and director of teacher education at Drew University and the founder and director of the Digital Literacies Collaborative. She can be followed on Twitter: @teachKHT.

Rob Williams is a media/communications professor and new media consultant who lives and works out of Vermont's Mad River Valley. In addition to teaching a wide range of media and communications classes at the University of Vermont, Champlain College, and Saint Michael's College, he has edited and authored a host of articles, essays, and book chapters on critical media literacy education. His most recent book is *Media Education for a Digital Generation* (Routledge, 2016).

Robert Williams, Professor of English and Interim Director of Interdisciplinary Studies in the Liberal Arts for Radford University, teaches English and Welding. His interests always condense to issues of literacy, writ large, and always include writing and reading whether in language or metal, or both.

Dan Woods is an Associate Professor of English at Radford University. Dan received his Ph.D. from Virginia Tech majoring in Curriculum and Instruction with a focus on English Education. Before pursuing his Ph.D., Dan taught middle and high school English in Roanoke City and Montgomery County. He earned his M.A.Ed. from Virginia Tech, as well as a BS and an MA in English from Radford University. His research interests include teacher education, critical literacy, and social justice.

Printed in the United States
By Bookmasters